O Beloved Kids

RUDYARD KIPLING'S LETTERS TO HIS CHILDREN

RUDYARD KIPLING

Edited by Elliot L. Gilbert

Published in 2007 by Max Press,
an imprint of Little Books Ltd,
48 Catherine Place, London SW1E 6HL

10 9 8 7 6 5 4 3 2

Text copyright © Sandra Gilbert

Design and layout copyright © by Max Press

A CIP catalogue record for this book is available from the British Library.

ISBN 978 1 904435-80-8

Retypeset by Decent Typesetting, Swindon 0870 350 2930

Printed and bound by Mackays of Chatham plc, Chatham, Kent

CONTENTS

ILLUSTRATIONS

INTRODUCTION

But Who Shall Return Us The Children?

The Secret

"Ducky Dicky-Bird", Rudyard Kipling begins one of his letters to his twelve-year-old daughter Elsie in July 1908, the next moment cheerfully conceding that the salutation is *"quite* the lowest title for you that even *I* have invented. Please tell me how angry it made you."

It would be hard to imagine a passage more characteristic of Kipling as a writer for children. On the one hand, its opening phrase caters to youthful delight in word play and general silliness; on the other, the apology that follows, with its half-serious invitation to anger, gracefully acknowledges the pride and dignity of young people, their dislike of being patronized by adults. Such an ability to think simultaneously like a grownup and like a child has always been considered a key to Kipling's success in the *Just So Stories*, the *Jungle Books*, and *Stalky & Co*. But that sensitive double vision, that intuitive understanding of the deep contradictions of childhood, may be even better expressed in the letters the author wrote to his own children, Elsie and John. And it is these letters, just recently made available, that appear here as the first new book by Rudyard Kipling in nearly fifty years.

Such a book was not what anyone was thinking about when Elsie Kipling, by then Elsie Bambridge, died in the late spring of 1976; instead, with her death the literary world eagerly prepared itself for the revelation of a long-concealed scandal. "What Did Kipling's Daughter Want to Hide?" demanded a typical headline of the day, this one in the June 13th *Sunday Times*, hinting darkly at suppressed family secrets and their imminent disclosure. It was a question, to be sure, that Elsie herself had done as much as anyone to provoke. For during the four decades since the deaths of her parents, Rudyard Kipling's only surviving child had made herself notorious by severely limiting access to her father's papers, allowing just a handful of carefully screened scholars to examine the contents of the archive she so devotedly guarded at Wimpole Hall near Cambridge.

Inevitably, such reticence awakened suspicions that there was

1

something in the history of the Kiplings requiring concealment. And when in 1949 Lord Birkenhead, the first authorized biographer, was forbidden by Elsie to publish his Life of her father, a project on which he had been engaged for three years, rumours about scandal in the family became even more persistent. Was it not well known, after all, that Caroline Kipling, Rudyard's wife and Elsie's mother, had destroyed hundreds of letters and other documents in the collection within a few weeks of her husband's death? And did not Birkenhead claim to have found, through his examination of the archive, materials of whose existence Elsie herself was unaware? No wonder that when a second authorized biography, by Charles Carrington, was published in 1955, critics concluded, with a logic worthy of Lewis Carroll, that the complete absence of scandal from the book only proved how really bad the true story must be. No wonder, too, that the death of Elsie aroused eager expectations that that story was now at last going to be told.

Some delay in the telling would, of course, be unavoidable. The will, by terms of which the archive was to go to the University of Sussex, would first have to undergo probate. And then the documents themselves would have to be catalogued and filed by the University librarians. It was in the midst of these preparations that the Birkenhead biography, revised by the author two years before his death in 1975 and now freed from Elsie's ban, was finally published and immediately put an end to the more melodramatic speculations about Kipling family secrets. For although the book was a frank and critically independent study, it contained little of significance that had not already been reported by Carrington, and it could certainly not be considered an exposé. Under the circumstances, the opening of the Kipling archive at Sussex was something of an anti-climax. The absence of any scandalous materials among the many letters, press cuttings, business papers, and photographs did not, it is true, prove that no such materials had ever existed. But as Charles Carrington summed up the matter succinctly at the time of Elsie's death,

before Kipling's papers passed to Mrs. Bambridge, Mrs. Kipling had already destroyed everything she didn't like in them. The secret in the Kipling archives is that there is no secret.[1]

But why then all the circumspection, all the suspicious reticence on Elsie Bambridge's part over the years? Paradoxically, the answer to that question involves one of the few matters about which the Kiplings never made any secret. An unusually retiring family, they despised what Rudyard called "the Higher Cannibalism", with its prurient exploitation of the private lives of public men and its commercial trafficking in draft manuscripts, domestic documents, and other literary souvenirs. Carrie Kipling did her best to frustrate such commercialism by exercising strict control over any potential literary commodity, routinely destroying most incoming letters, regardless of their source, and suppressing every scrap of handwriting that might otherwise have passed from RK's workroom into the marketplace. And it was no doubt in this same spirit that Elsie, when it became her turn to control the archive, chose to withhold her father's papers from all but a few scholars, thus unwittingly prompting rumours of scandal.

Given the family passion for privacy, however, the very existence of the archive raises a new question: how is it that any Kipling papers at all survived? Perhaps John Burt, cataloguer of the Kipling collection at Sussex, is correct when he remarks in his "Foreword" that "it is not now possible to be sure upon what principles material was chosen for preservation in the archive", a judgement with which Charles Carrington agrees. But even a cursory inspection of the catalogue suggests at least one likely principle of choice. For ignoring the business and legal papers and the literary manuscripts that bulk large in the collection, and concentrating instead on the letters by Kipling himself, we quickly discover that no group of these letters constitutes a more sustained or notable series than the 643 written by the author to his children: 223 to Elsie and John from 1906 through 1915, from which the present selection has been made, and 440 to Elsie as an adult from 1921 to 1935. If, then, there was any policy at all, conscious or unconscious, shaping the content of the archive, it may well have been the determination of mother and daughter that as a private person Rudyard Kipling should be presented to history principally in the role of father.

Next to his life as an artist, this was clearly the role Kipling himself cherished most. Playing the great man in literary company did not particularly interest him; neither did being the recipient of formal public honours, though such occasions were always brightened for him by the prospect of describing their solemnities in very unsolemn letters home to the children. The high-spirited account of degree awarding at Oxford, for example, written to John on June 27 1907, is amusing evidence of this. Even letter-writing appealed to him chiefly as an opportunity for domestic communication ("I hate writing letters except to you and Mother and Elsie", November 6 1907), but there was no phase of his life or work that was not at its most attractive when he was at his most fatherly. And if the archive holds any secret, it probably lies in the remarkable portrait these letters create for us of the parental Kipling, a sensitive Edwardian *paterfamilias*, so unlike the forbidding figure of popular judgement, who brings up his young son and daughter with imagination, tenderness, comic exuberance, deep affection, and the lightest possible touch.

"Why Can't You Frivol?"

In one sense, the world has long enjoyed "letters" from Kipling to his children. The *Just So Stories*, we know, were addressed directly to them, first to Josephine and, following her death at the age of seven, to Elsie and John. "During the long warm summers," Angela Thirkell, grand-daughter of RK's "Aunt Georgie" Burne-Jones, records in *Three Houses*,

Cousin Ruddy used to try out the *Just So Stories* on a nursery audience. Sometimes Josephine and I would be invited into [his] study ... [and he would] tell us about the mariner of infinite resource and sagacity and the suspenders – you must not forget the suspenders, Best Beloved.[2]

Elsie recalls her own early encounters with the stories in Cape Town, where they would be "read aloud to us for such suggestions as could be expected from small children".[3] Significantly, in the nursery copy of the book the phrase "For Little Children" on the title page has been changed, in RK's handwriting, to "For Elsie and John", and the authorial "By Rudyard Kipling" is replaced with "By Their Daddy", almost exactly as if the tales were being given the salutation and close of a letter.

From the first, indeed, there was always something of the intimacy of direct address, the immediacy of correspondence, about the stories, qualities that emerged most clearly from Kipling's own reading of them. "The *Just So Stories* are a poor thing in print," Thirkell continues her reminiscence,

compared with the fun of hearing them told in Cousin Ruddy's deep unhesi-tating voice. There was a ritual about them, each phrase having its special intonation which had to be exactly the same each time and without which the stories are dried husks.[4]

But other elements too link the stories with the children's letters. Both tales and letters, for example, are imaginatively decorated by Rudyard with pen and ink drawings (on February 10 1909, RK congratulates

John for continuing the family tradition of illustrated correspondence); both employ interpolated verses and fanciful descriptions of exotic places; most particularly, both delight in comic and/or ritualistic naming, with the stories' "Yellow Dog Dingo" and "Tegumai Bopsulai" parallelling the letters' "Ploomp" and "Ducky Dicky-Bird" and favourite signature "Daddo", and with the incantatory "O Best Beloved" of the tales becoming, in the letters, "O Beloved Kids".

If there was a key to Kipling's genius for communicating with children, nothing more graphically reveals it than an unprepossessing snapshot we have of the author telling one of the *Just So Stories* to a group of young listeners. (Ill. 3) The photograph, taken in 1902 aboard a ship bound for Cape Town, shows half a dozen children clustered around Kipling, who is seated among them on the deck. This arrangement of figures creates a quite curious effect, for while we can see that with his moustache and straw hat Rudyard is an adult among children, yet because he is rather disconcertingly the same height as the others, there is a momentary confusion about his true role in the group. It is precisely in this confusion of roles that the secret of his appeal to children lies. Conventional wisdom may instruct a man that the best way to be a father is never to forget having once been a child. But the Kipling of the *Just So Stories* and the letters to Elsie and John declares more audaciously that the best way to be a father is never to stop *being* a child. "You're awful growed up all of a sudden," he writes in 1890 to Amelia Clifford, alias "Turkey", the young daughter of friends, on whom he liked to practise his paternal skills before he had any children of his own. "Why can't you frivol and be a baby now and again as I am always?"[5]

Such a statement, whimsical as it is, draws deeply on the philosophical and literary resources of a whole century. In particular, it can be traced to the Wordsworth of a poem like "We Are Seven". Certainly, no other work of Wordsworth's argues so convincingly for the supreme value of the child or reassures us so warmly that as long as we maintain the vitality of the child within us we need never know death. The idea, a powerful and influential one, passed from Wordsworth to Dickens ("'I'm quite a baby,' said Scrooge. 'Never mind. I don't care. I'd rather be a baby.'") to Lewis Carroll, and much of its resonance in Kipling derives from its century-long history. But for Kipling, the idea had a personal source as well: the life-saving store of early childhood memories he cultivated to help him survive years of exile from his family. This commitment to a visionary childhood never wholly faded. In the charming drawing he made of John, for example, all bundled up in his 1907 Christmas coat, we see, beyond the amusing sketch, the perennial Kipling allegory: a child's spirit peeping eagerly out of its ungainly adult body to ask, "Why can't you frivol and be a baby now and again as I am always?"

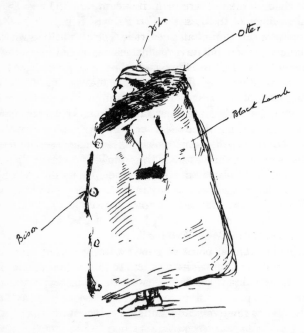

Kipling's own "frivolling" took a number of forms, from his Mr Toad-like mania for cars, touched on occasionally in the letters, to his impish waving of gaitered legs in the air to signify his decision not to dress for dinner, to his unhostly delight whenever guests fell into the Bateman's fish pond, which appears to have been frequently. It was a rough, boyish, sometimes painful hilarity, not always very attractive, as his more sadistic revenge comedies suggest, and in part persisting from the "Soldiers Three" days of his own adolescence. "The lighter side of army life", writes one commentator, "is mostly to be found in practical jokes. There was a bit of Kipling that never quite grew up and that always rejoiced in such jokes."[6]

More often, however, the part of Kipling that "never quite grew up" expressed itself in a notable rapport with the concerns of childhood.

Remembering, for example, the joy of being released for several weeks each year from what he called the House of Desolation by visits to his Aunt Georgie's at Fulham, he "begged for and was given" the Fulham bell pull for the entrance at Bateman's "in the hope that other children also might feel happy when they rang it."[7] He deeply understood, too, the delight children take in form and ritual and repetition, as his own ceremonial readings of the *Just So Stories* suggest, and for Elsie and John he drew up an illuminated charter, full of extravagant legal language, granting them full navigational rights to the Dudwell Brook that flows past Pook's Hill and through the Bateman's property. It was just that elaborate legalese of the charter, he knew, like the comic sesquipedalianism of the *Just So Stories*, that children would find so attractive, a kind of forbidding adult façade, moustached and bespectacled, from behind which piped the voice of a child, issuing invitations. They were invitations the moustached and bespectacled Kipling was himself always ready to accept, though at times he looked for them in vain. "Children could play with me today," he writes in the letter of July 15 1908, when Elsie and John are both away, continuing with painful prescience, "I wish I had one now – or even two kids."

"How the First Letter Was Written"

From the bibliographical point of view, two of the most interesting questions we can ask about Kipling's letters to his children are, first, why do we have as many of them as we do? and second, why aren't there more?

As to the first of these enquiries, it is reasonable to wonder how so many of the 223 items in the 1906–1915 group to Elsie and John could have survived. Most of them were written, after all, to a young schoolboy, only ten when he first went off to St Aubyns in Rottingdean, and we might question how careful a preserver of correspondence a child of that age would be. Yet the fact is that we seem to have all – or nearly all – the letters Kipling sent to John during his first school year, as well as those for most other years.

Of course, this achievement may be less remarkable than it looks. At St Aubyns School today, for instance, where telephoning is restricted and letter-writing encouraged, many of the boys, school officials report, carefully preserve their letters from home. So we might easily imagine John Kipling doing the same with his father's letters, under additional orders, perhaps, to guard them from devotees of the Higher Cannibalism. Packets of letters, then, grouped by academic year, would have been brought back to Bateman's every summer by John, stored among his own things, and after his death taken into the archive.

There are also some late letters to John that perhaps have entered the archive since Charles Carrington examined the correspondence in the early 1950s. At least, the index to Carrington's 1955 biography refers to Kipling's letter of August 22 1915 as his last to John, whereas the collection now contains seven later items. In her long stewardship of the papers, Elsie Bambridge regularly added new materials, and these seven letters may have been among her contributions, though what their source could have been we can only speculate. Certainly, Elsie did her work of preserving and developing the archive well, whatever her insistence on restricting access to it. One of her most valuable ideas was to have typescripts made of nearly all the letters in her father's often difficult handwriting. These transcripts, prepared by Cecily Nicholson, RK's last private secretary, differ from the originals only in their regularizing of erratic punctuation, a practice I have followed in this edition.

The second and more complex question to ask about the letters is why there are no more of them. It is a question suggested in particular by two year-long gaps in the chronology, the periods from October 11 1910 to October 18 1911, and October 21 1913 to September 28 1914, for which no letters to the children have been preserved. That each gap is precisely the length of an academic year, and that the years are those during which John was changing schools, suggest that the letters for these periods may have been mislaid in the confusion of moving. But whatever the explanation, the loss is a serious one since the two blank years cover such dramatic moments in Kipling family history as the deaths of RK's father and mother within a few months of each other, John's move from St Aubyns to Wellington College and later from Wellington to an army crammer in Bournemouth, Rudyard's efforts to get a commission for his son from Lord Roberts, John's baptism into the Church of England, his efforts to enter the army as an enlisted man, and his eventual assignment to Warley Barracks as an ensign in the Irish Guards.

A second major gap in the collection is the nearly total absence of letters by family members other than Kipling himself. About this, at least, there was nothing accidental; the family's desire for privacy might occasionally yield to the claims of literary history as far as RK's own papers were concerned, but all other correspondence was systematically destroyed. In fact, the removal from the archive of every

8

Kipling but Rudyard was so ruthless that where in one of RK's letters to the children Carrie Kipling had added a few words, these words have been carefully covered over with a paper label. There were few exceptions to this rule of silence. A dozen and a half of John's letters have survived from his last months, obviously preserved as a memorial, and most of them are printed here, full of boyish energy, poignantly self-confident, and hilariously confirming everything RK has warned us to expect about their spelling. Ironically, the censoring of the archive has, at least in this case, produced a dramatic effect. For, although we may regret the sacrifice of all the schoolboy letters, it is just that long, enforced silence that makes John's sudden appearance late in these pages so moving.

A last important gap in the archive is the lack of any really significant number of letters to Elsie; just about a dozen addressed directly to her are included. The obvious explanation is that Elsie, living and studying at home as many girls of her age and class did in those years, seldom required writing to. Only when she was away on a rare visit, like her swimming holiday in London in 1908, or when Rudyard and Carrie travelled without her, as they did in Egypt in 1913, did RK have any chance to correspond with her. (Later, and especially after her marriage, Elsie would receive hundreds of letters from her father, but those, addressed to an adult, are outside the scope of this volume.) Kipling doesn't seem to have written in different voices to his son and daughter; certainly, he treats Elsie to the same kind of earnest advice and the same affectionate ragging as her brother. But he did have a tendency to see his few letters to her as opportunities for discussing John, and especially – as in the letter of September 28 1914 – for expressing a. pride and love he was unable to state quite as openly to his son.

Considering what is and what is not in the archive, it is inevitable that John should be the centre of attention in a correspondence that is, more than anything else, the record of a typical Edwardian boyhood. Rudyard Kipling is not, of course, a typical Edwardian father, as the lively drawings, the impromptu poems, the wit, the energy, and the imagination of the letters testify. But clearly in these letters he appears as a father much more often than he does as a famous literary man, conscientiously encouraging better school grades, exchanging anecdotes about sports, describing family adventures, giving good advice. In this respect at least Carrington was right when he said that the secret of the Kipling archive is that there is no secret. For it is precisely the familiarity, the ordinariness of most of the experiences recorded here

9

that makes them so appealing, that gives the charm and strength to what is, finally, Rudyard Kipling's informal biography of his son John.

"My Boy Jack"

Biographies of Kipling don't have much to say about John. Most speak well of his high spirits, his quick wit, and his good nature, but Birkenhead goes on to comment that "at seventeen his character was still unformed",[8] Carrington's judgement is that he had "no marked talents",[9] and Angus Wilson refers to him as "a typical public schoolboy officer of those years".[10] As the letters from RK make clear, John was anything but an academic success, and even his greatest athletic triumph, winning the Young Cup for runners at Wellington, occurred when he got the best aggregate score in two heats without coming in first in either of them.

Still, it would be a mistake to dismiss John as wholly unaccomplished; in fact, his achievements at the time of his death compare favourably with those of his father at the same age. Where, for example, Rudyard at seventeen was sub-editing a newspaper and enduring the Indian hot weather, his son was single-handedly delivering a draft of new recruits from Ireland to England and leading twenty-mile forced marches through a record heat-wave. As for John's insistence, much to the astonishment of his parents, on being baptized at sixteen, there is no equivalent show of initiative in RK's early career.

In the letters that record the curtailed history of this young man, Kipling is at his most sensitive when he is dealing with such rivalries between the generations, and especially with the difficulties created for his children by his own fame. One of the first letters to John at St Aubyns reminds the boy of his good fortune at going to school in the town where he was born and still has many relatives and friends. Delicately unmentioned is the fact that Rudyard's own appearances in such a place will cause little excitement. Later, Kipling's apologies for having made his son uncomfortable at school with "The Children's Song" are nearly abject, and when at Wellington the boy is in danger of being asked to leave for failure to advance quickly enough, his father only very reluctantly points out to him that the event will be a newsworthy one.

Even after a real competitiveness between father and son begins to appear in the letters during John's last months, with RK boasting of his visits to the front and giving expert advice about the use of rabbit netting in trenches (advice John spiritedly rejects), the old delicacy persists. Rudyard refuses, for example, to wear the uniform he is entitled to as a war correspondent in France, knowing that he will be photographed in it and recognizing the priority of John's claim to the honour. (Ill. 9) He even sacrifices what proves to be his last chance to see the boy out of a similar sensitivity, writing to Carrie from Troyes that John "wouldn't like to have me tracking him yet".[11]

Such delicacy also characterizes the occasional fatherly admonitions the letters contain. As an artist, Kipling understood that parents, like poets, must instruct with a light touch if they don't want their lessons ignored, must realize – as he puts it in his poem "The Fabulists" – that "unless they please they are not heard at all". This recognition produces some of the highlights of the letters: the comic drawing of the huge toothbrush and mouthful of teeth to remind John of his hygienic duties, the wildly misspelled paragraph to encourage greater care in letter-writing, the amusing parody of the Swiss jeweller whose obsessive refrain is the admonition not to take the back off one's watch. The almost feminine indirection with which Kipling undertakes to teach his son in such passages will perhaps surprise some readers, and we may even wonder whether Virginia Woolf's well-known deprecation of RK in *A Room of One's Own* for "writing only with the male side of his brain" might not have been modified a little if she had been able to examine these letters.

To be sure, the letters can also be seen as confirming many traditional judgements of Kipling. RK's casual use of words like "nigger" and "gollywog", for example, or his near-hysteria at the schoolboy homosexuality he calls "beastliness" and whose practitioners he dismisses as "contaminating swine" will be offensive, or at least troublesome, even to the reader who can place such matters in the context of their time, a time when boot polish could be purchased in English shops in a shade called "Nigger Brown", and when productions of *The Importance of Being Earnest* at public schools were not permitted to include the author's name in their playbills. Even more lamentably Kiplingesque, many readers will find, is the encouragement these letters offer to John to pursue the military career that will destroy him only six weeks past his eighteenth birthday. But in this matter at least, the issues are complex and problematical.

What would seem to be the clearest statement of the Kipling position on the mystique of military service occurs in the letter to John dated March 23 1915. The Kiplings had been visiting novelist Rider Haggard and the children's old French governess, and in the course of a conver-

11

sation about the war, the question had arisen: "*If* there is no compulsion, why should John enter the army?" To which Carrie had replied, "Precisely *because* there is no compulsion." RK reports this answer to John with obvious approval, as if the whole matter were quite an easy and settled one. But after he and Carrie leave, Haggard, who had long known and worked with Rudyard and could read his moods as well as anyone, writes of the Kiplings in his diary:

Neither of them look so well as they did. ... Their boy John, who is not yet eighteen, is an officer in the Irish Guards and one can see that they are terrified lest he should be sent to the front and killed, as has happened to nearly all the young men they knew.[12]

The gulf between Kipling's ideals and his profound pessimism could not be more starkly presented. Those ideals, frequently expressed to John in the simple, unambiguous spirit of "If" (see, for example, the letter of June 16 1909), reject compulsion as the controlling principle of life and instead celebrate self-reliance and meaningful choice. Such a view would explain everything from Kipling's delicacy and reticence in the education of his children to his horror of the "contaminating swine" who, abdicating their own moral responsibility, yield to the compulsion of the "beast". But the Kipling of Haggard's diary entry is a man with a darker vision than this, the vision of an immense fatality mocking such illusory ideals. Realistically speaking, a young Englishman, born, as John Kipling was, in the year 1897 – the year of Victoria's Jubilee; the year, too, of the admonitory and prophetic "Recessional" – was fated to die on the battlefields of France beyond all possibility of human choice or control. And it was this knowledge Haggard saw in Kipling's face that afternoon.

In this sense, the particular stations of the cross in John's brief life – from St Aubyns to Wellington College in Berkshire, from Wellington to a Bournemouth crammer to prepare for the Sandhurst examination, from Bournemouth to Warley, and from Warley to France – are almost irrelevant, since no alternative course could reasonably have been expected to lead to a different result. Rudyard compulsively explores such alternatives in his "Epitaphs of the War" in couplets like "The Coward":

> I could not look on Death, which being known,
> Men led me to him, blindfold and alone.

and "Bombed in London":

> On land and sea I strove with anxious care
> To escape conscription. It was in the air!

and perhaps it comforted him to think that his son's death had at least come in the line of duty.

In any case, it came quickly. John reached France precisely on his eighteenth birthday, August 17 1915, and not quite six weeks later he was writing his last letter home, confiding, with a touching faith and self-importance, that

this is *the* great effort to break through and end the war. . . . They are staking a tremendous lot on this great advancing movement as if it succeeds the war won't go on for long.

The anticipated action was the Battle of Loos, an indecisive struggle that began on September 25 as a small gain along a section of the German front and faded out not long after with little to show for having consumed 20,000 British lives. On September 27, John's division of the Guards, withheld as a last reserve, was rushed in to shore up a crumbling portion of the line but was no more successful than previous units and, like them, suffered heavy casualties. The War Office telegram declaring John wounded and missing in action reached Bateman's five days later, but it would be another two years before Rudyard and Carrie knew for certain that he was dead. The body was never recovered.

"A Heart by Fifty Years Made Cold"

The Kiplings already knew what it was to lose a child. When Josephine Kipling died at seven of the pneumonia that had almost killed her father, the effect of her death was a devastating one from which Rudyard never fully recovered. For the departure of this much loved first-born daughter was accompanied by the dramatic diminution in Kipling of the interior child, of that "frivolling" baby whom the writer had long recognized to be a major source of his personal and artistic strength. Others could see this change in RK very clearly. Angela Thirkell, for instance, comments about him at this time:

Much of the beloved Cousin Ruddy of our childhood died with Josephine and I feel that I have never seen him as a real person since that year.[13]

The elegy Kipling wrote for his daughter, the poem called "Merrow Down" that follows "How the First Letter Was Written" and "How the Alphabet Was Made" in the *Just So Stories*, significantly uses the

13

metaphor of physical separation, of the withdrawal of the child from the father, to describe what Thirkell sees as her cousin's striking loss of authenticity.

> For far – oh, very far behind,
>   So far she cannot call to him,
> Comes Tegumai alone to find
>   The daughter that was all to him!

The death of John completed the devastation Josephine's had begun, the more so because it raised serious questions about Kipling's own culpability. When, for example, in an "Epitaph of the War" called "Common Form", Kipling wrote:

> If any question why we died,
> Tell them because our fathers lied

he was certainly referring to men of his own generation whom he had often criticized for failing to confront political reality. But he would have been the last to deny that the word "father" applied to himself as well, and he did not need the many gloating letters he received holding him accountable for his son's death to consider the possibility of his personal guilt. Had he not, after all, intervened with Lord Roberts to get John a commission? Had he not given the required parental consent for the boy to be shipped to France? More important, had he not, in dozens of stories and poems, celebrated the subaltern experience and shaped a whole generation's ideas about the excitement and glamour of war?

That RK could not entirely dismiss the thought that he was implicated in John's death is suggested, paradoxically, by his frantic search for scapegoats. The Radical Party, the Irish, the Jews, the unions – all felt the sting of his vindictiveness; indeed, here if anywhere is the long-sought scandalous Kipling. Yet over both his own feelings of guilt and his convictions about the guilt of others there broods his even profounder fatalism. Writing to C.R.L. Fletcher, for example, about what he sees as organized labour's profiteering during the war, he comments sardonically:

> For this cause my boy died at eighteen instead of between nineteen and twenty, as he ought.[14]

It is his old sense of the blank inescapability of things, the driving necessity which, as an artist, he had once courted and called his "Daemon" and which had now returned, demoniacally, to collect its wages.

No doubt Kipling's most characteristic response to his son's death was a sometimes too deep reserve. For while in the letters John is routinely discouraged from expressing pain – "I am only *very* glad you didn't show that it hurt," RK writes on November 16 1912 after the boy had received a beating at school – the emotional anaesthesia of the post-war Kipling approached the pathological. The off-handedness, for instance, of the passage in his history of the Irish Guards describing John's fate would seem callous if we did not know the agony it conceals.

Of the officers, 2nd Lieutenant Pakenham-Law had died of wounds; 2nd Lieutenants Clifford and Kipling were missing, Captain and Adjutant the Hon. T.E. Vesey, Captain Wynter, Lieutenant Stevens, and 2nd Lieutenants Sassoon and Grayson were wounded, the last being blown up by a shell. It was a fair average for the day of a debut, and taught them somewhat for their future guidance.[15]

Elsie for one was concerned about her father's suppression of feeling – about "the heart by fifty years made cold" RK speaks of in his poem "A Recantation" – fearing the consequences of such self-denial. "The two great sorrows of their lives," she writes in her memoir, "my parents bore bravely and silently, perhaps too silently for their own good."[16] And in fact it was following John's death in 1915 that Rudyard first began to experience the painful gastric symptoms that were to torture him over the next two decades and that not even the famous surgeon John Bland-Sutton could diagnose or relieve. In a sense, the pain, inconsolable, filling the void left by the departure of the children, was beyond diagnosis or relief. For like the speaker in Wordsworth's "We Are Seven", Kipling had irrecoverably lost the magical childhood secret of life, and had now embarked on a more sober career of witnessing for death.

There is no question but that in the pursuit of that career, and out of the debilitating silence and ruinous self-control of his daily life, RK produced some of his finest stories and poems; as Azrael, the Angel of Death, puts it in "Uncovenanted Mercies", "I have seen wonderful work done – with My Sword practically at people's throats." For Josephine he had written the elegiac "Merrow Down" and "They", a dream of lost children; now for John he composed "The Gardener", full of details from his work on the War Graves Commission, "My Boy Jack", tender and almost too painful, "A Recantation", with its touching reference to the phonograph records mentioned in the letter of December 3 1912, and perhaps most tormented of all, "The Children –

1914-1918", its imagery as graphic and bitter as anything in Wilfred Owen –

> That flesh we had nursed from the first in all cleanness was given ...
> To be blanched or gay-painted by fumes – to be cindered by fires –
> To be senselessly tossed and retossed in stale mutilation
> From crater to crater. ...

– and its refrain the question that haunted so much of the writer's later life and work: "But who shall return us the children?"

Helpless before that question, Kipling could never quite move beyond it. His genius was, as this collection so poignantly illustrates, to be the father of children; his tragedy was to be deprived of them and permanently scarred by their departure. The letters gathered here preserve that genius but cannot postpone the tragedy, and it is no doubt fitting that the last word we hear in these pages is John's emblematic goodbye. Rudyard was not there to see the young man's actual departure from Bateman's, having already left for France on a journalistic assignment. But Carrie describes the scene in her diary with a power unusual for her, a power that afterwards might have brought to Rudyard's mind the bitter-sweet Keatsian image he knew well of "Joy, whose hand is ever at his lips bidding adieu." "John leaves at noon for Warley," Carrie's entry for August 15 1915 records, capturing the last moment of childhood for all of them.

> He looks very straight and smart and young, as he turns at the top of the stairs to say: "Send my love to Daddo."

[1] Philip Knightley, "What Did Kipling's Daughter Want to Hide?" *Sunday Times* (June 13 1976).

[2] Angela Thirkell, *Three Houses* (London: Oxford University Press, 1931), pp. 87–88.

[3] Charles Carrington, *Rudyard Kipling* (London: Macmillan, 1978), p. 587.

[4] Thirkell, p. 88.

[5] The letter is owned by the Henry W. and Albert A. Berg Collection, The New York Public Library, Astor, Lenox and Tilden Foundations and is quoted here with permission.

[6] Katharine Moore, *Kipling and the White Man's Burden* (London: Faber & Faber, 1968), p. 32.

[7] H.L.L. Denny, "A Kipling Shrine" (Burwash Church, 1967), p. 8.

[8] Lord Birkenhead, *Rudyard Kipling* (London: Weidenfeld & Nicolson, 1978), p. 270.

[9] Carrington, p. 487.

[10] Angus Wilson, *The Strange Ride of Rudyard Kipling* (London: Secker & Warburg, 1976), p. 305.

[11] Kipling Papers, University of Sussex, Letter from RK to CK, August 21 1915.

[12] Morton Cohen, ed., *Rudyard Kipling to Rider Haggard* (Rutherford, N.J.: Fairleigh Dickinson University Press, 1965), p. 81.

[13] Thirkell, p. 86.

[14] Quoted in Birkenhead, p. 291.

[15] Rudyard Kipling, *The Irish Guards in the Great War*, Vol. II (London: Macmillan & Co., 1923), p. 17. Compare John's equally cold-blooded response to the death of his friend Oscar Hornung. "Isn't it awful about poor old Oscar," he writes on July 16 1915. "There is another of the 'old Brigade' gone. Many thanks for the laces, etc."

[16] Carrington, p. 595.

WHO'S WHO IN THE LETTERS

Here, briefly annotated, are the names that figure most prominently in Kipling's letters to his children. Casual acquaintances, Sussex neighbours, and servants whose functions seem sufficiently clear from the text are, with a few exceptions, not identified.

Aitken, Max: (see Beaverbrook, Lord)

Angy: (see Thirkell, Angela Mackail)

Aunt Cissie: (see Baldwin, Lucy Ridsdale)

Aunt Georgie: (see Burne-Jones, Georgiana Macdonald)

Aunt Louie: (see Baldwin, Louisa Macdonald)

Aunt Trix: (see Kipling, Alice; Mrs John Fleming)

Baden-Powell, General Sir Robert S. (1857-1941): Celebrated as the "hero of Mafeking", he first met RK in South Africa. Today he is perhaps best remembered as founder of the Boy Scout movement, a project, inspired in part by the *Jungle Books*, in which Kipling actively participated.

Baldwin, Louisa Macdonald (1845-1925): Kipling's "Aunt Louie" and the fourth of the Macdonald sisters, she married wealthy ironmaster Alfred Baldwin, later a Member of Parliament. It was Louisa who suggested that Alice and Lockwood Kipling name their son Rudyard after the lake at which the couple became engaged.

Baldwin, Lucy Ridsdale (1869-1945): Wife of Stanley Baldwin, RK's first cousin, whom she married in 1892. Extroverted, strong-minded, sports-loving daughter of a prominent Rottingdean family, "Aunt Cissie" bore four daughters and two sons: Diana ("Di"), Leonora ("Lorna"), Margaret ("Margot"), Esther ("Betty"), Oliver ("Ollie") [q.v.], and Windham ("Little").

Baldwin, Oliver (1899–1958), later 2nd Earl Baldwin of Bewdley: Son of Stanley Baldwin and Lucy Ridsdale Baldwin. Educated at Eton, he became a Labour MP and from 1948 to 1950 was Governor of the Leeward Islands.

Baldwin, Stanley (1867–1947), later 1st Earl Baldwin of Bewdley: Only child of Alfred Baldwin and RK's aunt Louisa Macdonald Baldwin, "Uncle Stan" was Prime Minister from 1923 to 1924, 1925 to 1929, and 1935 to 1937. Though he and his cousin Rudyard came to differ politically, they remained personally close, and there is evidence that RK wrote or revised a number of his speeches.

Balestier, Anna Smith (d. 1919): Married to Henry Balestier, RK's mother-in-law was early widowed and lived with her four children, Caroline, Josephine, Wolcott, and Beatty, in Rochester, NY. She often visited the Balestier family home in Brattleboro, Vermont, however, and was living there at the time of Rudyard's and Carrie's trip to Canada in 1907. In 1891, RK co-authored *The Naulahka* with Wolcott Balestier, and in 1892 he married Caroline.

Bear: Pet name for Caroline ("Carrie") Kipling.

Beaverbrook, Lord (1879–1964): Max Aitken, a Canadian journalist and politician, whose friendship with RK dates from the latter's 1907 trip to Canada. He was raised to the peerage in 1917 and in the same year helped persuade Kipling to undertake his history of the Irish Guards. The friendship cooled over political differences during the 1920s, after which the two men did not meet again.

Beresford, George Charles (1865–1938): The original of "M'Turk" in *Stalky & Co.*, he wrote about his former fellow student in *Schooldays with Kipling* (London: Gollancz, 1936).

Blaikie, Miss: John and Elsie Kipling's governess until 1911. She remained a good friend of the Kiplings after leaving their employ and occasionally visited them at Bateman's.

Bland-Sutton, Sir John (1855–1936): The Kiplings' eminent family physician who attended RK during his last years of declining health. At Rudyard's urging, he wrote a volume of reminiscences called *The Story of a Surgeon* (London: Methuen, 1930).

Brassey, Lord Thomas (1836–1918): Entered Parliament as a Liberal in 1865, the year of RK's birth, and for the rest of his long career was principally interested in naval affairs. In 1917, Kipling, who was opposed to the Liberal position on the war, described Lord Brassey to Stanley Baldwin as "vehemently ga-ga" and "an old imbecile".

Burne-Jones, Lady Georgiana Macdonald (1840–1920): RK's "Aunt Georgie", she married Pre-Raphaelite painter Edward Burne-Jones (1833–1898) in 1860. As a child, RK often visited his aunt in North End Road, London, and thirty years later at "North End House", Rottingdean, she looked after John Kipling, enrolled in nearby St Aubyns School.

Cecil, George (1895–1914): The son of Lord Edward and Lady Violet Georgina Cecil, he died in France a year before John Kipling under strikingly similar circumstances. See RK's "The War and the Schools" in *A Book of Words*, a talk delivered at Winchester College, December 1915, to commemorate Cecil's death.

Cecil, Lady Violet Georgina, (1872–1958), later Viscountess Milner: Married first to Lord Edward Cecil and afterwards to Lord Alfred Milner, she was a neighbour of the Kiplings both in South Africa and in Sussex and Caroline Kipling's closest friend in England. Editor of the *National Review* for a number of years, in 1951 she published a volume of autobiography, *My Picture Gallery 1886–1901*.

Clemenceau, Georges (1841–1929): French physician, journalist, statesman, and Academician, he was Premier from 1906 to 1909 and from 1917 to 1920. As a friend of Lady Edward Cecil, he visited Bateman's on several occasions where RK concluded that he was "an amazing human explosive".

Di: (Diana Baldwin; see Baldwin, Lucy Ridsdale)

Doubleday, Frank N. (1862–1934): A publisher whom Kipling first met in Vermont in 1895, he became a close personal friend (F.N.D. – "Beloved Effendi"), especially after his devotion to the family during RK's illness in 1899.

Dunsterville, Major-General L.C. (1865-1946): The original "Stalky" of *Stalky & Co.*, he published a memoir under the title *Stalky's Reminiscences* (London: Jonathan Cape, 1928). In 1927 he became the first president of the Kipling Society.

Feilden, Colonel H. Wemyss (1838-1921): Friend and confidant of the Kiplings at Burwash, with whom RK went fishing and shooting, made plans for developing his estate, talked village politics, and consulted in domestic emergencies. Feilden had run the Northern blockade during the American Civil War and had been an aide-de-camp to Robert E. Lee.

Grayson, Rupert (b. 1896): Fellow officer of John Kipling's in the Irish Guards, he was wounded but survived to visit Bateman's after the war and supply details for RK's history of John's unit.

Gwynne, Howell Arthur (1865-1950): Journalist who met RK during the first year of the Boer War and afterwards became a close friend. From 1911 to 1937 he was editor of the Conservative *Morning Post*, in which Kipling's work frequently appeared.

Haggard, H. Rider (1856-1925): Author of *King Solomon's Mines* and *She*, Haggard first encountered Kipling at London's literary Savile Club in 1889, and the two soon became good friends and collaborators. Kipling's letters to Haggard and Haggard's diary responses have been edited by Morton Cohen in *Rudyard Kipling to Rider Haggard: The Record of a Friendship* (Rutherford, NJ: Fairleigh Dickinson University Press, 1965).

Hely-Hutchinson, Richard Walter John, 6th Earl of Donoughmore (1875-1948): Under-Secretary of State for War, 1903-1905, he continued afterwards to be prominent in government affairs.

Hornung, Oscar (1896-1915): A friend of John Kipling's, he often stayed at Bateman's, and his death in France in July 1915 only made John more impatient to see action. Hornung's father was E.W. Hornung, creator of the fictional thief A. J. Raffles, and his mother, Constance Doyle, was the sister of Arthur Conan Doyle.

Jameson, Dr Leander Starr (1853-1917): Best known for his 1896 "Raid", a dramatic if unsuccessful foray into the Transvaal with four hundred and seventy men that led to his capture and imprisonment. As South African Premier, he lived in Cecil Rhodes' house at "Groote Schuur", where he and R K, at the neighbouring "Woolsack", became acquainted. Kipling states in his autobiography, *Something of Myself*, that his poem "If" was based on Jameson's character.

Joffre, Field-Marshal Joseph Jacques Césaire (1852-1931): At the time these letters were written, he was Commander-in-Chief of the French armies.

Kerry, Lt.-Col. Henry William Edmond, the Earl of (1872-1964): Commanded the 2nd Battalion of the Irish Guards during the time John Kipling was in training with the unit at Warley.

Kipling, Alice; Mrs John Fleming (1868-1948): R K's younger sister "Trix" was herself a talented writer, co-authoring an early volume of verse parodies with her brother (*Echoes*) and later publishing her own fiction, including her 1897 novel *A Pinchbeck Goddess*. At the time of these letters, however, she had become mentally ill and, except for occasional periods of remission, remained so for the rest of her life.

Kipling, Alice Macdonald (1837-1910): R K's mother. The eldest of the Macdonald sisters, she married John Lockwood Kipling in 1865 and soon afterwards accompanied him to India. As a witty, strong-minded woman she was an important influence on her son's life and work. Once berated by R K for the unmaternal rigour of her response to some of his verses, she is reported in *Something of Myself* to have replied, "There is no mother in poetry, dear".

Kipling, Caroline ("Carrie") Starr Balestier (1862-1939): A capable, strong-willed American woman whom Lockwood Kipling rather maliciously called "a good man spoiled", she first met Rudyard through her brother Wolcott Balestier, who was collaborating with R K on a novel, *The Naulahka*. The couple were married in January 1892, shortly after Wolcott's premature death, with Henry James giving the bride away. The Kiplings had three children: Josephine (1892-1899), Elsie (1896-1976), and John (1897-1915).

Kipling, Elsie; Mrs George Bambridge (1896-1976): The second of the three Kipling children, Elsie ("Bird", "Phipps") was the only one to survive past her teens. She married Captain George Bambridge in October 1925, was widowed in 1943 without having had any children of her own, and for nearly forty years after the death of her parents acted as custodian of the Kipling archive at Wimpole Hall near Cambridge.

Kipling, John (1897-1915): The last of the three Kipling children, John ("William") attended St Aubyns School and Wellington College before joining the Irish Guards in 1914. He died on September 27 1915 in the Battle of Loos.

Kipling, John Lockwood (1837-1911): RK's father. From a family of Yorkshire Methodists, young art student Lockwood Kipling went out to India in 1865 with his new wife Alice to take up the post of Architectural Sculptor in the Bombay School of Art. Author of *Beast and Man in India*, he later illustrated many of his son's works and until his death performed for RK the function of literary adviser.

Kipling, Josephine (1892-1899): The first of the three Kipling children, she succumbed in New York at the age of seven to the pneumonia from which her father also suffered and nearly died.

Kitchener, Field-Marshal Lord Horatio Herbert (1850-1916): Hero of Khartoum in 1898, Secretary of State for War from 1914 to 1916, he was appointed Colonel-in-Chief of the Irish Guards after the death of Lord Roberts in November 1914. As a popular verse of the post-Boer War period put it, "When the Empire wants a stitch in her/Send for Kipling and for Kitchener."

Landon, Percival (1869-1927): A correspondent for *The Times* during the Boer War, he became one of RK's most intimate friends, often travelling with him and, between journalistic assignments, living at Keylands, a cottage Kipling kept for him at Bateman's.

Law, Andrew Bonar (1858-1923): A Canadian politician, in 1917 he was appointed Chancellor of the Exchequer in Lloyd George's coalition government, at the collapse of which he himself became Prime Minister. During these years, the Law and Kipling families often met socially.

Lorna: (Leonora Baldwin; see Baldwin, Lucy Ridsdale)

Madden, Lt.-Col. G.H.C. (1872-1915): For a time Senior Major of the 2nd Battalion of the Irish Guards, "Jerry" Madden took command of the 1st Battalion in France in August 1915, was badly wounded the following October, just two weeks after John Kipling's death, and died a few weeks later in England.

Margot: (Margaret Baldwin; see Baldwin, Lucy Ridsdale)

Milner, Alfred, 1st Viscount (1854-1925): Journalist and colonial administrator, he brought Kipling into his Cape Town circle in 1898. The two men admired one another, frequently exchanging views and eventually working together on the War Graves Commission, of which Milner was Chairman. RK's poem "The Pro-Consuls" may be read as a tribute to Milner.

Ollie: (see Baldwin, Oliver)

Osler, Lady (Grace Revere): Related through the Balestiers to Caroline Kipling, Lady Osler was the wife of Sir William Osler (1849-1919), famous Canadian physician and Regius Professor of Medicine at Oxford. It was as a result of his friendship with Osler that RK acquired an interest in the history of medicine evident in such stories as "Marklake Witches" and "The Eye of Allah".

Pearson, John Yardley "Pompey" (d. 1915): A much-admired master at Wellington College whose house John Kipling entered in 1911.

Ponton, Dorothy (1884-1975): She replaced Miss Blaikie as John and Elsie Kipling's governess and teacher in 1911. A privately printed memoir of her experiences is entitled *Rudyard Kipling at Home and at Work*.

Poynter, Edward (1836-1919): A popular Victorian painter, now largely ignored, he was for the last two decades of his life President of the Royal Academy. In 1866 he married Agnes Macdonald (1843-1906), RK's "Auntie Aggie" and third of the Macdonald sisters.

Poynter, Hugh (1882–1968): The second son of Edward and Agnes Poynter, he was, as a boy, RK's favourite among his many young cousins.

Price, Cormell (1835–1910): Macdonald family friend and first Headmaster of the United Services College at Westward Ho!, in which RK was enrolled shortly after his twelfth birthday, "Uncle Crom" is affectionately portrayed by his former pupil in *Stalky & Co*.

Roberts, Field Marshal Lord Frederick Sleigh (1832–1914): As Commander-in-Chief of British forces during the Boer War, he invited Kipling, who had first met him in India, to join the staff of the Bloemfontein *Friend*, an army newspaper. RK accepted and the favour was later returned when Lord Roberts, the "Bobs" of Kipling's complimentary verses, procured a commission in the Irish Guards for John Kipling.

Stanford, C.E.F.: In 1895, together with Vaughan Lang, he established St Aubyns School in Rottingdean, where John Kipling became a student in 1907.

Thirkell, Angela Mackail (1890–1961): Daughter of RK's cousin Margaret ("Margot") Burne-Jones and herself a novelist, she has left a record of her early childhood experiences with Josephine, Elsie, and John Kipling in *Three Houses* (London: Oxford University Press, 1931).

Uncle Crom: (see Price, Cormell)

Uncle Edward: (see Poynter, Edward)

Uncle Stan: (see Baldwin, Stanley)

Vesey, Captain the Hon. Thomas Eustace (1885–1946): Adjutant of the 2nd Battalion of the Irish Guards, he was badly wounded in the same attack in which John Kipling was killed. In 1918, by this time a Lieutenant-Colonel, he was awarded the *Croix de Guerre*.

1906–1908

During these years, Kipling and his family wintered – or rather double-summered – in South Africa, living at the "Woolsack", a comfortable Dutch colonial house built by Cecil Rhodes next door to his own "Groote Schuur" estate outside Cape Town and placed at the disposal of the Kiplings for as long as they might wish to use it. A trip by John and Elsie in March 1906 to the beach resort of Muizenberg occasioned R K's first extant letter to the children.

These were also years when Kipling accumulated honours, including degrees from Durham, Oxford, Cambridge, and McGill, and the 1907 Nobel Prize for Literature. At the same time, he was completing work on *Puck of Pook's Hill* and beginning a second set of Puck stories, tales in which John and Elsie appear as Dan and Una and the geography of Bateman's,[1] the seventeenth-century property in Burwash, Sussex, which the family acquired in 1902, plays an important part.

In September 1907, John entered a boarding school (St Aubyns or, more familiarly, Stanford's) in Rottingdean, the small village a few miles east of Brighton where he had been born ten years before, where the Kiplings had occupied "The Elms" from 1897 to 1902, and where R K's "Aunt Georgie" Burne-Jones still lived. Within a few days, Rudyard and Carrie sailed for Canada on a month's tour, a trip that provided Kipling with material for a series of travel articles, "Letters to the Family", charmingly counterpointed by his private reports home to the children. The Canadian venture, John's first year at school, and an extended visit to London by Elsie in the summer of 1908 were the principal occasions for letter-writing to the children during this period.

[1] See illustration 1

Dearly Beloveds,

It is a very hot day but Mummy is not so uncomfy as she was yesterday. She is very tired and is now lying on the couch in my study. She ate an egg for breakfast and it agreed with her. It was a fresh egg from Groote Schuur laid by a kind fowl on purpose. I think that if the weather gets cooler Mummy will soon get better. We are waiting for the doctor to come and tell us how she may behave. She misses you very much and, tho' you might not think it, so do I.

We saw in the paper that there had been a *very* heavy gale of wind at Muizenberg yesterday. I hope you didn't bathe. The weather here was only a little blowy.

I went down to post my letter to you yesterday at 3 o'clock, and I never saw so many people before at Rosebank station. They were all coming to the Show. It took all the time from my coming in at the far gate of the station, walking to the telegraph office, sending a telegram, and posting your letter *and* walking back again, before the people got off the bridge. Just think what a crowd that means? And there was a huge crowd round the gate of the Show.

Now I am coming down to see you on Sunday morning so please don't go to church. I shall get to Muizenberg by an early train and if Miss Howard will give me lunch I'll come home directly afterwards.

I haven't been doing anything except looking at Mummy who says that she loves you a lot and hopes you are enjoying yourselves and behaving respectably. Mummy is now going to have something more to eat. She has gruel without any rice in it but she does not have so much pain.

> Always your loving Dad.
> For John   For Elsie
> xxxxx   xxxxx
> xxxxx   xxxxx
> xxx   xxx
>   x   x

Õ Family –

I am writing to you in ténder and löving áccents. They look rather pretty, don't 'em. – here I stopped and filled the stylo. You can see a portion of the consequences at the bottom of the page – just the fringe of it – but you can't see my blotter or my left hand, which are truly Beautiful. Well, I never *did* like stylographs.

This morning we went to attend the ceremony of unveiling a monument to the Cape Town Volunteers who died during the war. It was rather a hottish day. The memorial is a statue of a volunteer in full fighting kit standing behind a seated figure of Hope, something like this!

We went in by the 9.28 train, and there were lots of volunteers. The statue is at the end of the parade-ground close up to Cape Town. When we arrived it looked like this, all veiled in a large linen sheet.

There were not many people except the volunteers themselves. A few benches were put down before the statue but hardly anyone sat in them. Sir Walter Hely-Hutchinson arrived just as the clock struck 10.15. He made a speech which I couldn't hear; at the end of it took off his hat and pulled the cord which released the sheet. Down and off came the sheet and his A.D.C.s had just time to skip aside or it would have flopped on top of their heads. I was highly delighted.

Then we went across to the City Hall to hear a service of prayers and hymns and a sermon. I don't think you have ever been in the City Hall. One end of it is filled up with the hugest organ that ever you did see – something like this.

Steps descend into the hall and all the steps were crowded with men in uniform. But I kept my eye on the organ because it was so vast: and I expected to hear Noises! I did! I never knew anything could growl and thunder and bellow so splendidly. It just shook the hall. Being of an enquiring turn of mind I looked to see who was making it perform and just in the centre where I have drawn a thing like a dead wasp I saw the shoulders and hands of the organist.

There was some sort of mirror reflecting him. He was dressed in a red gown but one couldn't see the keyboard of the organ. All one saw was these mad hands pawing in the air and every time they came down the organ squealed or hooted or howled. Mad – quite mad, my dears, but *most* interesting. We sat next to Dr and Mrs Smartt and drove home with the Strubens behind their new tall high fine horses which John saw in the stable.

I am a provident person. Yesterday on my way into Cape Town to buy baccy I left two empty baskets as a delicate hint at Strubenheim.

When we reached Strubenheim this morn I took back – a full basket of figs and grapes. Also I ate two pears *just* before lunch which ruined my meal. I now understand J[ohn]'s delicate appetite. Pears is filling. You've no notion how well a basket of fruit goes with a black coat, a top hat *and* one grey glove.

this is the gloved hand

I don't think there is much else to tell except that Mother and I are buried in Queen Victoria's letters. We read 'em to each other aloud and sit up till all hours to finish our volumes. It beats any novel I've ever read. There is a dear delightful Prime Minister, called Lord Melbourne who was always helpful to the Queen and loved her like a father and gave her good advice. One time the King of Sardinia (the island belongs to Italy now) got stuffy because he was invited to dinner with the Queen by a *card* instead of a formal note. Lord Melbourne wrote to the Queen and said:— "This may seem a very little matter to Your Majesty, but Your Majesty will remember that he is a 'very little king'!" Wasn't that nice.

To-morrow I hope to golf. Ah me! Those who have not seen me golf have indeed missed the Delight of the Age!

Which reminds me that I cleaned my cleek with sand-paper and Ada's plate-powder till it shone like silver. I haven't done no work. Mummy is better I think every day than she was (perhaps because two yellingly pestiferous brats are away) but strictly between you and me we find the house quiet – yes, rather quiet. Be good! *Try* to behave! Don't stuff! Dry yourself (this means John) thoroughly after you bathe; wear flannel next your skin and wash behind your ears. Give our love to John and Cecil and Miss Howard and Miss Blaikie (who eats) and believe me ever your

> obedient
> Father.

13, Norham Gardens,
Oxford.
Thursday. June 27. 1907.

My dear John:

I was very glad to hear from Mrs Clarke that you seem to have been behaving yourself decently: but I don't think much of the postcards you send. They are short and small. However in a very few days I myself will be able to get your news at first hand.

Sorry about the weather. It has been most disgusting in our parts of the world too and coming down from Durham on Tuesday afternoon it was Unusual Vile. Yesterday was dark, windy and warm. We went down to Oxford by an early train which reached there at 10.30. On the platform a man met me with my scarlet and grey gown. It's rather like an African parrot. Then we drove in a carriage till I came to a wonderful hall – a sort of baronial hall. Mummy went away with Mrs Osler and I was left among a crowd of men all in gowns of all colours – red, black and grey. I knew a lot of the men, and a butler handed round biscuits and wines. Presently we formed a procession – two by two – and were put into order like boys at school. Then we all walked out into the streets and for 20 minutes we "ceased not to advance in our stately procession" through the streets. They were crowded with people and all the people cheered Mark Twain who walked in front of me. And when they weren't cheering and shouting you could hear the Kodak shutters click–clicking like gun locks.[1] That was great fun. Then we were walked through wonderful quadrangles and halls and archways into another and most enormous baronial hall with marvellous windows and there we were told to wait till we were asked for. We sat about on old oak benches and waited – and waited – and waited. Every now and then a splendid person in a gown would come in and lead away several of us, along a great stone passage into the shadow of a dark doorway and then we who were left behind heard the roars of applause and shouting from a multitude in the distance – exactly like prisoners on a desert island hearing savages eating their companions. This was very fine. If we looked along the stone passage into the dark hall we could just see a figure all in gold, like a Burmese idol, sitting high on a throne. That was the Chancellor of the University in his robes of office, sitting on his stately seat, ready to welcome the men who were getting their degrees. And we waited, *and* we waited, AND we waited and talked to each other. At last a man I knew at the Club said:—"D'you think we can smoke?" and a fine person in a gown said:— "Not *here*! You can smoke under that archway." So we went out and Mark Twain came with us and three or four other men followed and we had a smoke like naughty boys, under a big archway.

Last of all – about 12.30 we were sent for – in a batch of seven. When I say "we" I mean me and the men who were getting my particular sort of degree.

We came into a huge round hall,[2] packed with people up to the ceiling. I looked about and saw Mummy looking very sweet and beautiful and then I didn't mind. All the young undergraduates sat in the gallery and shouted remarks. A very old man, with a small voice, made a speech in Latin about each of us and the boys shouted to him to speak up. When he couldn't one boy said:— "Hush! You'll wake the baby!" And another said:— " 'Tisn't polite to whisper in public." And another said:—"Try Mother Siegel's Syrup." When Mark Twain went up they shouted like anything and they cheered and they asked him nice questions. I was the last of the lot and the man who spoke about me in Latin was very tired and he could not be heard, even by me. Then one of the undergraduates said in a nice confidential voice:—"You'll tell us about it afterwards Rudyard". Then the Chancellor shook hands with me and said a nice thing in Latin and then all the boys sang: "He's a jolly good fellow!" And so I was made a Doctor of Letters.

While we were waiting I met an old school-master of mine who had been my French master and while he was talking to me I was introduced to a great French musician, a Monsieur Saint-Saëns, and I talked to him, no end – in French! I was awfully proud of that. Then I saw my own dear Headmaster, Cormell Price, and a lot of people I knew and when we all came out of the hall to go to lunch who should I meet but the Pater![3] He'd seen all the ceremony and wasn't a bit tired. Then we lunched in a wonderful room, and then I went to a garden party and then I went out to dinner. Mummy wore her blue silk dress and looked simply *lovely*. I had to wear my gown at the garden party and I felt as if I'd forgotten our bath-sponge on the way to the bath aboard ship. Gowns are funny things. They flop about one's legs.

You can imagine I was *very* tired. Mummy stayed here, in this delightful house, and went to bed early. She is resting to-day but we want to go to see the Oxford Pageant this afternoon. Then to-morrow we come home and I think on Saturday you'll see me coming along to haul you out of Rottingdean by the slack of your breeches! Hurrah! I hear all you pug-dogs are having high old times and that you went over and played in our piece of land. Glad you got the key. Give my love to Larry and my specialest and most particular thanks to Mrs Clarke for writing to us so fully about things.

Perhaps some day we'll get some summer weather. Meantime I am

Your affectionate
Dad.

[1] See illustration 6
[2] The Sheldonian Theatre
[3] John Lockwood Kipling

My Son:

I have just got back from Rottingdean. It was a drive full of careless dogs. We nearly killed one in Lewes coming down the steep hill and another only just saved his silly life at the end of the Broyle. Strange as it may seem I did not sing very much on the road home. No – it was not a cheerful drive. However I bucked up when I thought of that par-tic-u-larly interesting dormitory of yours and I hoped you had got hold of *The Cruise of the Cachalot*[1] and were settling down to read it till the boys came. It did not seem to me that you would want a *specially* large tea after what you tucked away at Aunt Georgie's. Mummy and Elsie and Miss Blaikie were waiting for me in the hall – awfully keen to know how you had got on and whether I was sure I had taken you all over the school. I answered:— "By Allah, we ceased not to walk up and down and round and about that school till we had examined every apartment thereof"; and I related to them all that I had seen and I ceased not to narrate till Elsie went to bed. (I am not changing for dinner to-night. Hurrah! I wave my gaitered legs with delight.)

Elsie was most excited about the dog-baskets at the end of the beds but Mother most wanted to know whether you had eaten a good tea at Aunt Georgie's. I said you had indeed eaten an enormous tea. I did not tell about your having to unloose your waistcoat!

This is not exactly a letter but merely a note full of no news just to tell you of things in general. Also, I want to know whether I have written plainly enough for you. IF NOT I CAN, OF COURSE, WRITE LIKE THIS BUT IT TAKES ME EVER SO MUCH LONGER TO WRITE. KINDLY LET ME KNOW WHICH ONE OF THE TWO STYLES OF WRITING YOU PREFER. I think myself that the easy flowing hand is the best. I have told Miss Blaikie to send you your telescope that you may view the ships at sea.

8 p.m. The bell has just gone for dinner and I must stop. I expect you have been asleep for this last half-hour – but no matter. I will continue my letter to-morrow.

Thursday.

Another lovely day. All the house is very busy with getting things ready for the journey [to Canada]. Mr Lusted is doing things with a hammer in the storeroom which, as you know is to be turned into a special room for Mummy. I have decided to call it The Bower. We got the telescope out ready to send to you but we are so afraid it may be broken in the post that Miss Blaikie and Elsie will bring it over when they come to see you on the twelfth of next month. That is only about three weeks to wait. I expect that by the time this letter reaches you, you will have been examined about what you know and will have been given your desk in the class-room. I don't think you will be put in the lowest class but if you are it does not matter as you won't stay in it for very long. Now I have got to do dozens of little things – such as oiling my gun: going to see Daunt about taking up the flood-gates when a flood comes and so on and so forth.

Just write us a line on Sunday to tell us how you feel. I will send you letters twice a week from Canada and I will also draw you pictures of events on the voyage. They won't be as wild as the events in *The Cruise of the Cachalot* – I hope!

Remember to ask Mr Stanford to let you go over to Aunt Georgie's on Wednesdays and Saturdays – or whenever the half holidays are – if you feel you would like to go.

Mother and Elsie and Miss Blaikie send heaps of love and I rest and remain

> Your specially affectionate
> Dadd-o!

[1] F T Bullen's account of a voyage around the world in search of sperm whales (London: Smith and Elder, 1905)

> s.s. Empress of Ireland.
> *Monday morning. September 23rd* [1907]

A cold grey foggy morning with a south-west swell; the ship pitching a little and a great many chairs empty at breakfast.

Very dear Family,

This North Atlantic ocean is a silly thing. I left it ten years ago in a thick fog with a lumpy grey cold confused sea and now I have come back to it, it is doing the very same things as it did then. The same old fog-horn is making the same husky throaty noise and the decks are all damp and dripping. Mother is telling you in her letter how we were shifted out of Cabin 123 – the one Elsie wrote the labels for. It was really very funny. I was lying in my cabin reading when my cabin steward came with a piece of paper in his hand and said: – "The Purser says that you are to shift". I was almost asleep and naturally I grew angry. "Shift? Shift?" I said. "What the deuce for? Where the deuce to? Confound your shiftings." "Please, Sir", said he, awful humble, "it's a Suite." ("Suite" means a set of rooms, and is pronounced like "sweet".) Then he showed me the piece of paper, on which was written "Mr Kipling to shift to 119–121". Then it was my turn to grow humble and I followed him to the port side of our deck and we opened a little door marked "private" – and this is the plan of what I saw.

1 = bedroom
2 = sittingroom
3 = bathroom

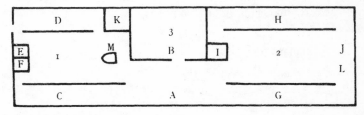

A. Beautiful little hall – leading into
B.   ,,   ,,   bathroom with private bath etc.
C. Sumptuous bunk for Mummy and one above for me: ornamented carved ends to bunk – not common iron
D. Large and splendid couch under window – furnished pale green.
E.F. Washstands for Mummy and me
K. Magnificent white wardrobe with large mirror.
    2. Sitting-room – white wall paper
H. and G. Two superb pale green couches – one with ornamented wooden ends.
I. Writing table.
L. Real chair.
M. Another real chair in bedroom.

Talk about luxury! Just think of the joy of having your own private bath at any hour you want instead of having to cut about the passages in your dressing-gown the minute that the Bath Steward tells you that your bath is ready. I feel like the Duke of Connaught and Mummy feels like the Duchess.

The ship is a wonderful concern. I went all over her with the Captain at Inspection this morning. She has one deck more than the Walmer and she carries about one thousand third class passengers. I am sorry to say that most of them are sea-sick. I was nearly sick myself while I was going over their quarters. There are decks deep down below where the men passengers lie in iron bunks three deep – no, two deep. Not exactly a nice place. We went over the kitchens and saw the machine which takes a barrel of flour and turns it into dough for bread, and an electric machine for washing dishes (Nellie would like that) and an electric machine for roasting meat. It was all more wonderful than you can imagine – and so were the smells – THE SMELLS – THE SMELLS!!!

Last night I went up to see the Captain in his cabin on the boat deck. It wasn't like the Cape Boats. The wind blew; there was a cold moon and a chilly wrinkled sea and I wrapped myself up in my great coat and felt cold.

[no signature]

Place Viger Hotel,
Montreal.
Sunday night. Sep. 29. 1907.

Very dear Family,

We have been in Canada now since Friday morning: and our adventures would fill a book. Just as soon as we got up in the morning when the steamer had reached Quebec, I heard a voice outside our cabin door saying that there was a private car waiting for us to take us to Montreal. I was just a little surprised: Mummy and me being small persons and private cars being a little longer than the pullman car on the London train. Well – no matter. We left the ship and found this stately splendour of a private car – its name was Dumfries – tacked on to the end of the passenger train. A stately negro received us with the airs of an archbishop: called us "Sir" and "Madam" in a deep resounding voice and whenever we dropped anything on the floor he noiselessly and swiftly picked it up. This made us feel rather like bad untidy children. It was a fine day and the sight of the beautiful country – the maple leaves are just turning red – cheered us. We laughed with joy at the sight of the queer narrow French farms, which are only a hundred yards wide and run back from the river for two and a half miles.

Each has a little wooden house and a pilliwinky windmill. We danced about in the lonely glory of our great long green velvet and mahogany palace of a car with 29 sleeping places and two bedrooms and at last we came to Montreal after a run of four hours. A lot of people were waiting to meet us but helped by our noble nigger conductor we somehow managed to slip past them and arrived quietly in a cab at the hotel whose picture you see on the paper. Then Mummy met *her* Mummy[1] and she was glad to the limits of gladness and rejoiced to the uttermost extent of rejoicing. In less than ten minutes Grandmother was ordering Mummy about like anything and calling her "child", ("Come here, child! Don't do that, child!") while I laughed to see Mummy taking it all so meekly. Mr Doubleday and Dorothy were at Montreal to meet us. Somehow or other they missed us at the station. They sent heaps of love to you. Altogether it was a most wonderfully happy evening, and you ought to have seen Mother's eyes dance.

Our only trouble was our Car. (I fancy you'll hear a good deal more about that car.) When we left it at Montreal, the Noble Nigger said:— "What would you like done with your car, Sah?" Then I began to realize that the thing was our own to keep as long as we liked, and the nigger gave me a ticket saying that Mummy and me and anyone we wished to invite could take that car anywhere up and down Canada for the next six weeks!!! Well, *I* didn't know what I ought to do with a private car – whether I ought to order it to be oiled, or pushed up and down the railway line to keep it warm till I came back so I tried to look as though I were quite accustomed to private cars and I said:— "Oh – eh! – err! I'll see about it!" Then the Noble Nigger (I fancy you'll hear more about that nigger) said reproachfully:— "I thought I was going through all the way with you, Sah!" Even *then* I did not understand what he meant till the Vice-President of the Railway himself said he thought we might perhaps like to run up the line a bit (it is only three thousand miles long) and look at Vancouver and the Pacific Ocean and a few trifles of that sort. Anyhow we could do what we liked with the car. We could fasten it on to any train we chose; and stay behind at any station we chose and join on again to any train that we chose and the Noble Nigger would be our guide, philosopher and friend.

All these things happened and befell us on Friday afternoon. In a very short time it seemed to us that the sooner we were on our private car the better would it be for us. Everybody sent us letters; everybody wrote and wired asking us to dine, lunch, tea, hunt, play and generally to lark about everywhere: and all the other people asked me to make speeches and deliver lectures and address addresses to the towns, cities, villages, hamlets and prairies of the Dominion of Canada. It was a hectic time! To cut a long story short we decided to flee out of the kind-hearted city of Montreal in our private car (of which doubtless you will hear more) on Monday morning. At first Mummy's Mother said she would go too but later on she decided she was too old for such a journey (6000 miles there and back) so she said she would go back to Brattleboro[2] again and wait till we came back from our trip and we would have a quiet five or six days together before Mummy and I sailed back to you. Mummy and she have had a splendid visit: chattering most awfully: all about everything we do or think or say or eat or wear at Bateman's and all about you and everything relating to you and your doings.

On Saturday (that was yesterday) I saw callers and wrote letters. I ought really to have brought Miss Lilian Blaikie along. I never needed a secretary so badly before. On Saturday afternoon Mummy went out to visit a Society of Ladies who teach the French girls and the Indian girls to make embroideries and boxes and such things. She had a fine time and she bought a sort of counterpane and the Society – which is called the Guild of Canadian Handicrafts – gave her a box of scented grass ornamented with patterns in porcupine quills and lined throughout with birch bark. We had a nice quiet dinner at the Hotel (I could tell you yards and yards about that Hotel) and on Saturday evening Mr Doubleday left for New York. He and Mrs Doubleday are coming over to England in the Lusitania, sailing on October 19th, and they will stay in England till November 15th. This means that we shall see them in England. Oh be joyful for they are dear people. To-day is Sunday. Mummy and I have been out to lunch at the Mount Royal Club. It was a Snipspus Lunch. We had the famous Montreal melons to begin with;

gumbo soup; Canadian haddock which is one of the finest fishes that ever you did eat; roast wild duck and green corn! Green corn, my dears, in September! We met most interesting people. One of them took us off to his house which was just round the corner and showed us the loveliest collection of pictures, rugs, old Dutch models of ships and Japanese pottery that I have ever seen in a private man's house. Indeed it was finer than most museums. We did not get away till half past four o'clock.

It has rained heavily all to-day and the streets are in a filthy state. To-morrow morning at ten minutes past ten we hope to go down to the station with all our luggage, and get into our private car the Dumfries (certainly more will be heard of that car) and sail away across Canada towards Winnipeg. Our letters will be sent after us by various trains as they come in and they will look out for our car wherever she happens to be lying and they will give us our letters. I confess it strikes us both as a gay and a joyous adventure. If we find that it bores us we have only to catch on to a train going the other way and come back to Montreal again.

I fear that I may have to make some speeches at various places which is an operation that does not agree with me.

Mother has packed and unpacked herself into fiddle-strings but she says as long as she hasn't you two horrid little brats to look after she can stand most things. Seriously, she lies down for an hour in the evenings before going to sleep and you don't know how large and long the days are without you two. She sends you tons and tons of love and I am writing for her. I imagine I shall do most of the writing from us two to you two.

Now, good-night and good-bye for a little. Here are some postcards. My next letter will be written to you in pieces from various places all along the line. It will be dated from our Private Car (you may have noticed that I am proud of this), but wherever and however it comes I am always and ever

Your loving
Pater.

[1] Anna Smith Balestier.
[2] The Vermont town where the Kiplings too had lived from 1892 to 1896.

41

Dear Sir – My esteemed Son – O John, etc.

We reached this place last night and found your first letter from school waiting for us. It had been sent on from Montreal. You can just imagine how delighted we were to get it and how we read it over and over again.

I am very pleased to know that you like school – I feel sure that you will like it more and more as time goes on and you settle down and make your own friends. But I know exactly how homesick you feel at first. I can remember how I felt when I first went to school at Westward Ho! But my school was more than two hundred miles from my home – my Father and Mother were in India and I knew that I should not see them for years. The school was more than two hundred boys of all ages from eighteen to twelve. I was nearly the youngest – and the grub was simply beastly.

Now with you, you are not thirty miles from home – you are by no means the youngest chap there – and they look after you in a way that no one ever dreamed of doing when I was young. Likewise you have the pull of living in the village where you were born, full of all the people you have known all your life with Aunt Georgie round the corner. And that reminds me. To-day is the day when you should see Bird and Miss Blaikie so we have sent you a cable from here just to tell you that we were both thinking of you. There is a difference of about eight hours in time between where we are and where you are because you are so far East that you saw the sun rise while our side of the world was still in darkness. This means that though I sent the cable at eight o'clock in the morning by our time, it will be somewhere about tea-time before you get it.

I am rather pleased with you about one thing. You know I never mind jumping on you when you have done something I don't like – the same way I generally tell you when you have behaved decently. Well, from all I can discover, you behaved yourself like a man when you felt homesick. I understand that you did not flop about and blub and whine but carried on quietly. *Good man*! Next time it will come easier to you to keep control over yourself and the time after that easier still.

Now for our adventures. I have written a long account of them and sent them to Bateman's but I could not print them properly because the

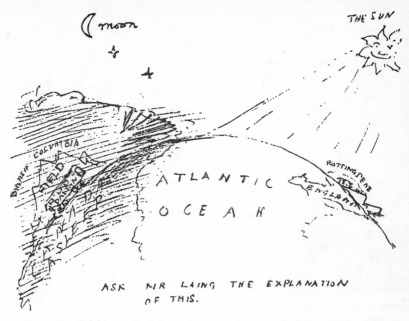

ASK MR LAING THE EXPLANATION OF THIS.

train jiggled so. I wrote them in running hand – and they are so vilely written I could scarcely read them myself. I recommend you to ask Miss Blaikie to print them out for you. Some of the adventures are interesting.

Here is a tale that I want to tell you myself. As I was in the steamer that runs from Victoria to Vancouver – a distance of about seventy miles all among wonderful wooded islands – we saw dozens of whales spouting and blowing in every direction. Some of them rose up and showed their backs like this.

They call that kind hump backs. Then – to my amazement – two monsters reared up and leaped clean out of the water together. They were fighting.

43

I AM RATHER PLEASED WITH YOU ABOUT ONE THING.
YOU KNOW I NEVER MIND JUMPING ON YOU WHEN YOU HAVE
DONE SOMETHING I DONT LIKE. THE SAME WAY I GENERALLY
TELL YOU WHEN YOU HAVE BEHAVED DECENTLY
WELL, FROM ALL I CAN DISCOVER YOU BEHAVED YOURSELF
LIKE A MAN WHEN YOU FELT HOMESICK. I UNDERSTAND
THAT YOU DID NOT FLOP ABOUT AND BLUB AND WHINE
BUT CARRIED ON QUIETLY. GOOD MAN! NEXT TIME IT WILL
COME EASIER TO YOU TO KEEP CONTROL OVER YOURSELF
AND THE TIME AFTER THAT EASIER STILL.

NOW FOR OUR ADVENTURES. I HAVE WRITTEN A LONG ACCOUNT
OF THEM AND SENT THEM TO BATEMANS BUT I COULD
NOT PRINT THEM PROPERLY BECAUSE THE TRAIN JIGGLED SO
I WROTE THEM IN RUNNING HAND — AND THEY
ARE SO NIFLY WRITTEN I WILL SCARCELY READ THEM
MYSELF. I RECOMMEND YOU TO ASK MISS BLAIKIE TO
PRINT THEM OUT FOR YOU. SOME OF THE ADVENTURES
ARE INTERESTING.

HERE IS A TALE THAT I WANT TO TELL YOU MYSELF.
AS I WAS IN THE STEAMER THAT RUNS FROM VICTORIA
TO VANCOUVER — A DISTANCE OF ABOUT SEVENTY MILES ALL
ALONG WONDERFUL WOODED ISLANDS — WE SAW DOZENS OF
WHALES SPOUTING AND BLOWING IN EVERY DIRECTION
SOME OF THEM JUST BLOWING WHEN THEY CAME
UP THUS.

THEY ALL THAT KIND HUMP BACKS
THEN — TO MY AMAZEMENT TWO MONSTERS REARED UP
AND LEAPED CLEAN OUT OF THE WATER TOGETHER.
THEY WERE FIGHTING.

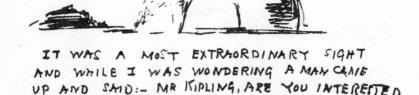

IT WAS A MOST EXTRAORDINARY SIGHT
AND WHILE I WAS WONDERING A MAN CAME
UP AND SAID:— MR KIPLING, ARE YOU INTERESTED
IN WHALES?
 I SAID :— I WANT TO KNOW EVERYTHING
 I CAN, ABOUT THEM

PART OF A LETTER FROM THE CANADIAN TRIP
IN KIPLING'S CAREFUL PRINTING FOR HIS YOUNG READERS.

It was a most extraordinary sight and while I was wondering a man came up and said:- "Mr Kipling, are you interested in whales?" I said:- "I want to know everything I can about them." He said:- "Then you have come to the right man. I am in charge of the whalery here." I had heard of whale-fishing but I had never heard of a whalery. It seems that the man had a sort of place on the beach where they cut up whales. And he kept two steamers cruising about doing nothing but hunt whales. They use the bomb-gun - you have read about it - a harpoon fired from a small cannon. The harpoon sticks into the whale and then a charge of powder in the head of the harpoon explodes. The whale dies very soon but the man said that it makes terrible and sorrowful noises. "You ought never to hear a whale die, Mr Kipling," he said. Then the steamer has a patent air-pump and pumps the carcass (that means the body of the dead whale) full of air so that it won't sink for hours. Then she goes off and looks out for more whales and at the end of the day she collects all the dead whales and tows them to the whalery. One steamer came in the other day with four dead whales in tow. Rather hard on the whale to blow him up first with powder and then to blow him up with air! The whalery is a regular factory where they rip off the blubber, boil it down into oil (a lot of what is sold as cod liver oil is only whale oil, the man told me). They use his bones for manure and they dry his flesh to sell to the Japanese who are very fond of it. They tan the skin of his bowels into leather for boots. They can't do anything yet with his outside skin - it is too thick for boots - but they hope to be able to turn it into some sort of floor-cloth some day. Every bit of the whale that isn't used for food, oil or leather is ground down to make artificial manure. Here is a sort of sketch of the whalery.

There is a sloping platform going down to the water from the whalery. The steamer tows the whale's body to the foot of it and it is hauled up exactly as a boat is hauled out of the water on a slip. Then men with knives and saws and things hack at it as it passes along and all the rubbish is ground into manure at the back of the factory and is loaded straight into railway cars! They very seldom get a sperm whale and I don't think they have ever yet found a right – a whalebone whale – in those waters. A whalebone whale would be worth five or six thousand pounds to them. Most of the whales are what they call hump-back or sulphur-bottoms. Nice name that. I do so wish you had been along to hear the man talk. He was so funny and in earnest about his blessed whale manure and the high prices the Japanese paid for his beastly dried whale meat!

We have stayed at this place – four thousand feet up in the mountains – since five o'clock last night and our car will be fastened on to the five o'clock train this evening. We spent this morning in a buggy going out to see a lake called Emerald Lake. It is a wonderful, splendid deep emerald green. Enormous mountains capped with snow and covered with pine stand all round it and their reflections in the water are all tinted green. It is exactly like an emerald. The road there was awful bad with precipices on one side. At a turn in the road we met a red and white speckled pack horse with a blue eye. He was leading a train of pack ponies and I saw two women whom I took for Indian squaws. They wore beaded jackets and rode cross-legged. They were quite brown and tanned. As I passed them they looked at me and I felt they were white women. They were two ladies who had been camping out for three months with their ponies and a guide. I thought to myself and Mummy thought so too that after a few years, if all goes well, you and the Bird will have a month's camping with us in this wonderful land.

Now I must end for a little. Lots of love and my best assurances of respect,

> Ever your own
> Daddo.

> Bateman's,
> Burwash,
> Sussex.
> *Wednesday morning.* [Nov. 6 1907?]

Dear old man –

It is a still foggy day just after breakfast (porridge, eggs and kippers). Elsie has gone down the garden to take something (I don't know what) to the cuckoo and I am up in my study writing just a line to you which your Girlie will take up the hill to the pillar-box.

We came home in the motor all right. It was very dark and very foggy in places – specially at Ringmer village. But Baldwin [a servant] drove beautifully and got us to Bateman's in exactly one hour and a half – which is his usual time for the run. All the maids were glad to see us and the first thing they did was to ask after you. So did both Miss Blaikies and they just were pleased to know that you were getting on so well. I think I never saw Girlie so pleased. I told her about the football and the drills and the shooting and everything else that you told me. We sat up talking till nearly eleven o'clock.

Yesterday was beautifully fine and warm. I hope it was the same with you. I went out for a walk with Elsie at ten o'clock. I had to go up to the village to see old Mr Jarvis the butcher about something he wanted done to Dudwell Farm where Daunt lives. On the way up we saw old Mr Howells in the fields by Little Bateman's. He told us that old Mrs Howell his wife had been very ill but she was better now. Before I went away I told Jim Lusted to mend the roof of Little Bateman's and also to whitewash the ceilings of two rooms. Old Mr Howell had always been worrying at me to have this done. Well, Jim Lusted mended the roof all right and whitewashed one ceiling but just as he and his men were beginning to whitewash the other Mrs Howells took ill and they had to stop the work. Old Mr Howells said to me:—"She just took and tumbled right out of bed and I thought she was dead – but it turned out she wasn't." Although I was sorry I could not help laughing at the way he told it.

Then we went on up the village and saw Jim Lusted outside Brooks' shop talking to young Brooks and he took us up to the loft – where you and I went to ask about the tools – and showed us a lot of old oak panelling which he has done for the big guest-room. It looks awfully jolly. Elsie was pleased to get into the shop – because she saw the Canon – Whittaker – coming down the street on his bicycle. Elsie doesn't like the Canon. Then I spoke to Jarvis and then we went on to Colonel Feilden and he showed us all over the little house next to his own which he has bought and he gave us a pheasant and walked home with us. The pheasant's crop was all full of acorns. We could feel them wobbling about underneath the feathers on the breast. Jarvis came to see me in the afternoon. I had a long talk with him and answered tons and tons of letters. I hate writing letters except to you and Mother and Elsie.

Mother was tired yesterday and stayed in bed: but she is gay and festive to-day and is going to explore all round the garden and see what Martin has done. Ernest is working in Colonel Craddock's garden at Southover. He gets ten shillings a week and comes home every night. I

47

do think that a boy of fourteen might begin to stay away from home a little. The dam is full of dead leaves and Martin rakes them out in lumps and takes them to the leaf-mould pit behind the garden wall. All the same there are lots left and if he doesn't take care they will clog the turbine.

Mother is sending you the sort of stick that the Indian tribes send to each other when they declare war. You will notice that it is shaped rather like a bone. I suppose in the old days they sent a real bone – just to show their enemies they would make bones of them. I wrote the inscription on the sides so if your footer team wishes to challenge another team you have only to send them the challenge stick and they will know what it means.

Here is a mystic picture writing that you can tell me the meaning of;

TT IS A REMINDER TO YOU TO WASH YOUR TEETH!!

I can't think of any other news just now. Mrs Doubleday and Dorothy Doubleday are coming down for the day to-day. I have had a letter from my Pater and am writing to ask him to write to you and send you drawings in the letters. I hope the old Zugger football was a success – and will give you many goals.

Now – my son – I've got to work – all same one piecee nigger – at my beastly letters, so I bid you farewell and I rest and remain

Your loving
Daddo.

If is *awful* hard work to print a letter all through. Do hurry up and learn to read my ordinary beautiful clear hand-writing.

IT IS A REMINDER TO YOU TO WASH YOUR TEETH!!

I CA'NT THINK OF ANY OTHER NEWS JUST NOW
MRS DOUBLEDAY AND DOROTHY DOUBLEDAY ARE
COMING DOWN FOR THE DAY TO DAY. I HAVE HAD
A LETTER FROM MY PATER AND AM WRITING TO ASK
HIM TO WRITE TO YOU AND SEND YOU DRAWINGS IN
THE LETTERS.
I HOPE THE OLD ZUGGER FOOTBALL WAS A SUCCESS.
– AND WILL GIVE YOU MANY GOALS.
NOW – MY SON – I'VE GOT TO WORK – ALL SAME ONE
PIECE NIGGER – AT MY BEASTLY LETTERS SO I DID
YOU FAREWELL AND I REST AND REMAIN

YOUR LOVING DADDO.

IT IS AWFUL HARD WORK TO PRINT
A LETTER ALL THROUGH. DO HURRY
UP AND LEARN TO READ My ordinary
beautiful clear hand writing.

KIPLING COMBINES HUMOUR AND INSTRUCTION IN
THE LETTER OF NOVEMBER 6 1907.

Grand Hotel,
Stockholm.
Dec. 10th. 1907.

Tuesday: 2.30 p.m. (just getting night)

Dear Babes–

We reached Stockholm this morning at 9.47 just after it got light. Stockholm is even more wonderful than Copenhagen. (I am writing with a Swedish pen and I don't know which way the beastly thing prefers to write. It won't write the proper way of pens.) Now I have found another pen which is even quainter. It is pointed and ornamented with a royal crown. But to continue the story of our journey. We left Copenhagen at 7 last night in a little steamer which crosses from Denmark to Sweden (I believe this pen is trying to write Swedish by itself). Then we took a train – a queer corridored sleeper lighted by a gas that smelt most wonderful strong and bad. There was no food on the train but at about 8 o'clock a kind man we met got us a glassful of steaming hot coffee with two straws like you drink lemon squash out of! That coffee saved us! Also he gave us a delicious kind of sweet bread with pats of butter melting on it. I never had so delicious a meal but if you had seen Mummy sucking hot coffee out of a straw you would have laughed. Stockholm was hot and wet, with streaks of meltified snow. Solemn men in top hats of great glory received us at the station and escorted us to a carriage largely made of plate glass and silver mountings. The inside was pearl coloured silk. In this glorified bridal-coach Mummy and I sat and behaved beautifully. We reached a splendid hotel and were shown a suite of stately apartments and the important men in the top hats explained to us that owing to King Oscar's death all the ceremonies of the Nobel prize-giving would be cut down. There would be no banquets; no speeches; no large assemblies. At this news I looked properly grave and sad but I was *very* glad to escape from the speeches and the banquets. Then I was taken to call on the head of the Swedish Academy and then I went to call on the British Embassy and in a little time I am going to be taken to a meeting where a Nobel prize will be given me. It means a gold medal and a parchment certificate and to-morrow they give me a lot of money. All the flags here are at half-mast for King Oscar's death and the whole city looks mournful under these gloomy grey skies.

Mummy has done nothing but work hard all the day but she is going to the ceremony too. There will be only two ladies present. If the King had lived he would have given the prizes himself. There are three other men besides me getting prizes. Sir Rennell Rodd – young Rodd's father – is the British Ambassador here. He is, as you know, in England just now but he will have to come back for the King's funeral.

Stockholm is built on and about and round all sorts of canals and harbours crowded with all sorts of little steamers. Our windows look out on one broad canal where three ferry boats cut about every few minutes. It's a sort of Venice up in the north.

I can't think of anything more to tell you except to give you our dear dear love.

Ever your most affectionate
parents.

Grand Hotel,
Stockholm.
Dec. 10th. 1907.

5 p.m. (Still Tuesday: still darker)
Dear People –

I continue my letter from where I stopped it at 3.25 p.m. Well, at that hour came the bridal carriage – Cinderella's glass coach I am going to call it – and Mummy and I and two professors piled in and drove through the dark shiny wet streets where all the lamps were reflected on watery pavements and harbours and canals – so that moving steamers' lights were mixed up with shop lights. Everyone in the streets seemed to be in black and the shops were full of black dresses. We stopped opposite the door of a place that looked like a theatre – with iron inner doors and stone staircases. It was the school of the Academy of Music. We went up stairs, after I had left my hat, coat *and* go-loshes with a door-keeper and came into a room ... It was all bare and white with semi-circles of chairs whose seats tilted up with a spring when you weren't sitting on 'em. Behind the platform about eight feet up were three white plaster busts of three great scientific men. (That is why I can't understand their calling the place the Music-room. Perhaps it was the science lecture room after all.) Only the professors of the Swedish Academy were there – not fifty all told. The galleries were empty. Most of the chairs were empty and there was a general feeling of emptiness all about. You see on account of King Oscar's death *all* the big public

51

functions were stopped and all the professors were in deep mourning. The four Nobel prize winners sat in four chairs thus:—

| Professor Nicholson from Chicago who had found out things about light | Professor Buchner, a German who had done something scientific | The Chancellor of the Swedish Academy | A French doctor who had found out things about fever & sleeping sickness JE! |

I felt rather like a bad boy up to be caned. Different professors got up, went to the reading desk on the platform and talked to each man in his own lingo. The American got it in English: the German in German: the Frenchman in French: and me in English. It is an awful thing to sit still and look down your nose while a gentleman who talks English with difficulty pays you long compliments. As each oration was finished, the victim got up from his chair, the schoolmaster (I mean the Speaker) came down from the platform and shook hands with him. At the same moment a tall young man with a leather rosette in his buttonhole presented the victim with his diploma and gold medal. You have no notion how difficult it is to shake hands gracefully when one arm is full of a large smooth leather book on top of which is a slippery slidy red leather box – like a huge Tiffany jewel case. Try, with a blotter and the case of my silver key and see what happens. I felt like this:—

playing a 15-30 puzzle! The air seemed full of friendly hands all rushing to clasp mine! I had made a bet with myself that Mummy should be the first person to look at the diploma and play with the medal. So I handed them both over to her. The diploma is a beautiful hand-painted book.

The medal weighs about half a pound. It is pure gold and represents poetry listening to the voice of music! Never you dare to say I can't sing again. I thought it was a picture of Mowgli listening to a woman playing on a lyre. He has nothing on to boast of but he is sitting on a bath-towel and saying:– "Now where *is* the rest of my week's wash. I have it all written out." Seriously it is one of the most lovely pieces of work which I have ever seen.

That was all the ceremony. It took less than an hour and then we went into another room to get our money. I liked the American professor awfully! He was younger than I but the rest were pretty average old. Then we climbed into Cinderella's coach again and came back to our hotel. That is the full account of all just *as* it happened. Everybody kept assuring me that if the King had not died the ceremonies would have been four or five hours long and there would have been banquets! I don't want banquets. However a few professors are giving Mummy and me a quiet dinner in this hotel to-night and we dine out to-morrow night with the Secretary of the Academy. He has a white porcelain stove in his house eight feet high. I saw it when I went to call this morning. After that, on Thursday night *unberufen – unberufen – unberufen*[1] – we come home – home – home!

The only thing I don't like about this part of the world is the dark. The sun begins here at 9 and stops at 2.30 and as we have had heavy grey skies, rain, mist, and snow ever since we started, you can faintly guess how dark the days are . . . Swedish grub is interesting but pickle-ish. They pickle pretty much everything they can catch before it goes bad. And they catch a lot of things. They have eels in jelly and pickled herring and lobster and crabs and raw ham and dried raw salmon – none of which will our Lady Mother let me eat. Isn't it a shame? To-morrow we hope to steal out and do some shoppings together.

      Ever your loving
      Dad.

[1] "touch wood"

53

Bateman's,
Burwash,
Sussex.
May 8. 1908. 8 p.m:

My dear Son John,

This is my first note to you in your second term at Stanfords – please observe how beautifully it is written. To-day has been a beastly wet day – I suppose you had it too at Rottingdean – but in the evening after tea the rain took off and it was warm. So I went up to the village with Elsie and bought two penn'orth (short for pennyworth) of peppermints which we sucked all the way home round by the church. It was amusing but not exciting.

By the way yesterday the new pigs came – they are both black and the smallest we've ever had. They cost eleven bob each and I assure you, Sir, they don't look much bigger than kittens. I haven't any news except that, as you know, we both have colds but I think the colds are improving. Mother's is better and mine is much better. Mother has been bringing down books from the attic for her new room. We use your clothes basket – cram it full of books and lug it down the stairs. It is mighty good exercise.

I have written a lot of letters and tried to do some work but I haven't succeeded in doing much. I hope to be down with Gunhilda on Saturday next and maybe I shall bring a gun-metal hunter with me. I believe you wanted a hunter.

Miss Blaikie told us that you had been shifted to a new dormitory but that Beresford was in the next bed to you. It's curious to think, Sir, that in the days when my school number was 264, there was a Beresford (No. 157 I think) next bed to me for years and years.

I do hope that you will go up a form this term on the strength of your Latin and Mathematics. You are *quite* all right if you will only think; when you don't think you ought to be kicked. I regret I have not kicked you enough. I'll look out for the next number of the *Captain*[1] as I promised; you look out for your school work.

All the house and specially Mother sends lots of love, and I am as ever

      Your superiorly affectionate
      Dad.

This is rather a measly letter but truly there is nothing to tell.

[1] A boys' magazine, published from 1899-1924.

Bateman's,
Burwash,
Sussex.
Monday. May 18. 1908.

Dear old man,

Just a line before I go up to London by the 9.34 train to try on a lot of beastly new clothes and to get you a leather watchguard.

I was awfully pleased to see you on Saturday and, though I didn't tell you at the time I was *very* pleased with your going downstairs in the night when Beresford thought he saw "a ghost". That's the sort of thing that a man who means to get into the navy ought to do. Don't you bother too much about your eyes. They will come all right and a good deal of your lack of appetite just now is because you are settling down again to work after a long holiday. It is always beastly to settle down to work at first but after a few days one gets used to harness.

This is a lovely day – I hope it is so with you – and I hate having to waste it in town. There are hundreds of things waiting to be done in the garden. Elsie and I got two pounds of mushroom spawn the other day and planted it all about Stella's field – in the hope that it will grow mushrooms later.

Yesterday Mother and I went over to Lady Edward Cecil's at Great Wigsell. She has bought two of the very smallest Iceland ponies you can imagine. One of them comes up a little above my *knee*! They were so small that they were sent in packing cases – like dogs! They are covered with hair six inches long and in the field they look like mad black sheep. They are only for pets – not for use.

On Thursday I have to go up to town again and make a speech.[1] Which is a thing I hate but it has got to be did. Now I must put on my Sunday go-to-meeting boots and my stiff hat and go and frowst [wallow] in a railway train. Oh cuss!

Dear love from us all to you and remember that among those who love you is

Your esteemed
Dadd-o.

P.S. I awfully liked the quiet way Larry Clarke handled his engine. There's a lot in Larry. Remember me to the cheeksome Oliver [Baldwin].

[1] Banquet of the Royal Literary Fund, May 21 1908. RK spoke on the burdens of authorship.

Bateman's
Burwash
Sussex
June 5th. 1908

Dear old man –

Here's a piece of news that will cheer you. Gwynne and Mrs Gwynne came down yesterday and this afternoon, just after lunch, Mr and Mrs Bland-Sutton, who had come down to lunch from London were walking round the pond, and Gwynne was in the birch-bark canoe. He asked Mr Bland-Sutton to come in and see how easy the canoe was to guide. Mr B.-S. said. "No thank-you", so Gwynnie went paddling round the pond just to show how easily he could manage her. He sat at the stern, and, as you know, the canoe cocked up her nose – like this:

Well, that was all right till in turning the lower corner the canoe's bows slid out on the bank – like this:

You can easily understand, then, that with only one third of the canoe water-borne, and *that* the sharpest end, Gwynnie ought to have crawled cautiously forward or got someone to push her off the bank. Instead of which he began to wriggle about in his seat and then – you can imagine. The canoe shot him out:

and Gwynnie went in! Mrs Gwynne, Mr and Mrs Bland-Sutton and I laughed till we couldn't laugh any more. I sent him to my room to change. He was wet from head to foot, and he wants me to tell you about it. So I have.

Ever your loving
Daddo.

Bateman's,
Burwash,
Sussex.
June. 9. 1908.

Dear Bird [Elsie],

The house is four times emptier and five times larger than it was at 11 o'clock this morning. Can it be possible, said Mr Campbell,[1] that the departure of a F-t P-rs-n in a pony-cart has had anything to do with this surprising change? I think so.

This afternoon after lunch I nobly weeded the peony bed under the wall with a knife. I am indeed an energetic worker. I was getting on splendidly till Mummy came and helped me with a spud. Then we quarrelled and fought about our different systems of weeding. Mine was the Delicate and Refined (how like *me*!) Hers was the Careless and Slap-dash (how like *you*!) Anyway betwéen us we weeded the peony bed.

After tea I went out with my Papa up to the village to enquire after Colonel Feilden. He is a great deal better – has slept during the day and his breathing is easier. Aren't you glad? As my Papa and I walked up the footpath that leads to Ten Oak Shaw we saw a she-child about two foot high and a he-baby about eighteen inches high climb over the stile. There were a lot of cows in the meadow. The cows were naturally interested in the small things and that made 'em afraid. They stopped, hand in hand, and moved by little rushes at a time. Naturally the cows were more interested. Equally naturally the babes got more frightened. Though I had no daughter to protect me against the fierce onslaughts of the cows (they gurgled in their throats) I advanced alone to those small panic-stricken babes and escorted them past the ferocious cows, several of which whisked their tails. As soon as they got to the other stile the kids scuttled over like rabbits. This is a tale of noble heroism!

There isn't any other news so I send you a few simple rules for Life in London.

1 Wash early and often with soap and hot water.
2 Do not roll on the grass of the parks. It will come off black on your dress.
3 Never eat penny buns, oysters, periwinkles or peppermints on the top of a bus. It annoys the passengers.
4 Be kind to policemen. You never know when you may be taken up.
5 Never stop a motor bus with your foot. It is not a croquet ball.
6 Do not attempt to take pictures off the wall of the National Gallery, or to remove cases of butterflies from the Natural History Museum. You will be noticed if you do.
7 Avoid late hours, pickled salmon, public meetings, crowded crossings, gutters, water-carts and over-eating.

That is all I can think of at present: but if you ever feel doubtful about your conduct, you have only to write and I myself will instruct you further, said Mr Campbell.

> Dear love from us both.
> Ever your
> Daddo.

[1] Mr Campbell: the name under which RK gives good advice or makes arch comments in the letters to the children.

> Bateman's,
> Burwash,
> Sussex.
> *June 11. 1908.* 12.45 a.m.

A letter just in from Miss Blaikie announces that you sleep like a pig and eat like one. This is perhaps not quite the way Miss B. puts it but it's the general sense of the remark. I am glad to hear it, said Mr Campbell. Sleep and nutrition are good for the young.

Bateman's is full – quite full. My papa and my mamma[1] and my Aunt Louie and my Aunt Louie's maid Phoebe are all here. My mamma and Aunt Louie came over yesterday in the motor. Baldwin drove 'em from Rottingdean. He went over on Monday to take Aunt Georgie back, and stayed till Wednesday afternoon. He saw John on Wednesday having a bathe. John instantly said:– "Are they here?" "No, Master John," said Baldwin. "I'm afraid you'll be disappointed this time." Poor old John. Anyhow he had a good bathe and B. reported he swam about more than he did last time.

Sir William Van Horne has sent John a bowie-knife – a perfectly devilish thing, my dear. Of course he can't have it at school. He'd rip young Beresford or Bingham or someone up the tummy. So I shall keep it till he comes back.

Mrs Kipling desires me to thank you for your care and consideration in marking such rhododendrons (how the dooce d'you spell rhododendron?) as you thought might be useful for Bateman's garden hereafter. A taste in practical botany (said Mr Campbell) is always laudable.

Just swiped Mummy's stylo! while she was out of the room. (I'm writing in her office.) I'm glad to hear about the lunch at Mrs Wheler's. I always want you to enjoy yourself. Here comes the parcel of brushes for Pater and your dear little letter. Thank you ever so for going to get 'em for me: but you don't praise the [Army and Navy] Stores as you should. I prefer 'em to Harrods, I've never been to Harrods, so of course I'm right.

It's a dull grey day and old Moon is working in the garden. We are going out in the motor to Scotney Castle this afternoon. My stomach cries cupboard. We send our love.

Your Dad.

[1] Alice Macdonald Kipling.

Bateman's,
Burwash
Sussex.
[June 23 1908]

Oh my Bird!

We took John over to school last night at 7.30. (That was when we reached Rottingdean.) We pulled up opposite the school. John jumped out. Some Stanford boys came in at the gate. One of 'em said:— "Hullo! Is that a Daimler?" "Yes," said John – grabbed up his little suitcase and disappeared. It was just like chucking a trout into a pool. But I expect the little chap had a good deal more on his mind than he cared to say. He enjoyed every minute of his time up to the very last and it was a dear delight to us to have him home. I see from Miss Blaikie's long letter to-day that she was of the same opinion. The vision of Miss Burns assuaging (that's pacifying) the wrath of Mademoiselle with a paper somehow filled me with mirth. I had a vision of her waiting your arrival, her toes quivering with indignation.

Talking of trout, I got a big one out of the pond to-day on a bit of paste and put him into the brook. We want to clear the trout out into the river; put the goldfish into the pond, run the water off and then get the weed out, so as you can have some bathing in your holidays. At the present rate of catching it looks as tho' I'd take till Xmas to get out the trout alone – and Lord only knows how I'm to get the goldfish. We'll have a campaign next Sunday with the dinghy or the canoe.

It's a red hot day to-day – everyone cutting or carrying hay – and I'm sorry for you in London, my darling. Never mind, on Thursday you'll go and wash yourself in the Paddington baths and on Thursday evening – *unberufen! unberufen – unberufen*! I see you, *all clean*, at the Leonards. This thought so paralyzes my pen that I can write no more. Mummy has gone to change to go out to the village – she will make me walk up with her.

I have drunk beer for lunch. I wish (*désirer*) to go to sleep. Why (*pourquoi*) must I go up to the beastly village. This is indeed (*vraiment*) a cruel world.

> I am your loving
> Daddy.

Oh! I forgot to say that Colonel Feilden came down this morning – his first walk since he has been ill.

> Bateman's,
> Burwash,
> Sussex.
> *Wednesday, June 23rd. 1908.*

Dear old Man –

Another hot day, but there is a bit of an east wind which is keeping things cool. Mother sent off your grey clothes to you last night, and wants you to wear them if it is hot, till your real thin things which Miss Blaikie has ordered come down from town. Please see that you do.

Elsie writes that she went to the Paddington swimming baths yesterday and the woman there said to her, before she got into the water:—"I suppose this is your first attempt". Elsie does not tell me what happened when the woman found that she could swim. (Do you notice that I am writing all this with the fountain pen that you and I cleaned in my dressing-room? For some mysterious reason or other it works beautifully now.)

Colonel Feilden came down to see us yesterday morning – his first walk since he had his cold. He says as soon as you settle what sort of stamps you are going to collect he will be able to give you lots more. Of course it is impossible for any chap to collect all the stamps of the world, but I think if I were beginning again I should try first to get a good simple collection of modern stamps of all the countries in the world – say two or three of each and then go on to really work up the stamps of the British Empire. Did you know that the native states of India have stamps? I never did till I saw the Army and Navy price list. Colonel Feilden told me to tell you that stamp-sellers generally charge twice as much as a stamp is worth: and that one ought not to deal with them till one has tried everyone else for exchanges.

The new hive which we ordered for the swarm of bees has not yet come, but Mr Coppard got them off the apple tree where you saw 'em swarm and has put them in a straw skep [beehive] just at the foot of the tree. I went and looked at them this morning and they seemed very happy. They will be rather startled when they are turned out into the new hive.

No other news to tell you except that I am and always will be

> Your loving
> Daddo.

> Bateman's,
> Burwash,
> Sussex. Wednesday morn.
> [June 24 1908]

[To Elsie]

Yes – that was all very fine but what did the swimming woman say when she found out that it wasn't your first attempt? You broke off just at the interesting part of the story. Did she say:— "Law!" or "Come along, my darling!" or what?

STUDY OF THE PADDINGTON STRIPED WHALE. *NOT* IN THE
NATURAL HISTORY MUSEUM

However I'm awfully glad that you liked it and I hope whenever you
feel hot or dirty you'll repair to Paddington and blow and wallow to
your heart's content. There really *is* a great deal in washing.

I am going on with a new Puck tale – told to Una while she is milking
in the pasture by Philadelphia Bricksteep a girl of fourteen.[1] Now you
can guess what the tale is about. I'm not quite sure myself but I am
greatly enjoying writing it.

It's a beautiful warm day with a touch of east in the wind and
everybody round us is haying. The valley *churrrrrs* with the noise of
hay cutters just like S. Africa with locusts.

Yesterday at 3.30 your *Ma* went up to the village to see Mrs Lusted,
Mrs Hayley and some others. Says she to me:–"D'you think we'll have
a thunderstorm?" "Oh yes," says I, who am always cheerful. "Very
good, then *you* can carry this coat," she says, and she gives me a hot,
long, hairy, heavy, blue coat which in that still sticky weather weighed
about two tons and three quarters. We went up the hill through the
fields: me sweating under this beastly blue burden. In the field just
below the Bear Inn I says to her:–"And what are you going to do with
this dear nice light coat of yours?" "Oh," she says, "I shan't want it.
You carry it down again." So I left her at Mrs Lusted's and solemnly
walked through the village bearing this superfluous blue coat. Miss
Hylands' retriever was asleep in the road but the sight woke him up
and he had to bark. I don't blame him. She wasn't back till 5.20 when
we had tea in the garden and watched the roses, reflected in the pond
and it was lovely. I caught two goldfish and put them into the little
fountain. They were much surprised.

It's now 9.15 a.m. This letter ought to catch the 10 o'clock post, and it will tell you that I am always and ever

> Your loving
> Dad.

P.S. I wrote the same thing to John. Ain't it odd.
P.P.S. Thank you for reminding me about Howell's fence. I'd clean forgotten!

---

[1] "Marklake Witches", *Rewards and Fairies*.

> Bateman's,
> Burwash,
> Sussex.
> *July. 8.* [1908]

Ducky Dicky-Bird (This I consider *quite* the lowest title for you that even *I* have invented. Please tell me how angry it made you.) There is nothing whatever to record: so I sit down to write it out at length.

The wind is in Leg Trouser (you know where that is) but no rain has come: though Mummy and I nearly broke our backs last night watering the roses round the pond. I had a bucket: she had a watering pot and the pond was almost a foot below the brim. So you can guess that we had to stoop. Also I got wet.

Yesterday was a beautiful lazy day. No beastly daughter to make one play tennis, so I simply loafed. I remember distinctly that I washed when I got up (one should always wash) but after that I did nothing. We took the motor at 3.30 and went to Netherfield Quarry to order some more stone. We intend to continue stoning the path past the tennis court from the garden. We found the quarry and an intelligent foreman who knew everything except the price of the stone and he said – pointing to a cliff – "We shan't get at *your* kind of stone for a fortnight *at* least." It was as though a small ant had said:–"Wait till I've pushed down this mountain." Then we came home by Battle and Robertsbridge and as I have told you watered plants all the evening.

To-day we aren't doing anything at all that I know of except going to look at the bees which may or may not be an exciting piece of work.

I am delighted to hear from Miss Blaikie's letter that you are swimming more slowly than you used to do. This is important because if you swim like this

it is not beautiful. Whereas if you swim like this

all the world admires you,

    and
     I
       am

                 A dull grey day but no rain.

     your
       loving
          Father.

                    Bateman's,
                    Burwash,
                    Sussex.
                    July. 9. 1908

[To Elsie]

Sorry to hear in your last that Ranelagh was too wet for the Striped Whale of Padington (It's generally spelt with two ds by the way) but I was afraid it would be. We had grey skies, soft weather, with flurries of rain that looked as if it meant to do the deuce-an-all of a downpour but which never amounted to much after all.

Glad to hear that Miss Blaikie is "lively" and feels better for her tonic. *You* don't seem very depressed in your young mind either. What you want is being sat upon, my love: and I'm only sorry that I haven't time during your week-end visits to deal with you as you deserve. Never mind, I'll try and make up for it during August. (That isn't very far off now.)

I went up and had a look at your garden at Nixie's pond but the rain doesn't seem to have fetched on *our* mushrooms. Remember, half those mushrooms will belong to me. I don't mind selling you a little ketchup.

All this morn I worked on my new Puck tale – "Marklake Witches" – which I think ought to be good. My only bother is I can't think of a place for Una and Philadelphia Bricksteep to sit in while Phil is telling her story. They can't sit on stools because Una has the only one – there isn't a shaw nearby and there isn't a cow-lodge. Can you offer me a suggestion? Sixpence for a good one. Angy and Miss Edith Struben came at 4.30. Angy is just as much of a dear as ever tho' I haven't seen her for two years. She tells me things about the Miss Burns and you. Miss Struben is very full of her painting in Italy. She says she has studied a lot there and means to go back to the Cape about September. We all went for a walk into Hook's upper field and home by the Rye Green footpath. Angy took off her hat and chucked it into the hall and went round bare headed – as usual.

I can't think of any other news unless I invent some and that's no good. I haven't fished since you left. I'm keeping the big trout for you, and I hope this week you'll cop him.

Now it is time to go and dress for dinner and such other disgusting things – like washing and hairbrushing. Oh, here's some pretty verses I saw the other day.

> I had a garden when a child
>   I kept it well in order,
> 'Twas full of flowers as it could be
>   And London Pride was its border.
>
> I had marigolds and hollyhocks
>   And pinks all pinks exceeding,
> And a splendid root of love-in-a-mist
>   And plenty of love-lies-bleeding.

I rather liked the swing of it.

> Dear love.
> Your Dad.

Me che-ild,

Children could play with me to-day – and I wish I had one now – or even two kids. You may have noticed that on Saturday and Sunday I was, as your dear French governess says, *deestray* – which is pure French for absorbed and worried. This was on account of your Mummy's pains in her inside which grew worse after you left. On Monday she was far – *far* from happy and in addition to pains she sat about and imagined the various diseases that that pain might mean. She counted up 97 of them – or three. I forget which.

So yesterday, Tuesday, I took her up to 47 Brook Street to see Mr Bland-Sutton: he being learned in people's insides. He has a beautiful house and I just caught a glimpse of the Wonderful Dining-room with the pillars. I didn't go in because I wanted you to see it first.

Well, then he saw Mummy and he punched and he whacked and he thumped her and did all those things which are necessary when one has a tummy, and he wound up by saying that there was nothing wrong with Mummy in the way of the five or six terrible diseases she had imagined herself to possess. She has *not* got Squiffamalosis, or Ventritis or lumps or bumps or other things. "Then what has she got?" says I. "Well, she's got a delicate alimentary canal," says he, (this is doctorese for "indigestion") "and on no account must she eat uncooked fruit; or salad or raw apples or pears. Isn't the water at Bateman's hard?" "Yes," says I. "Well, that's one of the things that has given her her Delicate Alimentary Canal."

Then, to Mummy's intense disgust, he prescribed a simple but loathsome medicine of one's childhood – nothing less or more than CASTOR OIL! When we got out into Bond Street and I wanted to dance in the puddles (it was raining) Mummy was furious! "Castor oil!" said she and went into a chemist and bought a little of it. "I want to know how I can be *cured* of my delicate alimentary canal," says she. "Don't eat uncooked fruit, my love," I said. "Avoid salad (which you're fond of) and apples and pears and nuts and bark and twigs and those things." Still Mummy wasn't pleased. She wanted an immediate cure. I said things about not working after meals and getting indigestion and resting when one was tired. It was all quite true and improving, and she was quite mad with me. But no matter. Her pain became less on the way down in the train (we took the 2.10) and she felt better in the evening. When it came to taking the castor oil at bedtime in milk (a filthy brew!) I stood and laughed while she capered round the room and called me names. To-day she is vastly better because she knows she has not got the 97 separate and fatal diseases which she thought she had. And that, my darling, is the reason why small children could play with me. I didn't want to have Mummy with 97 diseases or even one.

I saw by Miss Blaikie's postcard to-day that you have been diving and practising side stroke. Well, well. Keep your hair dry, wash yourself all over, don't throw boots at your preceptress, and believe me to be, my dear Miss Kipling,

> Very sincerely yours,
> Rudyard Kipling.

> Bateman's,
> Burwash,
> Sussex.
> *July. 29. 1908.*

My dear Miss Kipling,

Your Little Brother returned from school yesterday. I repaired to Rottingdean in the Motor via Brighton stopping at the Queen of Watering Places to pay a pleasant and instructive visit to a Dentist of my acquaintance who kindly walked round my Beaming Smile with spanners, wrenches, thumbscrews and similar pleasant tools.

At 3.30 p.m. I reached Master Kipling's seminary and found your Poor Brother dissolved in tears at the thought of

 His new "straw hat".

parting with his Dearly Loved Companions, his affectionate Matron and his Respected Head Master. When his sobs had abated somewhat, he flung himself at Mrs Stanford's feet and pleaded most eloquently to be allowed to Remain and pursue his studies – if necessary on Bread and Water! Such were his simple words. I carried him, still weeping, to the house of Lady Burne-Jones where at 4.15 p.m. he made a Delicate Tea of not more than six or seven slices of Bread and Butter, several hot tea-cakes and a few pounds of chocolate cake. At 5 he consented to get into the motor and with many a regretful glance at St Aubyns (the

home of so many pleasant Reminiscences) I carried him away, the prey of uncontrollable emotion. Seldom have I seen one so young so loath to revisit his Ancestral home. He complained that no time would now be allowed him to continue his studies in Latin and Mathematics – the objects of his deepest interest. He further stated that his sister was a Slacker and at Lewes (his sobs being less frequent) staggered to the Post Office to send her a telegram to this effect.

(The true version)

The young imp sang nearly all the way home and struck up "The church's one foundation" at the head of Lewes High Street! I had to remind him it wasn't the Heathfield road! When we got home he ran about till he got the bat and stumps and made me bowl to him. He sat up to dinner at 7.30 and went to bed at 8.30 about as blissfully happy a young mortal as I've ever seen. He is now (9 a.m.) rampaging round my room, after having washed out my old stilo, wondering what he shall do next. I foresee my days will be evil and hectic till you come back. I am trying to get him to send you a few lines but he shies off the subject. He has all his exam papers with him which he wants Miss Blaikie to look at.

Now he has hauled up a chair to my table and says he will write to you. Oh Lor! Don't you *ever* be a father, my Bird. He's shaking my table like an earthquake!

> With love,
> Dad.

P.S. I think he wants being kicked with love and forethought.

Bateman's,
Burwash,
Sussex.
Tuesday. *Oct*. *6*. *1908*.

Dear old man,

Your last letter was a beauty as far as its length but it was *vilely* spelt. I don't think I have ever seen quite so many mistakes in so few lines.

Howe wood yu lick it if I rote you a leter ful of mis speld wurds? I no yu kno kwite well howe to spel onli yu wonte taick the trubble to thinck?

Mother is writing you a line to-day and I expect she will tell you what we are going to do on Saturday. It has been most wonderful weather and to-day is the finest of all. I believe if you had been at home you could have played cricket every day.

We are going off with Elsie in the motor this afternoon to Hawkhurst to buy some more laurels and larches for the garden. I have been swopping off the heads of docks in the three acre.

Yesterday Colonel Feilden came and I took him out shooting. He got 7 (seven!) pheasants on the farm. He shoots most beautiful. He only missed one shot and then he got the bird with his next barrel. When you are a little older and can stand up to a 20-bore he says he will teach you how to shoot. He was awfully pleased because he did not expect to get any birds.

Now I have got to run out and speak to old Moon.

    Much love from us all
    Your Daddy

Bateman's,
Burwash,
Sussex.
Nov. 30. 1908.

Dear old man:

Your last letter is more than usually vilely spelled which I expect is because you skylarked with Bingham instead of looking up the Dictionary. (If I were you I should walk about chained to at least three dictionaries, like a suffragette to the Ladies' grille.) Why *can't* you spell?

Are you sick?

Are you underfed?

Do your shoes pinch?

Didn't you loosen your waistcoat enough?

Then why the *Doose* don't you spell?????????????????? Never mind. In a fortnight from the time you get this (*unberufen! unberufen!*) you will be speeding home in the motor.

By the way, I am getting the Daimler Co. to send us one of their new motors to try on Friday. It is called the *"Brighton Landaulette"* pattern and is supposed to be *quite* noiseless. *Nous verrons* as our friends the French say.

Mother is much better. She went out in the garden to-day and gave several orders. She did not leap stiles or gates but walked with a firm and collected stride. I hope in a day or two to take her out for a motor drive.

There is no news except that the weather is playing at being spring and the silly trees are budding. They will get a nasty knock when winter comes.

Bird and I planted a small oak this morning. Miss Blaikie is glad you liked your letter from her. I wish you wrote as neatly as she does. How many more watches do you want? Have you swallowed your last?

Love from us all,
Ever affectionately,
Dadda.

1909–1911

After 1908, troubled both by uncongenial developments in South African politics and by John's absence at his distant school, the Kiplings reluctantly gave up their winters at the "Woolsack". Instead, from 1909 until the outbreak of the war, they spent January and February of each year vacationing in Engelberg, Switzerland, following up winter sports with continental touring into early spring. For a few weeks each January, John would join the others in skiing, skating, and curling, but he would soon have to return to school in Rottingdean, and it is to these separations that we owe many letters from father to son.

Other of R K's literary activities during these years included publication of *Actions and Reactions*; writing "As Easy as ABC", "The Female of the Species", and a number of Puck and Stalky stories and poems; working with C.R.L. Fletcher on *A History of England*, for which he wrote twenty-three poems; and composing and delivering a series of lectures and after-dinner speeches, an obligation he more than once grumbles about in his letters to John.

The period was also shadowed by four deaths occurring within little more than eight months of one another. Most publicly dramatic was the demise of King Edward VII, whose burial day evoked a kind of set piece in the letter of May 20 1910. More personally significant, however, were the deaths of Cormell Price, the much-admired "Uncle Crom", Headmaster of Rudyard's College at Westward Ho!, and of both of Kipling's parents, the two latter taking place during the late 1910–early 1911 period from which no letters to the children have been preserved. The last major event of these years recorded in the letters to John and Elsie is the visit by Rudyard and Carrie to Wellington College in Berkshire, a school with - like Westward Ho! - a military background, to plan the next stage of John's education.

Hotels Cattani,
Engelberg.
Jan. 20. 1909.

(In the sitting-room, 10 p.m. A very cold night with a mist outside)

Dear old man,

Your passage across France must have increased the revenues of the Telegraph Department. First thing this morning came a wire from Mrs Dale Lace, saying that you had been met at Basle. (She had very kindly sent it off at midnight after she had seen your train go, I suppose.) Anyhow we were glad to get it. About 7.10 (just as we were going to dinner) Georgie's wire saying that you were off to Brighton in Mr Lang's car, gave us a good appetite for our meal. (How this beastly Onoto dribbles!) We said to ourselves:– "Well anyhow Lang major is kicking John up and down the saloon carriage. It will doubtless do him much good!" And about 9 o'clock while Mummy and I were playing Patience Mr Stanford's wire from R'dean, which was despatched at 6.55 p.m. came to assure us that you were safely landed. (By the way I send you the telegraph-form, in order that you may compare it with English telegraph-forms and see what the words mean.) Please thank Mr Stanford very much for sending us the wire. I have a vision of you almost falling across your bed from sheer fatigue to-night – unable to hold forth to the boys on the delights of the Swiss Alps – tired out by your travels over land and sea. Another time you ought to be able to take the trip alone. I will not conceal it from you that we all miss you.

This morning while I was loafing round the rink in the sunshine as usual, Mr Waddy asked me if I'd care to curl. So I went over to the back rink – the peaceful one – and not only did I curl, Sir, but I made (by accident) one or two good shots and I enjoyed the game so much that I am down for another game at 10.30 to-morrow morn. I'm rather glad you didn't see my efforts. Elsie sat on a *luge* (Mother brought her over from the Rink) and laughed abominably as I ran before the stones and "Soupit them up". None the less curling is a fine game.

I had my revenge on Ploomp [Elsie] in the afternoon. It was too hard for ski-ing so Mummy and Bird and I and Miss B[laikie] went out for a walk. You know what a perfect slackster B[ird] is on the foot – uphill or downdale. We went uphill right to the brown bare ground at the top of the toboggan run, only we got at it from the top of the Monastery field. Bird moaned and grumbled and shirked and slipped and behaved as tho' she had never seen a mountain and never wanted to see one again and I raged and stormed at her and urged her up (I couldn't prod her with the ski-sticks) and by the time we had come down by the side of the toboggan run and got home again, she confessed she had enjoyed it. But she didn't look like it at the time. We did *not* have chocolate at the shop (it seemed too soon after your departure) but went straight back to the hotel and the minute we got in (about 4 p.m.) it came off horrid cold and a deadly chill mist blanketed all the valley.

Well, you know the run of our lives and you can see how that – with Elsie's skating – makes up our day. I believe E. has had her head washed this afternoon (after tea) and removed her things into your room, where she is now fatly asleep. Mummy and Miss B. both together had to help tie up her bruised heel. She *is* awfully like you in the way she likes all the world to wait on her.

I spoke to Cattani to-day. He says that when you come here again it will only take you three days on the rink to pick up all your skating. He put it rather funnily. He said:– "In three days your son will be where he was before!" I couldn't see what he meant for a little while.

For a wonder there isn't a dance to-night. A Mr Capper (but I think you saw his advertisement) is downstairs in the big Kuranstalt hall giving a performance of thought-reading. I don't quite know how thought-reading is done because Mummy and I thought we'd quietly go up to our own room at 8.30 and avoid all the fuss. We found the stairs out of the hall blocked by people sitting there in rows, and I craftily led Mummy down the dining-room to the card-room and up the staircase to our floor again. Talk of B-P's Scouts! That is real Red Indian wood-craft. I bet the thought-reader never thought I'd do that.

The Professor[1] (I mean the Golliwog's) sister-in-law came to-day to help look after the Golliwog's wife. She wore a wonderful bonnet with a plume of feathers in it, and as they sat at breakfast this morning the Professor played with it. We saw it in the mirror. The Professor's sister-in-law looks a little like Lady Farrar.

Well, it is late now and I have a sort of feeling that by writing this to you on this particular evening I am keeping you awake at R'dean so I won't go on.

> With oceans of love from us all,
> Ever your own particular
> Dadd-o!

P.S. All good farmers are now pouring liquid manure upon the snow – even on the higher hills, and it *do* smell!

[1] F.A. Frolich, a holiday acquaintance.

> Hotels Cattani,
> Engelberg.
> *Wednesday Eve.* [Feb. 10 1909] 9 p.m.

(In the writing-room of the Grand. I don't think you've ever been there.)

Dear Man,

Your letter came to-day. I notice that you do not say anything about your great and grand jump up the form. But *we* notice it and are proud and glad and send you our best congratulations. It's a big jump – of four or five places and I can't tell you how pleased I am. We are delighted, also, with the news that you haven't had a cold so far. It may be that the other chaps get theirs by fooling about after their baths as you say. I hope that your three weeks in Switzerland stiffened you up. All the same don't *you* fool about after your tub. We are very glad that you are going to see Aunt Georgie again. Poor dear, she has had a bad time of it with the shingles but I hope you'll be able to send us good news of her and I hope that the toys will interest her.

Now I have come in from the writing-room to sit with Mummy in the big hall. We take all our meals in the Grand as the dining-room in the Kuranstalt has been shut up. But we have the same maid to wait on us as we had when you were here. I have a *great* secret to tell you. This afternoon at 2.30 I went out *to learn to skate*! I wore Elsie's old skates and the brother of the man who taught you to telemark on skis was my instructor. That is to say he held me by both hands and when I thought I was going to fall I hung on to him like a shark to a drowning nigger. (Have you ever heard that expression before?) Anyhow he didn't let me fall. It was great fun and I rather enjoyed it though all the muscles inside my legs are aching like anything. I rather wish that I had begun before. I am going out to-morrow at the same time. They are having illuminated skating on the rink tonight.

This afternoon the Professor steered a bob-sleigh down the road twice. The first time he nearly killed all his people at the bridge over the line at the Grunenwald Hotel, by running them into a pile of wood. The second time he got as far as the second hairpin bend and instead of taking the corner he ran the bob about ten feet up the hill. You were never at the bend. It is the next below the hairpin and twists. Well, *would* you believe it but after they had been spilt out twice the rest of his team refused to go on with him! He told us the tale just now after dinner and made us laugh. He is very pleased that you like the German book. Don't you think *The Warm Bath* is the funniest of all? I used to think so.

Elsie slogs away at her skating every day – half an hour with the Instructor at 11 a.m. and then goes on till 12.45. I mustn't tell you what Mummy has been doing because it is a secret but it would surprise you greatly if you knew.

We gave some prizes last night for the best disguises at a Fancy Ball. People played up splendidly and some of the disguises were awfully good. The Professor (now I have moved back to the writing-room again) got himself up to look *exactly* like me when I am on the rink.[1] I lent him my jersey, knickers, puttee, coat, cap and shoes and a hair-dresser came in and stuck a moustache and black eyebrows upon him and – you never saw anything so funny in all your life. We laughed ourselves nearly ill. A lot of people couldn't make it out at all. They saw me in evening dress at one end of the ball-room and at the other they saw me again slouching about in dirty outdoor clothes. Another man disguised himself as a mattress and went and lay down in the middle of the floor and people came and sat on him.

He got first prize. The Professor got second. There were Red Indian squaws, a scare-crow, a pile of baggage and rugs (I fancy you have seen something like it on the ships), two *very* good suffragettes and a man got himself up as a Spanish dancing girl and made us all laugh. We have just finished distributing the prizes and I am writing downstairs instead of going up to our room, so that we can give Elsie a chance to get to sleep.

I don't think there is anything much more to tell you. I am glad that you try to illustrate your letters with drawings; and I rather liked your bit of picture of the cliffs and the boat. Recollect that a Brighton fishing-boat always has an overhanging counter and a funny little stuck up boomkin.

Now my son I will bid you farewell. I am very pleased at your having gone up in class and so are *all* of us. I always said that you had an intellect somewhere up your sleeve.

       With dearest love,
       Your Daddo.

¹ See iluustration 7

                        Hotels Cattani,
                        Engelberg.
                        Feb. 24. 1909.

Dear old man –

Loud and prolonged cheering might have been heard from the valley of Engelberg when your last letter *and* the school list came in. To be third in one's form (and only a few marks below second) and to be second in Arith. is indeed Great! and La Famille Keeplon' was full of pride and joy. Likewise, to know that you had had no cold was cause for a fresh outburst of cheers. And you wrote us a ripping good letter, full of news, which we all enjoyed immensely.

Everything is being packed up to-day – we go to Lugano to-morrow – and now we know how *you* felt on your last day here. We had our last skate after lunch: then, with tears, we unscrewed the blades off our boots. (Mother sent hers upstairs boots and all.) We (Elsie and I) carried the naked blades upstairs in our hands. Ada greased them and wrapped them up in paper while Miss B. took Elsie's boots and mine to the cobbler to have the screw holes plugged up with bits of wood or leather. And so it is all finished till next year! But Ploomp *has* really learned to skate and to-day waltzed with the Instructor while the Band played. Next year she will be a jolly good waltzer and so will you be too. I can nearly do the outside edge. Sometimes I do it all right but unless the Instructor stands by ready to catch me I always feel that I am going to fall. Roller-skating seems to be quite the craze in England this year. I daresay you found that your work on the ice made it easier for you to get the trick of them. Elsie shall have a pair of roller skates (I suppose one can get them from Gamages or the Stores) and you two can cut about the Gym and all over the brick paths in the garden. Only don't ask *me* to take a hand – or foot – in the game. I don't mind steel blades but wheels that go round are more than I can manage.

I believe – though I am not sure – that the King's favourite type of car *is* a Daimler. If so, you were right in your guess when you saw him. It's nice having the King at Brighton because all the papers carefully describe the state of the weather there, and tell us how the King stood on Mr Sassoon's lawn to watch the sunset. Thus we know exactly what sort of weather you are getting at Rottingdean. The spring seems to be rather queer in England this year. Martin says we need rain badly.

We had a note from Aunt Georgie to-day, saying she had seen you. Poor dear, she says she still feels awfully tired, after her attack of shingles.

I *do* hope you'll qualify to shoot at the outdoor range. If you do and Stanford lets you, you can take over your own min. rifle to shoot with. It carries as true as a hair and has the regulation bolt action. You seem to have had a gay time at half-term. I wish I could have looked in for a moment. But by the time this reaches you, it won't be more than five weeks to the Easters! Hurroo! Look after yourself carefully, old man. You've got through the first half of the term without a cold. *We* think it was the good effect of Switzerland. Now don't you go and play about after your bath and get a chill. (You said you thought that was the cause of some of your men having colds.) Keep your inside in order. (I wish *I* could always.)

Mother is making you a new kind of tie. It is called a "Swiss Wintersport" tie, and it is a lively and anarchical red. Rather a beauty. I hope you liked the photos of Bird. I *very* carefully painted the one she sent you. She wasn't taken at the very best part of her swing, I think.

Now I must stop. Dear love to you from us all.

Ever your loving
Daddo!

Savoy Hotel,
Rome.
Tuesday. Mar. 2. 1909.

Dear old man,

How I wish we'd had the pleasure of your company for the last twenty-four hours! It was one of those happy little day *and* night performances (like the trip to Engelberg from Boulogne) for which the Famille Kaplon is beginning to be famous. I know Elsie wrote you to-day but I wonder if she described the full horror of our little jaunt from Milan to Rome. The Continental Bradshaw merely says "Leave Milan 10 a.m.: arrive Rome 10.50 p.m." – that is to say, makes it a thirteen hour trip all but ten minutes. *We* made it a twenty-four hour game, all but half an hour. It wasn't anybody's fault. It just snowed *and* snowed *and* snowed two feet deep on the flat all over Italy from Milan to Florence and, with our usual luck, of course, we got into the thick of it.

We left Milan at 10 a.m. yesterday. It was snowing a bit then, but nothing much. It got worse as we jogged along south and at Parma (where I suppose Parma violets come from) we noticed a lot of Italian peasants with wooden shovels and green brollies. Even then I was such an ass – not expecting snow in Italy – that I didn't realize what the shovels were for or why the people were out in such numbers. At Bologna (which the sausages are named after and where there is a famous University; thus supplying food for mind and body as Mr Campbell might say) – at Bologna we turned off south across the mountains to get to Florence *via* Pistoja. ... About half an hour out of Bologna, on the way to Pistoja the snow was a foot thick on the roofs, and on the trees. It was very wet, heavy, big-flaked, sticky stuff that even furred on to the telegraph wires and made 'em look like tails of excited cats. We got well in among the mountains and it rather reminded me of our run up to Engelberg. There was always a roaring river on one side and a steep hill on the other except where we ran into cuttings or through tunnels. I noticed that the men with the shovels were hard at work keeping the sidings clear at every station. (I'm tired of this beastly pin-point pen.) They worked under the shade of their green and yellow brollies. You never saw anything so funny. Some stuck the brolly-handles down their necks and went on shovelling. I must try to draw it for you.

The spades looked like gigantic spoons and held about a tea-cupful and a half of snow.

We went rather slowly but we were only ¾ of an hour late (which is nothing in Italy) at a little place called Porterra (river on one side and steep hill below as per usual). Then we went into a tunnel and just before we came out of it we stopped with a very complete and sudden jerk - stopped as though the engine had been hit on the head. This it turned out (I've exhausted my stylo pen - the little red one you gave me) was very nearly the case. The cutting in front of us had filled up with snow and as our engine came out of the tunnel a fresh avalanche (fine word to use for half a dozen foot of snow) had dropped on to it. *You* know how hard snow can hit. Our engine was hit three times and accordingly stopped. We didn't know this at first. We thought something had gone wrong with the air-brake: that the driver had clapped it on and jammed it, which sometimes happens if there is a leak in the pipes or couplings. All we knew was that we had stopped and that a person in authority armed with a long and dripping torch of resin marched down the tunnel sticking the torch in among our wheels. There isn't much room in an Italian tunnel for anything except the train: but little refuge holes are cut in the side of the tunnel for men to step into if they should happen to meet a moving train. When this man waved his flambeau you could see that the sides of the tunnel were marked and crusted in places with bosses and stalactites of frozen water – same as on the rocks at Engelberg. I think *they* made me feel colder than anything else. (Did I tell you by the way that we had left our dinner-car at Bologna after lunch at 12. noon. It was then getting on for five p.m.) Then the tunnel suddenly filled with the joyful roarings of demons, who yelled *avanti* and *pronti* and *Madonna* and anything else that came into their easy minds. They were the local peasantry – with the wooden shovels and the green brollies and they were going to tackle the avalanche in the cutting in front of us. But snow to the extent of two feet on the flat is scarce in Italy and wooden shovels *with* green brollies don't go well – one or t'other must suffer, and I fancy they didn't make much impression on the blocked-up cutting ahead of us. Meantime I had a queer feeling – about the centre of my stomach – that there was a nice steep cutting *behind* us at the beginning of the tunnel, which might just as well fill up with an avalanche as the thing in front of us. So I made enquiries. "Oh yes," said a man I asked (in French). He represented a Belfast firm in linen at Florence, and was rather an amusing chap. "Oh yes," he said, "there has already been one avalanche behind us, but it is not so bad a one. We are now trying to break through the snow before us to get to Pistoja. If we cannot, we shall try to get back to Porterra. Of course, if any more avalanches come behind us it will take time." After about an hour the workmen all scampered back into the tunnel with fresh yells of *avanti* or *avasti*, or whatever their loud and joyous shout is. They said they couldn't do anything with the line ahead of us except pull down more avalanches; so they were set to dig us out behind for the back end of the tunnel had filled up by that time – and it was an hour's job before we backed out of the tunnel and, slowly and cautiously, for fear of starting more avalanches, we retraced our steps to Porterra, which is about half the size of Etchingham – what we could make out of it. I don't know when I was ever so pleased to see the white blurr of the outside world again (it was all one smother of whirling snow) and I saluted the green brollies and the wooden shovels and the high peaked hoods that stood silent on the great mounds of snow at the tunnel mouth.

I wish I could give you any notion of it in black and white, but even when one can't draw one ought always to try to explain with an outline. There was a beast of a black river at the bottom of the embankment.

But – to return to Porterra. Everyone of course flung themselves into the little refreshment room to buy food as soon as we came there. No one of course knew whether we might not have to stay there the whole night. D'you remember the scene at Châlons-sur-Marne when we tried to get coffee? Well, multiply that by ten – for Italians are rather more excitable than French – flavour with gârlic and a continuous *crrrash* of evil words and you will realize what the little rush at Porterra was! I grabbed some rusks – like Boer bread – and a couple of oranges – in the crowd and you can imagine my joy when a great, fat, flobby thing of a woman in a brown gown simply rushed at me, pinioned me by the arms and regularly shook me. She was, I imagine, one of the waitresses in a wild fear lest I should cheat her. She even tried to howk [dig] the rusks out of my coat pocket but at this I objected and gave her a franc (about four times what her beastly rusks were worth) and she dropped me. Then we just hung about in the blinding snow – it was a couple of foot thick on everything – till the train got orders to go back to Bologna and try to get to Florence by way of Faenza. Well, then back we pounded and plowtered to Bologna in the dusk. It was then about 7.30, and we got in about nine! I was rather scared at one or two turns in the road where we overhung the river and the hill above was steeper than usual – because I thought that if a really big avalanche came it might knock us sideways into the water. And that same water – all full of ice-flowers – looked beastly cold. After a while I remembered that the snow was as sticky as clay and would not be likely to slide at anything short of a slope of 45 degrees or 50 degrees.

(As a side story. The week before we left Engelberg Von Stockar – the lean brown man with the big wife who skated so well – climbed, or tried to climb, one of the peaks beside the Hahnen and the weather changed suddenly and came on heavy fog and mist. He spent one night at the hut in the snow-field and the next morning his guide said they had better get down – if they could. So they left the hut, in dense mist and snow for the valley and when they had got about half an hour among the bare rock peaks and ice, the guide said they couldn't get back to the hut if they wanted and they *must* get down to Engelberg. They got down – goodness knows how, because half the time they couldn't see the length of a *ski* ahead of 'em and Stockar said it was rather sickening to lie on one's stomach trying to find out whether the next step would land one on snow, rock or a thousand foot of whirling mist – and *hearing the avalanches behind and before*. The snow was very restless that day, and Stockar never expected to get back to the Hotel alive. Mr Waddy went with him but turned back when the mists came. He tried his best to make Stockar come too, but couldn't.)

Well, we got into Bologna and mucked about there for half an hour, and then we pounded off for Faenza – thirty-one miles up the line. I have always had a great love and affection for Faenza. (Ask Aunt Georgie why. It is because of a quotation which says:– "I have known three and twenty leaders of revolts in Faenza".) So I thought, perhaps, Faenza would do us a good turn. And so it did. When we got there it was raining cats and dogs and I knew the snow would not slide any more. Faenza was dead asleep. I heard a man in the compartment next ours yelling for a bottle of fizzy water and tho' he shouted like a fog-horn no one answered him and he had to jump out into the wet and almost swim to the refreshment room to get it. At Faenza we turned south – precisely as we had turned south at Bologna and made another attempt to cross another range of mountains and get down to Florence *that* way. Luckily we were successful. It was raining on top of the snow and though we had to screw along above rivers that roared in the dark,

83

and to edge ourselves under steep snow-clad hills and to dive through scores of tunnels, nothing stopped us and we got to Florence at 4.30 a.m.

I won't say much about our sufferings. We were five in a second-class compartment. Elsie was stretched out and given a sleeping place but the rest of us had to sit and slouch and slummock as best we could. It was *another* six hours from Florence to Rome, which we finally reached at 10.30 this morning – just twelve hours late. But the run into Rome across the Campagna was wonderful. We saw the day break over Lake Thrasymene – "reedy Thrasymene" – and we saw Clusium and the restaurant Porsena, named in honour of Lars Porsena, and we saw huge oxen and high lean pigs, and grey olive trees and the outlines of Soracte – a mountain you will come to know about. But the most beautiful things were the towns on top of the hills – each hill had a town or each town had a hill – whichever way you like to put it, and everything was new and wonderful. We saw Father Tiber in full flood shaking his "yellow mane" because there had been a big storm the night before with any amount of rain (we, of course, had had snow up in the mountains) and the Tiber was a boiling mud torrent. Then at one turn of the line, about ten miles away from the city we saw the Dome of St Peter show up like a bubble. Think of the size of the building if it shows up at *ten* mile! Elsie hopped about and tried to look at both sides of the line at once and enjoyed herself awfully. It's no good wishing that you were with us because you've your own job to do, but some day we two will get off together and see a town if we have to tramp to it on our four fat legs!

It was a spring day with blue sky and bright sun when we reached Rome and there were great date-palms growing in the public gardens (at least I think they were date-palms) and for the first time in two months we saw brown naked earth. Did you realize that we had carried the snow with us from Charing X station on the 28th Dec. 1908 to within a few miles of Florence on the 2nd Mar. 1909? Oh it was jolly good to see daisies growing in the grass and irises and daffodils in the public parks. I put my foot on three daisies at once to be sure that spring had come, but Bird says you ought to put your foot on seven, and when I asked Miss B. *she* said nine! All I can say is they must have disgusting big feet.

Tired as we were, we three crawled out into the Borghese Gardens from 12 till 1.30. They are very beautiful in spots – with stone-pines and lots of eucalyptus and mossy statues. As we went home we passed a battery of Artillery going to barracks after exercise. The horses were a powerful lot but very long in the coat and apparently very badly kept. The guns were *not* quick firers and did not look to be much cared for. They had a silly sort of screw-brake (about strong enough to stop a perambulator) when they went down hill and the horses weren't trained to hold back properly. Perhaps they were *light* field artillery and the regular artillery are quick firers.

We are all dead tired and Mother looks as though she had a cold in the head. Bird slept like a pig all this afternoon. I slept a little and I'm all right only when I shut my eyes I see the snow whirling in front of them. I won't close this letter till to-morrow – to see if your weekly one comes on to us. Show this letter to Aunt Georgie (*my* Aunt Georgie), if you think it may interest her. Dear love, old man. Oh, I *am* tired, and my back is in eighteen pieces – none of which fit.

Wednesday, 3rd March. No letter from you so far. I hope it hasn't been sent to Engelberg by mistake. Remember our address is:–

Savoy Hotel,
Rome.

We are all better to-day, and all send you our love.

I am, my dear Sir,
Yours ffly,
Daddy.

Bateman's,
Burwash,
Sussex.
Friday, May 28. [1909]

Dear old man,

Just got your letter about Empire Day at the school. The entire family nearly fainted at the amazing fact of an extra letter from you. I also spent Empire Day in an agreeable fashion. Mummy and I went in the motor to Sturry – a village two miles beyond Canterbury to have lunch with Lord Milner. It's 46 miles and nearly every village along the road – Rolvenden, Tenterden, High Holden, Bethersden, Ashford, etc. – was decorated with flags and on one village green we passed a curate standing under a flagpole and exhorting a whole crowd of little kids. I am awfully pleased at the progress which Empire Day is making and I expect that in a few years even the Government will fly flags in its honour. Lord Milner has a delightful house at Sturry with a river at the end of his garden lawn. We saw an eel in the river more than a foot long – quite big enough to eat.

And talking about eating "my boy, my boy" let me impress it on your young mind that you wouldn't have been taken to the doctor if you had eaten properly in your youth. Now listen to me! When meals come round you must not start an interesting conversation with Ackroyd or anyone else who sits next you but you *must* devote yourself to the business of eating – and nothing else. There is not the least danger of your becoming a glutton so I council you to stuff your little tummy *in silence*. When you are my age doctors will tell you to mix talk with your vittles but now you are young, you are young and you should eat without talking. You are however too old to be suddenly sick at table (as the very young sometimes are), so swallow down your meat, even though it does not meet (that's a rotten bad pun. I swear I didn't mean it) with your approval. You are deficient in lime in your carcass, young Sir. Meat will give it you. Seriously, old man oblige me by eating. Otherwise you may have to take cod liver oil! *Then* – not to put too fine a point on it – you may cat [vomit] and no one will pity you.

I have been digging in the garden. Mother has been weeding in the garden. Elsie played tennis in the garden to-day. (This is not a French exercise but a story of our news.) After tea Elsie and Miss B. went fishing. They caught nothing (*rien*). Uncle Stan and Aunt Cissie come to-morrow but (*mais*) they do not bring any child with them. Your Angy comes to-morrow. My father left yesterday morning. I am in good health. I am stiff from digging in the garden. Your Mother's left knee is stiff from kneeling to weed in the garden. Your sister is annoyed (*fâchée*) because she did not catch any of my trout, *and*

> I am ever
> Your loving
> Dad.

> Bateman's,
> Burwash,
> Sussex.
> *June. 3. 1909.*

Dear old man!

"Oh what a surprise!" I was awfully set up by your letter and showed it to Elsie. She says she will "demand" one from you on the grounds that you were sent the St Nicholas (that's a good magazine too) by her.

I don't know about *your* weather. Here we are having a howling north-easterly wind with grey skies and a temperature to match – a regular late October day. I was weeding this afternoon on my hands and knees and felt as stiff as a Dutch doll when I had done. Did I tell you that while Uncle Stan was here I did a thing for which I should have beaten you if you had done it, with a golf-club. I was cutting off a dead branch with my knife (my father had sharpened it only a day or two before on *your* oil-stone; so you observe all three generations were concerned in the affair) and I drew the blade towards me. It cut the twig like butter and as my left hand was in the light (I don't know why) it cut the forefinger of the left hand from the nail end of the last joint to the middle joint. I don't know what the proper anatomical names are but it was a slash about two inches long and pretty deep.

Well, you can see from this that every time I tried to bend my forefinger the cut naturally opened. I had to go about for a day or two, stinking of iodoform (Mummy tied me up) holding my finger as stiff as a stick, and feeling rather a fool. It was an utterly silly thing to have done and, as I have said, if it had been you I should have chastized you with a cricket stump for handling a knife so clumsily. Since it is myself, I merely said that it was "an extraordinary accident". I couldn't tub for two mornings because I couldn't wet my bandaged finger.

Mother (she is knitting in front of the drawing-room fire) does nothing nowadays except knit. She knits when she walks in the garden or through the farms; she knits in the trains and when she rests in bed. I'm only glad she doesn't knit in her sleep. Her only explanation is that she is making stockings for you. When I sent you to school this term you had only two legs. How many more *have* you grown? You can't be a centipede like this?

Also collars are being made for you – hundreds of 'em apparently. Well, no matter. At half-term when we meet (Oh be joyful!) we will go into these matters at length, "my boy, my boy". Meantime learn to eat, study to stuff – enjoy life, accept my blessing – don't be a beast – receive our united best loves and believe me,

> Ever your loving
> Pater.

> Bateman's,
> Burwash,
> Sussex.
> *June. 16. 1909.*

Dear old man –

I wasn't going to write to you this week on account of coming over on Saturday but seeing that your sports begin on Saturday I just want to breathe a few moral maxims in your ear "said Mr Campbell".

You are now getting on in life – like Elsie – and I want your behaviour to correspond with your years. Therefore, O my Son, do all that you can to win, honestly and fairly the events for which you have entered. If you win, shut your head. Exalt not yourself nor your legs nor your wind nor anything else that is yours. To boast (not that you are given to it) is the mark of the Savage and the Pig. If you lose remember that you have lost. It doesn't matter one little bit but it matters a great deal if you go about jawing about your handicap being too heavy or your having had a bad start or your being tripped or put off. The man who explains why he lost and hints that under other circumstances he might have won is worse than the Pig and the Savage. Remember that, *mon ami.* We shall be equally delighted whether you win or lose as long as you do both of them, as you always have hitherto, decently and quietly. Only *don't* join the knot of little shrimps who always exist in every school, who always jaw and jabber and explain if they happen to have lost an event.

Elsie has a H A T! I haven't letters big enough for the article, but it is a

I don't know whether she will come in it. She can't if there is any wind or anyone else on the cricket field. Our plan is to come into Brighton early on Sat. morning and do an hour at the dentist's. Then to Aunt G's for lunch and then directly to the sports. Tea with you in the school and then home. Hurroo!

Did I tell you – or did anyone tell you – we came home by the Wick the other day? We'll try it again on Saturday – *unberufen*. Great and joyous love from us all,

> Ever your
> Pater.

P.S. Caught 5 fish to-day in the pond. Mother caught 4 – Col. Feilden 1. I lent my moral support. We are trying to catch the fish and then to poison the weed.

> Bateman's,
> Burwash,
> Sussex.
> *Sep. 28. 1909.*

Dear William [John],

Got your letter last night. There isn't much to tell in the first few days, is there?

Our weather has been simply filthy and to-day it is raining drearily and drizzlyly. Mummy and I went up to London yesterday and I lunched at my Club on soused mackerel (in vinegar) and fish pie which is rather a silly sort of food. Nobody much was there and I didn't hear any good stories.

I've been awfully busy on my last story – about the gipsy man in America[1] – and I think with care I shall make it rather good. Only it wants an awful amount of work.

Are you under any of the new masters for anything? Do write and let us know what they are like. Sorry to hear about the "Children's Song"[2] – for which I feel I ought to apologize deeply. All your fault for having a poetical pa!

Did I tell you that my old school-mate (Colonel Dunsterville) was here the other day for just the night? He was exactly the same as he had always been and we met just as though we had never separated. Although he is commanding the 20th Native Infantry, he says he feels exactly as young as ever he was and he finds it hard to keep a serious face when he blows up the young subalterns for being bad. He is going back to India in a little while; leaving his seven year old son behind him.

Miss Blaikie caught a chill yesterday and one side of her face is all swelled up. Elsie is doctoring her with hot bottles. She is lying on the sofa in the nursery and she sends her love. Elsie also sends the same and says she will write on Thursday. We met Miss Eckstein in London. Do you remember her and Bernie and Erminie?

I'm afraid my news is small and few and scarce but I'll write more when I get some more. I've tucked up the bees for the winter under extra thick quilts and have given 'em lots of syrup. Only got one sting and it didn't hurt after the first prog [poke].

expression of bee while stinging   expression of *me* – stung

Clemenceau, the chap who was French premier, came on Thursday – an awful interesting chap.

Love to Larry and Julia.

> Ever your
> Dadeeeeeeeeee

[1] "Brother Square Toes", *Rewards and Fairies*.
[2] Concluding poem in *Puck of Pook's Hill*.

> Bateman's,
> Burwash,
> Sussex.
> *Oct. 5. 1909.*

Dear William,

You've taken a leaf out of Oliver Baldwin's book - you young villain! D'you remember when he sent Mother the complete score of a county cricket-match? Your two page time-table of your studies rather reminded me of it. But, on the whole, I'm glad to have it because I wanted to know the subjects in which Stanford gives you extra-tu. Algebra and Math. seem to be the things you are getting most of. Sweet subjects? Did you ever know how, when I was your age, my dear boy, I used to get up at 5 o'clock on winter mornings and study by the light of a tallow candle such beautiful things as

$$(x^2 + 2xy + y^2)^2 = \sqrt{xy^2 - 2x^2}.$$

Yes. That was what really held my attention! But the truly exciting part begins when you get to such poetical delights as

$$(a+b)\sin\frac{c}{2} = c \text{ as } \frac{a-b}{2}$$

(Ask Mr Long what that means?)

91

Then you light two tallow candles, and utter shrill yells. Seriously, I'm very pleased with this week's report and your being top in arith. But keep it up, my son, and haul yourself to the top of the form.

No words – no mathematical formulae – will begin to describe the foulness of this weather. My thermometer by the bee hives marks 60°–63° – a dense, muggy, fuggy air, varied with gusts of sticky wind and torrents of warm rain. The brook [the Dudwell] is up two feet – just like cocoa and running eight knots. The ground is pulp where it isn't squog. *Of course* in the midst of this glorious state of affairs, a lot of yews and hollies which Mother is planting have arrived. Martin Holles and Drawbridge planted 26 four foot yews outside our yew hedge at the front of the house. Their boots when they had done were [very muddy]. But we got the yews in!

I have mildew all over me. Do you know that feeling when even baths don't make you feel clean? It's all this dull damp.

But none the less I've had some exercise. Yesterday, in despair at getting a walk Mother and I went down to the mill, and piled up and stacked in order all the different sorts of timber there – posts, logs, laths, boards and slabs. When I finished hauling and shoving and piling there wasn't a dry rag on me and I had a glorious tub. To-day she and I tidied up the upper storey of the mill and came on filthy pieces of rag and fur and general muckings which you and Elsie must have carried up to the mill attic ages ago. Dirty babes!

I'm busy with my tales but I do wish you were here to help me trim up the poplar and the willow tree. Never mind. Two weeks gone almost. Only a month more to half term.

Miss B. found your pen. A sweet hunt she had for it. It was at the back of one of Bird's drawers.

Mother joins me in dearest love, and

> I am, as ever,
> Your Dad.

Bateman's, Burwash, Sussex: Kipling's home from 1902 until his death in 1936.

Elsie, John and Josephine Kipling, 1898.

Kipling reading to a group of children aboard a ship bound for Cape Town, 1902.

…sephine Kipling, …895; she died at …ven, in 1899, of the …eumonia that almost …led her father.

…*low*: Kipling and …mily aboard ship *en …ute* for Cape Town in …07; Carrie stands just … front of him. Elsie …d John are sitting on … deck.

Kipling (in the foreground, his face partially obscured by Mark Twain's academic cap) receives an honorary degree in Oxford, June 27 1907. "Presently we forced a procession – two by two – and were put into order like boys at school."

Right: Kipling in the skating costume that he describes in his letter of February 10 1909.

Facing page: Three drawings from a letter Kipling sent to the young daughter of friends, Amelia "Turkey" Clifford, to whom he used to write before he had children of his own. In the summer of 1890, she had mumps; Kipling wrote to her in commiseration, parodying "The Cow with the Crumpled Horn". "This is *The* Mumps", "With her head in a band of fine thick flannel" and "A Regular Waggon-load" from "the chemist up the road").

This is The Mumps

with her head in a band of fine thick flannel

a Regular Waggon-load

Right: John Kipling in uniform, 1915.

Left: Kipling, as a war correspondent in France; he insisted on wearing civilian clothes.

Below: Kipling at Southport, June 1915, appealing for more recruits.

a there rest few days. This will be my last letter most likely for some time as we wont get any time for writing this next week but I will try & send. Field post cards

Well so long old dears

Dear love

John.

Love to Jerry

The postcard John sent Elsie on his eighteenth birthday. *Right:* the last page of John's last letter to his father, September 25 1915: "this will be my last letter most likely for some time...".

Rudyard and Carrie Kipling at the cemetery in Loos, scene of the battle in which John was killed in 1915.

Dear old man –

On Sunday I went by motor to see my father and mother – and came back on Tuesday. That was why I haven't written you my weekly letter.

It has been a gay and hectic week! When I left my father's house on Tuesday at 10 a.m. it was raining awfully: and it never stopped for an instant *all* the way. One hundred and twenty-eight miles of motoring in a downpour that wetted everything to the skin. The motor came back to Bateman's one solid clot of mud. Well! that was only the beginning of the fun! I had an idea we should have a bit of a flood in the valley but I had no notion that we should have the worst flood since 1852! Miss Coates came over at 7 p.m. on Tuesday night. She said the brook was pretty well up to the bridge. It was raining hard. At 8 o'clock it was out over the banks. By nine our square pond had backed up and was all across the lower lawn. The tennis court had been flooded long ago. By eleven o'clock the water was over a foot deep by the limes. I went out in my rubber boots to see. By midnight the water was *at* the south door of Bateman's – lying in one level sheet right across the garden. Then Mother and I rolled up the carpets in the hall and the drawing-room for fear it should come into the house. It was very odd to see only half of the yew hedges sticking up in the moonlight. At 1 o'clock I went into the kitchen to get something to eat. I opened the cellar door and this is what I saw! Bottles and eggs and apples floating about in a foot of water. Well, it didn't seem to be much good hanging about so we went to bed and in the morning the water had gone off the lawns and we put on our rubber boots and began to take stock of the damage. Here is a little of it:

1 Dynamo by the mill flooded out and made useless.
2 Little foot-bridge across to Cedar Island under-mined.
3 Fence of the field by the mignonette path laid down flat. The flood was within a few inches of the top of the iron fence.
4 *All* my bee-hives swept away from Cedar Island – with the tables they stood on. Nothing left except the top of one hive.
5 The path by the brook all knocked to bits and the brick ballast that it was made of blown across the fields.

6   1 teak seat carried off and set down among the roses by the pond. The other seat floated over among the laurels.

7   The sand road knocked to pieces along its whole length.

Well, thinks I, "this is gay. I wonder what has happened at Dudwell." I went over and found that two feet of water had swept through the house in the night! Mrs Whybarn was in an awful state. All the floor was covered with fine mud. I went up to the village and bought a broom and Colonel Feilden came down with me. The Whybarn's pig had been floated out of his stye and was running about very clean and washed and very hungry. Colonel Feilden scrubbed his back with the broom which so delighted the pig that he followed Colonel Feilden all about like a dog and kept rushing at his leg in a loving fashion. So the Colonel had to smite him on the nose with the broom handle. You never saw anything so funny.

It came on to rain again yesterday and we couldn't go out. I don't know yet the full extent of the damage but I have marked the highest places to which the flood rose. You won't believe it when you see it. It rose six inches above the bottom of the mill door. It was waist deep on the tennis court!

Well, this is only a line to send you all our love and greetings.

Ever thy loving
Daddy.

Hotels Cattani,
Engelberg.
Sunday 2.30 p.m. *Jan. 30, 1910.*

Dear old man –

Your postcard Friday (12.15 a.m.) got in here this morning. That idea of yours of giving the time of the despatch is a jolly good one. It shows you sent off your news *very* soon after you got in. Of course we had the wire from Miss Coates telling of your arrival at Charing X, and I'm awfully glad that, with your usual luck, you managed to slip through the floods without delay. I suppose you know that two days before you crossed the Folkestone–Boulogne sailings were hung up – suspended – on account of the gales. A thing that hasn't happened for twenty years.

Yesterday was a beautiful day and Uncle Stan and Aunt Cissie came by the 4.38 train (they were two hours late at Basle of course and so had to wait till the 8.33 train and spend half the day in Lucerne). I took

Uncle Stan off at once to the outfitter's shop to buy him a white cap – he wore yours down to the shop – and a pair of gloves. Then we went on to Berlis and hired a pair of *skis*. He said he was *very* keen on ski-ing. They had tea with us in our rooms (their rooms are 282 and 281 on the floor below) and Aunt Cissie told us how you had warned her against every possible contingency on the road here and had told her what to wear etc. etc. That was a great help to 'em because they knew exactly what they wanted and what they didn't. This morning the sun shone and by 10.30 a.m. Uncle Stan and Aunt Cissie were just ramping to go out. We were all on the rink by 10.45. They hadn't any skates, so I went over with Uncle Stan to the skate-shop (taking his boots with us) to get a pair. Aunt Cissie chose Mount Charles but I recommended Uncle Stan to have Dowlers (same as me) because the blades were broad. And he did.

Their skates were ready at 12 – and they went on the ice. Aunt Cissie wasn't so bad, but poor Uncle Stan said he had forgot all about everything and I laughed like anything when he started from the skateroom door. He didn't fall but he just sort of slid where his skates led him and complained bitterly of the way his legs hurt. After a while he got warmed up and then Elsie took him round and then she took Aunt Cissie round and then Uncle Stan again. He looked as earnest and as anxious as though he were fighting another election. Well, then we decided to have lunch on the ice. The clouds came over the sun and it was rather cold but we enjoyed it ever so. We had hot soup, cold chicken and sandwiches like we had at the Gerschni picnic. Then Uncle Stan and Aunt Cissie and Elsie and I went on skating while Mother walked round the rink. Uncle Stan kept it up till 2.30. He has just come into my room and proposes going out for a walk! An energetic cousin. I expect he will be out on skis this afternoon but it has just begun to snow.

I leave a little space here for Mother to fill up, and I rest and remain,

Ever your most loving
Pater.

Hotels Cattani,
Engelberg.
Thursday Feb. 3. [1910] 9.30 p.m.

Dear old man –

A line to acknowledge your first school letter. Oliver by the way wrote his people a letter on the same day in which he gives *heaps* more of school news than you do. It seems that some new scheme of rewards has been started by which chaps who haven't got marks during the week get off Wednesday prep – or something. I don't quite understand it: so please enlighten me. (Sorry about the "Children's Song". *You* know that I didn't write the darn thing with the faintest idea it would be so cruelly used against the young.) In return here's a bit of verse I tried to do about *skis*. You know what a telemark is because you can do it. This is called the *Ballad of the Telemark*.

> Two strips of brown, well-varnished board
> With rapture from the shop we bring –
> A fathom long, four inches broad,
> And graceful as an angel's wing.
> Gadzooks ... It seems a simple thing
> Yet why do *they* take charge of *us*
> When we attempt the sideways swing
> That Mentor taught Telemachus?*
>
> In vain we call upon the Lord,
> In vain we cringe and crawl and cling
> To any hand that may afford
> Us respite from our slithering.
> Across the snow ourselves we sling –
> Half rocket, half rhinoceros,
> Dear me! What was that sideways swing
> That Mentor taught Telemachus?

* As a matter of fact, Mentor did nothing of the sort. The telemark comes from a little village called Telemarken somewhere in Norway or Sweden.

Uncle Stan has gone *mad* about skis. He goes out with big Carli Hess – the man that taught you – and he wallows and plunges and dives and slides and enjoys himself enormously. He skates all the morning and skis the afternoon. We have had lunch out on the rink nearly every day since they came. I don't like gnawing cold chicken and garlicky sausage on the ice but it seems to amuse the others. Now hear what your Own Bear did to-day.

She *put on her skates* at lunch on the rink. She skated for nearly twenty minutes. She had lunch in the open. She went out straight after lunch to see the luging competition, and on the way home she went down the monastery slope on her luge. Then she gave away the prizes after dinner. She is getting better hurrah! You had better tell this to Miss Blaikie next time you write her. I hear she is sending you your regular Sunday letters again.

There is as you well know no news. Our weather keeps fine and bitter cold. The water in Bird's hot water bottle was frozen the other morning. She had kicked it out of bed on the floor. It didn't freeze *in* her little bed.

Everything seems better now that your Bear [Carrie] is getting better. She is sitting opposite me at our table doing a whole pile of letters which Miss Coates has just sent her. She sends her best and dearest love and says she can't skate at all. (All the same she did: Elsie was by her side, but she didn't fall down.)

I am, odd as it may seem, as ever
> Your most loving
> Pa.

There once was a man who said:– "I
Am no end of a fellow on *ski*."
> When they said:– "Those are *shees*"
> He said:– "Just as you please.
I sit on my bottom and fly!"

There once was a man who said:– I
"Am no end of a fellow on ski"
When they said:– "Those are shees"
He said" Just as you please.
"I sit on my bottom and fly!"

97

Hotels Cattani,
Engelberg.
Feb. 23. 1910.

Dear old man,

Your letter just in and we HAIL WITH DELIGHT (you will find this expression in the papers) the news that you are going to give us two letters a week. Be sure they shall be well answered. It must be rotten to be in the sickhouse but I am glad to note that your conduct is marked excellent. Now *my* conduct when I am sick is far from being excellent.

Our weather has become hot and fine and the rink melts at about eleven o'clock. Elsie had her lesson to-day at 10.30. Even then the ice was getting pretty slushy. Mother skated a good deal. The passage down to the rink is simply awful. You can hardly stand on it. Nearly all the people have gone away or are going and by Sunday next when we expect to leave for Vernet-les-Bains, there will be hardly a soul left. All right about Geneva. We won't be absent-minded "begars" (why not another g William, my love) and it shall be a half-hunter as you demand. Seems to me that it is about time somebody gave me something.

Mother and I went out for a climb this afternoon in hot sun. The other little Pig – I mean Elsie the Slacker – stayed at home. We climbed up beyond the monastery field, up past the reservoirs and at last got into a bare wood where we gathered flowers – hepaticas, they call 'em. This will show you how far advanced the season is. The sun hits into our bed-room a little after eight and does not go out of our sitting-room till after four! But all this makes the snow simply beastly to walk on and we roll about and perspire in the sun and feel that we are taking mighty exercise before the Lord.

Here's a bit of free-hand "translation" that made me laugh. You know the notice in the carriages "not to spit about". It's in four languages. The German is:– "*Man bitter nicht in dem wagen zu spucken*". Someone looked at it the other day and said:– "Oh, I suppose that means 'If a man bites you in the night, don't speak about it'". I wish I knew German. I tried to ask some kids coming back from school this afternoon, where the flowers grew, and all I could say was:– "*Wahr sind das blumen?*" I know "*blumen*" means flowers but the rest is simply awful. I don't wonder they made faces and walked away.

As you can imagine there isn't much news. It's too dirty in the streets to tail; the snow is too wet for *skis*; and we skate, as I told you, only in the morning. Elsie gets her lesson, gets chocolate, gets to bed, gets fat. I have quite a time changing books for her at the L-I-B-R-A-R-Y. I see, O my beloved William, you prefer to spell it "libery" which besides being totally wrong is heathen, offensive and intolerable. Amend this.

Sorry about old Ackroyd. It's my private impression that the whole of your school ought to be washed in Condy's for a week. You seem so diseased.

I read about the big gale at Brighton – it *was* a *Gieshübler* of a gale – but did you see how the wretched Boulogne boat had to make *five* shots at Folkestone pier before she could land her sea-sick passengers? She began trying to come alongside at 8.15 and finished at 11.40! They must have gone up to London feeling like a lot of wet-stockings.

Well, now I will conclude. Mother has had a bath after her huge mountain climb and is lying down in bed reading the *Spectator*. It is ages since I had a wash. I will invest two francs in one this evening.

Meantime I am
> Your most loving
> Pater.

P.S. Wish you were here to share the bath with me. We had some fun for our two francs then.

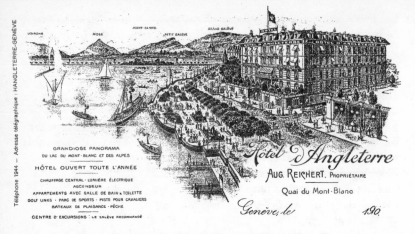

GRANDIOSE PANORAMA
DU LAC DU MONT-BLANC ET DES ALPES

HÔTEL OUVERT TOUTE L'ANNÉE

CHAUFFAGE CENTRAL · LUMIÈRE ÉLECTRIQUE
ASCENSEUR
APPARTEMENTS AVEC SALLE DE BAIN & TOILETTE
GOLF LINKS · PARC DE SPORTS · PISTE POUR CAVALIERS
BATEAUX DE PLAISANCE · PÊCHE

CENTRE D'EXCURSIONS · LE SALÈVE RECOMMANDÉ

Hôtel D'Angleterre

AUG. REICHERT, PROPRIÉTAIRE

Quai du Mont-Blanc

Genève, le 190.

Ordered a watch to-day, but it is being delayed while your initials are cut on back. It isn't a half-hunter because they are out of fashion but it's a real beauty. Don't open it to see the works.

To John Kipling Esq.   *Feb. 28. 1910.*

My Dear Sir,

Your excellent and never-sufficiently-to-be-praised Father has to-day bought for you a horloge of precision (see card enclosed) *c'est à dire* a new watch which I shall despatch to your address after it has been regulated and your initials have been engraved on its back. But first, *mon cher monsieur*, I would give you some advice as to the treatment of the watch. It is *not* a cheap watch. *Au contraire c'est un montre très expensif*! Therefore do not brutalize it – and on no account look into its stomach to behold its works. *C'est rigoreusement défendu d'ouvrir le montre.* You, my dear young sir, would not love that men should open you the stomach to regard therein. It would *bouleverser* your digestion. So it is also with a watch. Do you think that I, Golay Fils & Stahl (see card enclosed) manufacture watches of the highest precision *afin que tous les* dirty little *garçons* in the world should open them to see into their works? *Sapristi*! Non!

Your revered and most excellent father – who has paid enormous sums for this watch – tells me that you wanted a half-hunter. Half-hunters are now very seldom or never made. *Ils sont demodés, c'est à dire* out of the fashion but the watch which I send you represents our best machinery and will endure (if you do not brutalize it with evil treatment) till you are *un vieux. Mais – écoutez moi – Il est défendu –*

*verboten – prohibito, de soaker le montre en thé, ou le mettre dans les bains,
ou dans la mer, ou le laisser* on the cricket field, *ou le* chucker at other
boys' heads. *Mille tonnerres! Ventre-Saint-Gris!* One does not manufacture horloges of precision to be thrown about the shop (as you say in
English). There are few such watches. *Sac à papier!* There are very few
and I weep when I think of the gigantic sums which your admirable
and thoughtful father has paid for this watch. But you must treat it, *as*
a watch and not as an article of sport (I am not Gamage's) or amusement
or as a tool of labour. Your charming and accomplished father has told
me (*les larmes aux yeux*) that you have already massacred and assassin-
ated three watches! *Quel horreur! O Monstre!*

Receive, Sir, the assurances of my profound esteem,

s.a. Golay Fils & Stahl.

P.S. I think it only just to tell you that I overheard your imposing and
beneficent Papa say to your beautiful and indulgent Mother that
he would see you *fortement condamné* before he gives you another
watch.

P.P.S. *Prenez garde au montre.*

P.P.P.S. *N'ouvrez pas les works.*

Bateman's,
Burwash,
Sussex.
May 7. 1910.

Dear old man –

Your letter just in. Yes, it has been a beast of a week – nothing but
icy winds and squalls of sleet and rain with us. I hear the Downs by
Eastbourne were white with hail yesterday!

The King's death has been an awful thing. Curious to think that,
young as you are, you have lived in the reign of three sovereigns –
Victoria, Edward and George V. If his ministers had not worried him
over their squabbles and made him come up from Biarritz with a cough
on him, he might have lived for many years longer. Never forget that.
It is part of the debt we owe Lloyd George and his friends.

I went up to London to-day – the dreariest sight you ever saw. All
the flags half mast and all the people in black – crape bows to the bus
conductors' whips and bits of crape on the steering wheels of the motor
buses. The shops had one or two of their shutters up; the Clubs had all

their blinds drawn down and I had my lunch at the Athenaeum by electric light behind closed blinds. A very queer effect.

I went to the Stores to buy some puppy-biscuit for Jack and Betty and, of course, I went to the animal department. You remember that yelling black Pomeranian or Spitz that we saw? (when the lady spoke to us) He was yelling and yowling still, and a label in front of his cage announced that his price was three guineas, that he could "sit up and beg", was "quiet with children" and was "a good watch-dog". I don't care about the first statement; I thoroughly believe the last; but I think the middle statement is what you might call a lie. *I* shouldn't care to be the child he was quiet with. I spoke to the man at the counter about the difference between Jack and Betty. He said that they *were* full brother and sister out of the same litter but that very often one dog would be quite different from another. He showed me a couple of smooth-haired terriers – dog and bitch – as a proof of that. They were quite unlike each other but he vowed they were out of the same litter. He said that the dog-breeders wouldn't dare to cheat over such matters.

Jack and Betty are quite well and gay. Elsie and Miss Goode took them to Rye Green this afternoon but, I understand, they tried to chase ducklings and so were lifted up and taken home in a basket; they are an enterprizing pair of little imps. Betty is still the rowdier of the two but I don't think Jack will stand her going on much longer. Ellen calls her Miss Betty. If you don't know what Jack calls her you can guess from his growls. We will all do our best to have him in good shape when you come home.

Thanks for telling us about half-term. Odd as it may seem, you may expect us down about that date! Mother went to town with me to-day to get herself black clothes. They are hard to get. The Stores are full of black ties and black-edged cuffs. Isn't the Dead March a fine tune though it is so creepy.

Well, my son, God bless you. I am tired and these be stirring times. Dear love from us both. The grandparents and Aunt Trix went this morning and we have just had a wire saying they reached Tisbury after "a prosperous journey". So that's all right.

> Ever your loving
> Father.

Bateman's,
Burwash,
Sussex.
May. 17. 1910.

Dear old man –

Many thanks for your letter and the report which says you have done "an excellent week's work". Cheers! I am glad too to see that your handwriting is better. Only, *why* do you not put in capital letters at the beginning of your sentences? It makes it a bit difficult to read as one sentence slides into the other without warning. Rejoiced to learn that the bat is doing of its dooty. If it has the habit of knocking up "fours" encourage it and pat it on the back. Very few bats have that habit.

Uncle Stan and Aunt Cissie came down here, by motor, on Saturday and have just gone away this (Tuesday) morning. They brought Margot with them and she and Elsie had a high old time. I think the Bird is feeling rather tired after it. By the way she broke the copper binding off one of the dinghy's oars. I expect we shall have to get another pair.

Yesterday and the day before were beautifully warm and hot – just like summer. On Sunday a man called Lieuenthal, a Swiss, came to call on us. He is an inventor of flying machines and he showed me plans for a new airship which were the most wonderful things I have ever seen. He had bright blue eyes and he talked for two and a half hours without stopping. He showed me a little thing like a baby typewriting machine, only not much bigger than a Kodak which could transmit messages in cypher that no one could read and then translate the cypher back into plain English. The machine itself changes the cypher all the time as it goes on. I can't describe it till I meet you. He gave me a bit of the stuff that war-balloon skins are made of. I have never enjoyed myself so much before.

Elsie is awfully good to the dogs and gives them exercise and dries their little feet after they have been running in the wet grass. Moore gives them *great* care and dusts 'em with insect powder. Jack is very lively and frisky and can now knock Bet over. He grabs her by the hind leg when he does it. I think he will make no end of a fighter but he is a reserved and shy little beast. Bet is all jump and jip and ginger. We had them out just now after breakfast. In a little while we must put them on a leash and make them take longer walks.

Now I will stop. Thank you for your verses. They *were* primitive! I send you a pretty little poem that I have composed by myself. The only drawback to it is that Zug ought to be pronounced Zoog. Otherwise it is perfect.

Dear love from us all.

Pater.

There was a tall person of Zug
Who was found on all fours on the rug.
When they said:-"You've a fit!"
He said:- No! I've been bit -
"And I'm morally sure it's a bug!

Bateman's,
Burwash,
Sussex.

King's Burial Day. *May. 20. 1910*

Dear old man –

This has been one of the most wonderful days that ever I remember. In the first place it was the first day of *real* summer weather – hot but not too hot with a wind that drove away the thunder-clouds. In the second place it was more of a Sunday than anything you could imagine. Last night was hot and sultry with bright white lightning, winking and flashing far away towards the East: now and then one heard (I was up about 2 a.m. to listen to it) a low growl of thunder and then the rain fell in a steady warm drip, same as at Cape Town. I was afraid it might turn to storm by daylight and so spoil all the arrangements for the funeral procession through London: but it all cleared away by morning and from eight or nine o'clock everything was as perfect as it could be. *But* (I wonder if this was the case at Rottingdean) the stillness all over the fields and in the air was much deeper than the ordinary stillness of a Sunday. Nobody was in the fields: no one was driving sheep or cattle so one did not hear any distant lowing or bleating; nobody was driving a horse or getting a fallow ploughed, or packing pigs into market carts. It was absolute *stillness*. I listened long and often but except for the bees there was nothing. You see, all England – literally all our Empire – was getting ready for the King's burial. (The South-Eastern Railway had stopped its traffic and after a while as one listened one realized that what one was waiting for was a railroad whistle.) I expect it will be a long time before one hears all England as still as a Church. I couldn't help thinking that all over the world – in Canada, Australia, India and Africa work was stopped and held up till the King should have been buried.

We knocked off all work at Bateman's altogether. I only asked the men to attend the memorial service at one o'clock: with their medals. Hobbs wore both his; Drowbridge as a Territorial had to go to Ticehurst with his Company. He was in full uniform. Martin and Moore went in black and all the maids went too. The only one left behind was Mrs Martin. As we started for Church we met the Policeman. He had come down to keep an eye on Bateman's, while it was empty. That was kind of him. We went by the fields. There was nobody in sight: one could just hear the bell tolling, muffled (I wish you would find out how they muffle a bell) through the hot still air. The street was empty: every blind was drawn: all shutters were up. There wasn't a dog in the streets. We came half an hour before service. A few people were in their places then and afterwards they came in – they crept in, would be the proper description – one by one till there was not a vacant seat in the Church. There was a little purple riband on one or two places as a sign of mourning but really everyone was so much in earnest that mourning did not matter. Of course you had the same service as we had so I won't tell you about that. We sang:– "Peace, perfect peace"; "O God our help in ages past"; then we had "Crossing the Bar" as an anthem, and then Hymn 185 "The Saints of God". I don't think much of it myself. Colonel Feilden read the lesson. It was the one they always read when people are buried but never in all my born days did I hear it read as Colonel Feilden delivered it. I did not know it for the same thing – he spoke so beautifully, so clearly and with so much feeling. It is a splendid thing to read well! I had heard the chapter at Rottingdean when Uncle Crom was buried but this time, as the Colonel read it, it just went to my heart. He wore all his medals (except the Confederate medal for valour) the C.B.: one Mutiny medal: one Boer War 1881: one Polar Expedition with the snow-white ribbon: and one 1900–02 Boer War medal. I never saw him look so handsome or so young and as I have said, his voice was wonderful and his reading was perfection. The Service ended about 2.10. We all went out quietly and so home across the fields. No one spoke above a whisper in the streets as they went home. Talk of Sunday! Sunday wasn't in it for the Sundified feeling of the day. Elsie said she was quite shocked to see anyone knitting. She and Miss Goode walked together. The maids took up the whole of one pew – Georgine, Ada, Ellen, Long Nellie and Elsie Martin in a line. I don't know whether Nellie Beeching went. The Chapel people had their Memorial Service at 3 p.m. but most of them went to the Church service too. All the Sunday School children were there. As they settled down into their places one of the boys (happy boy!) managed to kick a tin under one of the benches with his feet, and instantly you saw all the boys' faces lighted with one grin of pure joy. I can't think what on earth the tin was unless it was a dustpan someone had left under a bench.

But seriously, it is a great day to have lived through. I expect it must have been impressive at your school service at Rottingdean. Out here in the quiet green country it was tremendously impressive. One saw just the ordinary everyday people, who after all make the world, just grieving for the loss of their own King and friend as they would grieve for anyone of their own blood and kin. The number of medals was astonishing. I won't afflict you with the moral of it, old man, but it's a gentle hint to us all to play the game and do our work, for the King did his and died in the doing of it just as much as if he'd been shot on active service. And he was a great King. We are too near to realize how big a man he was, but when you are my age you'll see it clearly.

All well here though Mummy a little tired, and the pups behaving scandalously. They are feeling gay and strong. They fight like fiends and Bet gets on the top of her kennel where Jack can't reach her and then he gives tongue like a Comanche Indian. I walked 'em over to Lost Meadow to-day and they followed me splendidly. They *are* good dogs and Jack has tons of character. Likewise he will make a hefty fighter. I don't think he knows fear.

Dearest love from us all – specially from Mother who has just gone to bed.

> Ever lovingly,
> Pater.

I hear Grandaddy has sent you the Bateman's photo. *Don't* forget to acknowledge it.

> Bateman's,
> Burwash,
> Sussex.
> *July. 12. 1910.*

Dear old man –

Thanks for your letter, but I can't understand your report. There you are, Sir, wallowing – simply wallowing – towards the bottom of the form and your form-master says you've done an excellent week's work – and your other master says you are very good. Why? Wherefore? But seriously I *am* glad that you are working. All your reports this term have been decent. When – oh when! – did your weather get warm? We had a bit of sun yesterday but most of the time it has been grey skies with a touch of East in the wind.

The pups are really splendid and Jack is becoming a finer dog every week. He follows one about like a shadow while Betty ramps and riots all over the shop. The other day there was a thrush in the strawberry nets. The two chased it up and down from outside till Betty drove it towards Jack who promptly and quietly killed it. He has a great mind that dog. I can drive him into fits of excitement by dodging round the trunk of the ash-tree. He quite understands the game – a sort of peep-o! – and that is the only time he barks. They fight much less than they did and are apt to go off together on excursions down the sand-road. The fence there has just been fresh tarred. You can imagine the rest. Moore has had to wash 'em twice a week. I suppose you know they have their new collars with *John Kipling Bateman's* and *Elsie Kipling Bateman's* engraved on the name-plate. They have also a leash like this:–

They do not like it one little bit. It's to keep them under control when one walks along a hard road, where motors are.

I've got to go to a beastly dinner to-morrow night and make a speech.[1] I detest speeches. Glad you liked the sermon about David and Jonathan. Did you ever read in the Bible how Jonathan got David out of rather a tight place when David was hiding from Saul in a field? They must have had high old times those two. A good friendship with a good chap is a fine thing.

Elsie tells me she is hunting up your ticka film so I suppose it will be sent on in due time. I don't mind telling you that I am counting the days till you come home. Odd – ain't it? It's just a comfort to think that I shall have a man about the place and not a kid. And – oh Cawsand! If only the weather is. fine! Now I will go on with my inky work.

> Dear love from us all.
> Pater.

I think the Eton match was a wonder! How sick and mad Harrow must have been. Like the Cambridge match it was a one-man show. How's your wickets coming on?

[1] Dinner at the Cecil Club, London, for Lord Charles Beresford, July 13 1910. RK spoke about the navy.

> Bateman's,
> Burwash,
> Sussex.
> *Monday night*, [Oct. 3 1910] 9.10 p.m.

Dear old man –

Your letter came in just now: the handwriting a little bigger which is a good sign. I don't want you to take after me in writing small. I'm very pleased to see that you are on your way to the top of the form which is a sound place to roost in: but I notice that Stanford in his report writes as though you were inclined rather to shirk difficulties when you come to 'em. *Don't* do that. It isn't a good habit and it grows on one. By the way Stanford writes me that you aren't taking much interest in your Greek and wants to know whether he shall put you on to German instead. Talk of the Devil and the Deep Sea! I am writing him to say that I want you to go on with your Greek. I think you'll agree with me that it's the best thing to do: for you'll need it if you go to a University and from *any* point of view a knowledge of Greek is worth gold and diamonds. I can ram enough German into you in six weeks on the continent for you to go on with, and these Xmas holidays in Engelberg you shall have some colloquial German, enough to conduct a small conversation in. So buck up and get on with your Greek: for a man that has acquaintance with that tongue has the key that unlocks half the real wisdom of the world.

Mother wrote you from that hotel at Farnboro' (which is really part of Aldershot) how we went to have a look at Wellington College. It's a simply glorious building with huge iron gates and quadrangles and inner courtyards standing in the middle of the most splendid grounds that ever you saw. The cricket and football fields are a dream of delight. By the way they play Rugby there. We saw a big-side team being coached to make a good scrum. The School Chapel is about three times the size of Rottingdean Church. It holds 500 boys, and they have a museum of relics of Wellington and other great Generals. It is in the school library. There is the cloak Wellington wore when he won the battle of Waterloo and there are arms and things. The big dining-hall is an enormous room – as big as the Chapel but the boys who live in the houses don't dine there. They dine at home. The school motto is *"Fortuna virtutis comes"* [Good fortune is the companion of courage] and inside the big gates are the words *"Filii heroum"* [Sons of heroes].

Pearson's House seems *very* delightful. There are about 30 chaps in it. They have each a cubicle to work and sleep in – with a big couch, desk, chair and any amount of knickknacks on the walls which are wood. They don't come up to the ceiling, but are like this:–

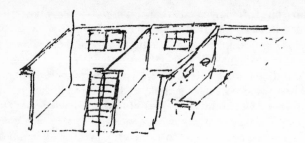

Of course each has a door which I haven't drawn. They look awfully jolly. They have a big form-room downstairs for the juniors to do prep in. The seniors prep in their own cubicles. The Head of the House can give you a licking, but Pearson says it happens very rarely. We saw young Seton Kerr there – much grown. The house is about five minutes' run from the College – through those glorious grounds that I have spoken of. One side of the house is on the edge of the road opposite a wood of fir-trees. It is a country of fir-trees and heather. I don't think you have ever been up in that part of the world before. They have a squash-racket court in the house on one side of it. If you don't look out the balls bounce into the road. There is no village anywhere near the College. You have a sort of big world of your own among trees and gardens and shrubberies and huge playing fields – more than a hundred acres. There is no half-term, but I saw lots of parents roaming around when we were there.

All the arrangements in Pearson's house seemed quite as luxurious as anything at Stanford's: and I confess the cubicles with their couches, easy chairs, private desk, photos, trophies, pictures and so on made me rather envious. I liked Pearson. The boys in the house didn't seem to be a bit in awe of him. Evidently it is a great thing to be in a good house. One's lessons and morning chapel are taken in the big College (where there are 300 boys) but one's meals are taken in one's house. I think this is about all I could find out. I was very delighted with the whole thing. It seemed to me quite like an Oxford College in miniature. Now you must buck up and go in with flying colours.

Glad to learn from Stanford's report that you are in good spirits but – don't give out letters in too flippant a style. It's awkward for a man to get letters not intended for him. Now I am going to read this letter out aloud to Mummy and she will tell me if I have left out anything about Wellington. So kindly wait a minute! No. She says she can't think of anything about Wellington. She notes your esteemed order for roller skates (steel-wheeled) which shall have her earliest attention, and she hopes she will be able to give satisfaction. She notes from your former letter that you require men's size – not juveniles. She also wishes me to say she has much pleasure in returning to your matron your winter knickers with a very superior patch on the knee, forming an elegant lozenge-slashed addition. These trousers have been washed and put into thorough repair and she trusts that later on they will be a comfort to you and give satisfaction when worn with a jacket that you very much like.

I've had the dogs out nearly all this afternoon. They certainly are the oddest little imps, and quite the most amusing companions, I've ever known. Did I tell you how Betty slew a field-mouse the other day? She is as quick as lightning. Now that they know you are not here they are rather sucking up to me as a sort of companion and I find that they do *not* turn back any more in the middle of a walk.

> Dear love from us all.
> Daddo.

Shelbourne Hotel.
[Oct. 18 1911]

9 p.m. (written on the top of a – well the neatly polished little cabinet they put on one side of a bed – because all the electric light is at one end of the room and I can't drag the table there).

Me daughter – O me daughter – (likewise, since you will probably send it on to John) me son!

Mother says she wrote you last night. If she did she must have been a pretty tired mother because, even when the railway is as good as the North Western nine or ten hours of travel do not make for peace or comfort. However, we both dropped into bed last night about 8.30 p.m. and were soothed by the noise of trams. (N.B. The Dublin Tram is the noisiest machine that ever growled round corners.)

We woke at early hours – much cheered by the thought that there were no beastly little – no darling children to be considered and did not descend to breakfast till 9 a.m.!!! The food was good and recherché; the waiters were all German. It was a warm, sticky summer day with blue sky and heaps of smoke in the air. Not *quite* as black as London. Then we went out for a walk. Such a walk! We trailed all round St Stephen's Square first, in a climate that rather reminded one of Madeira. *The*

111

astonishing thing to us was the absence of taxis. As I wrote John, the Dublin cab-driver will see himself blessed before he allows a taxi to be driven for hire. Result, Dublin is still in the horse-age and – stinks according! Then we loafed along through the pale sunshine till we reached the buildings of Trinity College – great blocks of grey stone houses and chapels and libraries, set in gardens and sheets of turf greener than emerald with youngsters and oldsters in College gowns all cutting about and now and then a girl graduate with her gown swinging coquettishly from her shoulders. Tell Miss P. that girls *wear* their gowns: boys just chuck 'em on anyhow. We went to the College Library and saw *The Book of Kells* – a most wonderfully illuminated old Irish M.S. as well as a heap of other volumes, *most* interesting to your parents. We just browsed along like camels on the loose through those heavenly still gardens for an hour or so. Then we strolled out and got into Grafton Street which is as you might say the Bond Street of these parts. At 76, Grafton Street is the Royal Irish Industries, where they sell Limerick and Irish point lace, poplins, linens, Irish tweeds and all that sort of flub-dub. Mother very kindly assisted the Royal Irish Industries. She assisted 'em from 11.50 till 1.25 p.m.! I won't tell you what she bought because she would beat me if I did – but she bought a whole floor full of things. How glad I am that I do not need collars of transparent muckings, or blouses that one can see through, or hankies that one can spit through. I *never* spit through my hankies praise be to Allah! But I daresay you will be pleased with some of the things. It's much more difficult to buy things for a man than for a woman. The only thing I could get John would be a trunkful of horse-dung. It's cheap in Dublin. Another funny experience is lying in bed and hearing the pat-pat of horses' feet. One very rarely hears the hoot of a motor.

Well, as I was saying, we shopped till lunch time and after lunch went out for a drive to Phoenix Park in a jaunting-car. My dears, jaunting-cars were designed by the Devil. You step on a step which is about as big as a stirrup. Then you sit sideways on a cushion, your legs hanging outside the wheels. The driver sits in front. Heaven knows how. But (Mummy says) one thing is certain. If anything happens the passenger falls out sideways. If there is any congestion of traffic in the streets the passenger's legs are hit. We were jerked and jolted along sideways at the awe-inspiring pace of at least 6 miles per hour. Mummy on one side – me on the other.

(I'm trying to get the blessed thing right. This is almost correct.) We drove along the banks of the River Liffey, which is a rich, pure black, stone-faced sewer that calls itself a river. Guinness' brewery is on one bank of it. Liffey water is the same colour as Dublin porter.

Well, in due time, say half an hour, we got to Phoenix Park – which is of enormous extent – about 1200 acres but in a jaunting-car this feels like 18 miles in circumference. We took an hour to jaunt round it so it must have been eighteen miles in pure exposure and suffering. There were hundreds and hundreds of fallow-deer in the park: all slightly sooty, like everything else in Dublin; and cows and sheep – and the horse (who was really a good little horse) lifted up one leg and put it down and lifted up the next leg and put it down, till I nearly wept with boredom. I distinctly saw the wool growing on the sheep's backs between every stride: and Mummy got cold and silent (like Lot's wife) and I grew cold and quite voluble (which is how cold affects me). And we wrote our name in the book at Viceregal Lodge; and also at General Lyttleton's house which was half an hour distant from Viceregal Lodge; and after two hours of jovial jaunting-car-dom we got back to our Hotel and urged our frozen limbs into half an hour's walk before tea to get warm. You, my dears, are young. When you meet a jaunting-car you may ride in it if you want to. But, be warned by me, *don't* ride for fun in Dublin. It's too like a funeral with you for corpse.

Then we had tea and a man came and talked to us for an hour about farming in Ireland and somehow we weren't grateful to him. Then your letter came for which we were grateful. You'll know by this time, Elsie, that we got your telegram – many thanks for same – and you will have got John's letter. It says much for the health of Wellington that, with all we've sent him in the way of grub, the little beast isn't sick. Perhaps four swims a week keeps it down.

This is all. Mums and I both send love. We are going to Belfast to-morrow in a *motor* – a hired one. It's a hundred miles run. We want to see Ireland: at present we have only smelt it.

Ever lovingly,
Dad.

1912-1914

Despite RK's deepening gloom about social changes at home (symbolized by the national coal strike of 1912), and accelerating war preparations abroad, life in the Kipling family went on much as it always had. "So far, Burwash, living on wood, knows naught of the strike," Rudyard informs John on March 13 1912, neatly summarizing the British genius for "business as usual" that the writer both admired and deplored. Certainly, the winter holidays in Engelberg continued, followed, in 1912, by a visit to Florence and Venice, and, in 1913, by an extended journey by Rudyard and Carrie up the Nile. The latter trip inspired a set of travel essays, "Egypt of the Magicians", on which RK's letters to John at Wellington and Elsie in Paris offer an amusing commentary, and concluded with one of the nearly annual motor tours through France.

Life at Bateman's also continued in its leisurely, domestic way, full of dogs and cars, visitors and squash courts. But the letters to John during this period sound a new, more anxious note. Emphasis is increasingly placed on the value of academic achievement; indeed, this is an important theme of "The Uses of Reading" (afterwards published in *A Book of Words*), the beautifully calculated talk RK delivered to the boys of the Wellington Literary Society on May 25 1912. And with the approach of war, additional questions arose about John's military future. Already rejected by both the navy and the army because of his poor eyesight, the boy was sent to a "crammer" in Bournemouth to be coached for the entrance examination to Sandhurst, while his father pulled strings with his friend Lord Roberts to secure the seventeen-year-old a commission in the Irish Guards. Regrettably, the letters between father and son during the months of this crisis have not survived; when the correspondence finally resumes, on October 21 1914, England is two months into the war and John is an ensign in training with the Guards at Warley Barracks, Brentwood.

Dear old man:

This is just a note sent out before receipt of your Sunday letter to let you know that on Wednesday 14th we leave here for Hotel Grande Bretagne et Arno, Florence, which we shall reach on Thursday 15th. Consequently if you are writing us a mid-weekly letter this week send it to that address; and of course send your next Sunday letter there. We expect to stay in Florence about three weeks but you will be duly told of any change in our address.

Yesterday there was a small Fancy Ball here and as so few people are left, Elsie and Lorna were allowed to go - in costume. They called themselves the Calico Cats and made their dresses with stuff bought from the shops. It was white calico with green paper spots for Lorna and red paper ones for Elsie exactly like the spotted china toy cats sold in shops.

They had red and green ribbons with bells round their necks and tails of cotton wool stuffed into a calico tube which I painted. Also I painted a sort of calico mask to look like a cat's face which they wore fastened inside their calico caps. Their ears were stuffed out with paper. The effect was splendid. No one knew who they were or whether they were boys or girls. And they got a special prize! They were awfully bucked! You never saw anything so funny as the sight of the two of them dancing together. To-day they are feeling rather washed out as they worked awfully hard all yesterday and did not come to bed till nearly eleven. They found or got or bought some awful glue to stick their paper spots on with. The result was that not only our rooms but the whole passage stunk like a bone factory.

You will be pleased to hear that we have had no skating for five days: there is no snow anywhere in the valley and the weather is spring. It is awfully queer to see the monastery slopes all naked and the whole valley green and brown. The last time I went up to the Scherond we saw a butterfly! A perfectly mad winter. I suppose there will be blizzards in March or April but we aren't going to wait for them.

Private. I got a note from Pearson telling me that you'd got the better of your cold and asking me if I knew that you were top of the form last week. Pompey [John Pearson, housemaster] is awfully bucked about it. Of course I didn't tell him I knew and I've never let on to him that I think you're clever but I chortled when he wrote. Do it again, old man. By the way let us know what your skates cost and we'll send you the money. Skates are not required to be paid for by the user when there is skating in England.

> Dear love.
> Ever
> Daddy.

> Hotel Royale,
> Grande Bretagne et Arno,
> FLORENCE.
> *21. Feb. 1912.*

Dear old man –

Your Sunday letter (with Eno) just received. Sorry for the Eno but proud to see that in spite of it you keep well up in form. You'll never know till you have a son of your own how indecently proud parents are of their sons' achievements. Of course I don't want you to be nothing but a clever swot (there isn't the least danger of that!) but every time I get news of your being top I throw a little chest and go out and smile at the world. The head waiter (who is uncommonly like Theo) will not know at lunch to-day why I am so dashed affable and grinsome to him. *Good* boy! And so your little noses were rubbed in the dirt by Sandhurst – big, hairy, hard-footed, young men! Well, cheer up! Perhaps if you do well and grow strong you may, some year, be strong enough to take on the Lower School Fifteen from Eton! Don't be puffed up at the prospect! Glad you got your ten bob all right. Don't make a beast of yourself with it. Spend it on Carter's Little Liver Pills and Cascara-Sagrada.

You ask what Florence is like. It's beautiful – miles more beautiful than Rome, and we'll send you some post-cards to prove it. It lies all among low hills at the foot of the Apennines (kindly consult Dicker to see if I have put in enough 'n's) and the hills are covered with white and pink and grey villas and cypress trees and olives, mixed up with vine-yards and cultivated fields and here and there an almond tree in blossom from head to foot. You know, the grass does not wither in winter at Florence. It just stops growing for a few weeks but stays as green as before. February here comes to about the same as April at home. There are great pink and white anemones growing wild in the grass, and the rose trees are sprouting, the lilac is in bud and yesterday we saw the first irises in full bloom, in the English cemetery. (*Note.* It may help you some time in form. Arthur Hugh Clough, English poet who wrote "The Bothy of Tober-na-vuolich", as well as some other dashed good poems died and was buried at Florence 1861. Also Eliza-beth Barrett Browning poetess and wife of Robert Browning died here in the same year and was buried in the English cemetery. That was why we went there. Also, Walter Savage Landor, eminent man of letters is in the same cemetery. I have a feeling you will find all those pieces of information useful before a month has passed. But to resume.)

The air is beautifully light and springy and on a fine day with a hot sun shining one feels as though one were drinking champagne that did not give one a head. The River Arno runs through the town and the houses come slap down into the river, just like the pictures of Venice. Our Hotel is on the river but separated from it by a narrow, stone-paved street which one does not see as one looks out of the window (we are on the first floor) so the effect is as though we were on a steamer. (I can't tell you how vile this ink is. If I don't half-print every blessed letter the stuff won't leave any mark on the paper.) There are no pavements worth mentioning anywhere but every street is laid down with large slabs of pale grey neatly-jointed stone and as most of the streets are not as wide as Bateman's Lane and as the city is full of cats, cars and trams we all float about together in an easy, good-natured, slow-moving crowd. Yesterday was the Carnival – the last big kick-up before Lent begins and people had dressed up as Pierrots with masks and were driving and walking about blowing absurd tin trumpets and chucking confetti at each other. One boy about your age had painted his face various colours instead of using a mask and had finished off the general effect with – a gilt nose! I had never seen a gilt nose before and it filled me with joy. (From the change in the colour of the ink you must realize that the waiter has just come in with a pot of fresh brew. Observe the effect on my handwriting!)

Of course Florence is full of the most glorious buildings – churches, cathedrals, towers, palaces and so on, each one of them crammed with horrible stories and murders. Our Hotel used to be the palace of a Cardinal who was murdered in it and one of the most awful attempts at murder on record was made a few hundred years ago in the Duomo, the Cathedral, just as the victim (he was a Medici) was going to Mass. The little game failed. There was a riot and before the day ended the Medici, who did not care for anyone except themselves to go in for murder, hanged an Archbishop (who had been mixed up in the attempt) out of his own window and generally played Hell with the City. Everybody in Florence in the Middle Ages always played Hell with everything when they could. Dante lived here till he was banished. He filled up his *Inferno* with characters whom he knew in real life in Florence and when you realize that Florence was then not much bigger than Tunbridge Wells, and when you read the list of crimes that Dante's neighbours were guilty of, you can begin to imagine what a cheery little Murder-and-Torture-Society old Florence must have been.

But one forgets all that as one loafs about in the sunshine and visits the wonderful picture galleries where all the pictures one has ever read about or seen in prints are hanging on the walls *quite* real. You and I have got to see this place together, some time, old man.

Well, I won't worry you with any more fine (and small) writing. We live very quietly in a suite of huge rooms. We go out sight-seeing for about two hours in the morning and an hour and a half in the afternoon and find that quite enough. To-day it is raining and, as you see, I am writing letters.

Dear love to you from us all. We are counting days till April 2nd thus:—

Feb 7 plus Mar 31 plus 2 Apr = 40

```
    7
   31
    2
   ──
 7) 40 (5 weeks!
   35
   ──
      5 days.
```

Ever your
Dad.

Grand Hotel Britannia,
Venice.
Mar. 13. 1912. 8.20 p.m.

Dear old man:

Your letter with news that you've had a chill (which is bad), and that the Coll. has beaten the "little boys of Eton" (which is good) has just come in. *Why* d'you get chills? They can't amuse you and they disturb us. I used to have 'em at school but I grew out of 'em. Sometimes (I say this with bated breath) chills can be caused by too much eating of tuck. However that's a thing which I don't believe is your failing. I'm sorry for it because it knocks you out of your work. But anyway Easter is a beastly term, and I shall be glad and grateful when it is over. I hope your gas won't give out. Pompey wrote me that he didn't see why you shouldn't all carry on till the end of the term. At any rate he has promised to let me know in time and then, as I think Mother told you, Moore will come over and fetch you to Col. Feilden's. *He*, by the way, is enjoying himself immensely, and says that so far Burwash, living on wood, knows naught of the [coal] strike. To-day's (Wednesday's) news seems more hopeful than anything we've had for a fortnight. Our idea is – as I think you've been told – to come home on the 25th.

Our news is of course *not* exciting. We go out into Venice, sometimes on foot, sometimes per gondola and each time we see something new and delightful. Yesterday we took a motor launch (6 h.p. Italian make 13 ks p.h. or say 8 miles) and went to see the glass-blowing factory at Murano about 2 miles across the lagoon. Mother bought some rather beautiful glass there – notably two white-ribbed decanters – for Bateman's. Then we went on to Burano, an island six miles away – where they make lace. Well, you wouldn't be interested in *that*, but you would have enjoyed the navigation of the little thudding motor-boat. The tide rises and falls about 2'6" in the lagoons. It was dead low when we left Murano and miles and miles of sands and shoals were uncovered. There were piles to mark all the trusty channels, and this was the general view of the landscape.

A more hopeless looking waste you never saw in your life. In a bee line Burano is about two miles, I should think, from Murano. At least it looked quite close but we had to follow a channel as twisted as a tapeworm. The water was a sort of oyster-shell blue and when we got among the islands we dodged in and out between narrow muddy banks and big fishing boats and on the way home got as nearly as possible between a fool of a tug and and a great barge that she was towing. I thought that the slack of the tow-rope would foul our propeller. But we got away by going astern just in time. Italians make an awful row, by land and by sea. Well, we didn't get home till nearly 6 p.m. having been out on the water five hours. About an hour before we got home something went wrong with our ignition. The engineer (there were two men in charge) had neglected her lubrication for about an hour and she knocked a lot. I *do* wish you'd been along.

Our window faces the end of the Grand Canal and the place where the big steamers come in and anchor. It is very like Havre in that way and we are always running to the window to look at the traffic. But words won't describe the beauties of the place. Now I will shut up.

> With all our best love,
> Ever your most affectionate,
> Pater.

> Bateman's,
> Burwash,
> Sussex.
> *Wed. May 1st.* [1912]

Dear old man –

Behold me recovering, though still in a drenched and drabbled condition, from my cold. My word! It was a beauty! Now Bird seems to have got something of the same sort and is in bed "enjoying" much the same treatment as I had. Her throat has been sore but is now better: but her nose and eyes are running no end and she lives on slops – not without protests and outcries! Poor old girl. Well, I only hope you haven't been following the family example.

The wind has gone round into the S. West and felt quite round and balmy to-day. I was out for nearly a couple of hours looking at the new land which Mother has decided upon buying. Otherwise I haven't done much except tried to think what sort of paper I shall read "The Twelve"[1] on the 25th May.

What really bothered me most was not being able to have a last jaw with you. I wanted to tell you a lot of things about keeping clear of any chap who is even suspected of beastliness. There is no limit to the trouble possible if one goes about (however innocently) with swine of that type. Give them the widest of wide berths. Whatever their merits may be in the athletic line they are at heart only sweeps and scum and *all* friendship or acquaintance with them ends in sorrow and disgrace. More on this subject when we meet.

The Leonards came over yesterday: with Bargee and my small goddaughter Meriel. Then came Sir F. Merrilees of the Union Castle Line with his wife and two long girls in a motor – so we had a lively afternoon. There isn't any other news.

Sorry you can't look at a cricket match without feeling faint and having to lie down in a four and sixpenny chair. Yah!

> Now I am going to bed.
> Lovingly ever,
> Pater.

The Challenge Rubber Co. keeps on sending me copies of the Motor Cycle (or whatever it is) which I send on to you. Dear love from us all. Landon comes to-morrow – fresh from the Persian Gulf.

[1] The Wellington College Literary Society, to which RK delivered "The Uses of Reading", later collected in *A Book of Words*.

> The White Hart Inn (or Hotel),
> Andover.
> *Wednesday night* [May 8 1912] 8.20
> p.m.

Dear old man –

We're on tour – Mum and I at least, for the Bird is at home – for two days. I had to see my sister (Aunt Trix) at Weyhill which is a few miles from Andover and Mother and I decided to have out the Green Goblin and make a jaunt of it. So far it has been great fun.

We left Bateman's at 2.15 this afternoon, came via Cross-in-Hand, Hadlow Down, Buxted, Newick, Chailey, Cuckfield, Bolney, Billingshurst, Petworth, Midhurst, Petersfield and Winchester and then across the Downs to here. A simply divine day – hot and sticky after the rain with everything rushing into flower or bud everywhere. The may was out; the horse-chestnuts were out; irises and wistaria were out in people's gardens and the whole hundred or hundred and twenty mile run looked like the English country in a picture. We had the motor open and enjoyed ourselves awfully. We stopped for tea for half an hour at Petersfield which made our running time about 4 hours. You will be pleased to learn that nothing passed us. You will further be pleased to learn that a Rolls-Royce Inspector (Hanbury) came down this morn at about a $\frac{1}{4}$ to 12 to overhaul the Goblin. Moore of course opened her up and jawed like sixty. Mr Hanbury was pleased to say that the Goblin was in excellent condition and needed nothing being done to her. We also had no complaints to make: so we gave him lunch and parted the best of friends.

He told me an awful story about a friend of his who had an American car and had just climbed with it to the very top of some big French pass near the Puy de Dome. Anyway, it was a ten mile climb. When he reached the top, it was lighting up time so he got down and lit the lamps and – owing to a leaky carburettor or something, the car lit too. There wasn't much available earth about – only terraced walls with tiny vineyards on top. And ten smitten miles from anywhere! And the car blazed and blazed! They scooped up earth out of the gutter: they dragged the bonnet off and used it as a scoop for getting a little earth out of one of the terraced little vineyards. But, as you can imagine, that didn't do much good. The man's wife picked up what she thought (it was dark by that time) was a clod of clay and wildly dumped it down on the engines. It turned out to be a healthy and hard piece of rock. Result – engines went pungo! They just had to wait by the blaze till the car was burnt out. Luckily the wheels remained so they piled into the still smoking carcass and coasted back, by gravity, ten miles down the pass to the place they had started from! That's a nice tale. *And* true. But can't you see the agitated woman in the dark dashing a big rock into the guts of the blazing engine?

And since we are talking of motors, I may as well confide to you that, when we went for a stroll round Andover while our frugal dinner was being got ready, I came on a motor garage with an 8–10 brand new Bedelia. I'd never seen a Bedelia close to before. The man in charge of the garage owned it and was very communicative. She was painted a rich *dark* blue and cost 103 guineas. Cheaper makes of lower horse-power cost between 60 and 70 guineas. *This* I consider a plain swindle. No side-doors. You step into a sort of canoe and the seats are hammock seats. But I expect you know that. The belts are apparently changed by hand or a stick. On the whole I'm glad I've seen her. I don't love her any more. A bug-trap and a rattle-trap, is my verdict, Sir. Nor do I like her steering gear so far aft.

Well, this seems rather a motorious letter but after sitting for so long in one I expected my mind is unconsciously full of 'em. You may care to know that a few days ago coming down from town we were passed by a 6 h.p Rex. It was all that the poor brute could do (he caught us at the foot of a hill). He kept his position for about ¼ mile and then very kindly let us go by.

I haven't anything more to say, dear man. This letter smells of petrol already. Dear love from Mum and me. Angy has been staying with us and I am quite sure would send you her love too.

        Ever,
        Dad.

                        Bateman's.
                        June. 5. 1912. 7 p.m.

Dear old man,

We did have a day and three-quarters yesterday! Words cannot describe the riot and confusion and crowded streets of Eton – one jam of parents, motors and gorgeously attired kids. As we moved slowly through the press at 11.30 a.m. Oliver [Baldwin] in white or yellow waistcoat, huge buttonhole and immaculate topper suddenly appeared on the foot-board. His hawk-eye had discovered us and he piloted us to a great yard roaring full of more parents and kids and glossy toppers where they were having call-over, which they call Absence. Here, *longo intervallo*, we picked up Aunt Ciss with Elsie, Di and Lorna who had come from town in Uncle Stan's motor (Uncle Stan was there too, of course) and then we found Oscar Hornung and Mr and Mrs Hornung. Then (of course: it's always the case on the 4th of June) it began to rain. We waited till it cleared up and moved off slowly to see the great cricket match.

You never dreamed of such superb playing-grounds as those of Eton – in summer. In winter they must be ghastly damp and rheumatic and influenzaish. It was close, and hot and sticky at first with heavy clouds and about 500 parents sat round the pitch in chairs while Eton played New College. Sir Guy Campbell's son (major) was playing for Eton and I saw Sir Guy and Lady Campbell. Also I saw Inigo Freeman-Thomas being talked to by his grandfather Lord Brassey (at which I fled). Also I saw (or rather Elsie saw) a Gibbs boy. I suppose I saw a lot more men but they were all so dead alike under their toppers that I could not tell t'other from which. Well, the girls sat on chairs and watched the match – Di and Lorna furiously excited. Elsie, I grieve to say, quite a heathen and unimpressed by the nobility of the game. But it was very pretty.

I *might* have gone to attend speeches in the Great Hall but as the first piece spouted was *"The White Man's Burden"* by R.K. – I did not. Then at 1.15 Elsie, Mummy and I went to lunch at the White Hart (strawberries and cream) while the rest of the party went to lunch with Oliver's tutor. Somehow it seemed to us we'd be happier at the White Hart: and we were.

And *then* it began to rain and when we got back to the cricket-ground things were damp and they were covering the Sacred Pitch with tarpaulin. Everyone sheltered under the trees like wet hens till it got too bad. Then there was a general break to go to the Memorial Hall and see the Chapel and the schools and similar things. Oscar Hornung was our pilot. It was very interesting but the form-rooms tho' old struck me as pretty frowzy and full of germs. Then we went back and had tea in Oscar's rooms with his people. A rather jolly room but, on the whole, the houses didn't strike me as being specially clean and the lavatory accommodation was not extra special.

Then the sun came out and Elsie insisted on staying on and we went to the big school-yard to attend Absence – general call-over. Every man raises his topper as he says "Here, Sir"! Then, in the car (with thousands of other cars) up a lane and across grassy fields down to the river to get a good place to see the procession of boats. We got a ripping place and saw the whole shoot – eight or nine boats: the rowers got up like ancient man-o'wars-men: the coxes attired as middies with dirk and belts, and with bridal bouquets of flowers on their knees. A very ancient and sacred ceremony but not exactly what you might call impressive. They rowed past us twice. Then at 7 we made a bunk across the dripping fields, not waiting for the fireworks and, leaving Windsor at 7.30 p.m., arrived at Bateman's at 10.30 p.m. – most of the time raining. A great day altogether and E. enjoyed it enormously.

I believe that Lorna and Margot are coming down by motor on Speech Day to join our party at Wellington, which I think will be rather fun. We shall make a fine and good-looking crowd. I *do* hope it will be decent weather.

I can't tell you what a joy it was to me to have that time with you. I hope I didn't bore you with good advice but it *is* good advice. Oscar Hornung who is only 17 is now on the edge of having a house to manage and I'd give a deal if some day I could see you head of your house.

Remember my council. Keep your tongue between your teeth: don't criticize aloud (write it out all to me!) and flee from the contaminating swine! More later. I hear the postman.

Ever,
Daddo.

Bateman's,
Burwash,
Sussex.
[June 25 1912]

Dear Warrior,

Many thanks for your campaign letter. I followed the war in the daily papers. You and Winchester seem to have been wopped: but, as *The Times* pointed out, your line of retreat lay directly towards the lunch tents. Hence, I suppose, the speed with which you retired and the zeal with which the enemy pressed you. One account said that "in vain did Wellington try to cling to the line of low hills by the S.W.Rly". I had a vision of you personally, lying on your belly in the heather embracing an ant-heap! What happened about the motor-car which, according to *The Times*, ran into the rear of your Company-formation as you were marching? It said that no one was hurt but it must have been a recklessly stupid thing for the man to do. Altogether I am *much* delighted by your field-day. It shows that you are getting tougher – for haversack and 20 rounds is no featherweight. I hope you were careful about *not* drinking water from the wayside.

We (Mother and I) spent the week-end at Mr Allen's at Free Chase. Bet has had another litter of 5 (three kept) by Nipper. They are delightful little beasts – about the size Jack and she were when you and I bought 'em. Rollo, Togo and Worry are their names – beautifully marked dogs. Bet literally howled with delight to see me. We met there Sir William Wilcox, the great irrigation expert. He built the Assouan dam among other things and has wandered through Babylon and Baghdad making dams on the Tigris and Euphrates. One of the most interesting chaps I have ever met. He and his wife came over here from Mr Allen's to have lunch and he gave us good advice about how to manage the brook. At the present moment we are trying to put in a 12″ exhaust pipe into the mill-dam and have drained the pond out to the dregs.

Only mud and eels are left and the men are wildly excited trying to catch them.

You will be pleased to learn that three sides of the squash court have been finished. The floor and the back wall have still to be done but I hope that won't take long. The size of the court is within a few inches *exactly* standard size. We are 29'8" long: standard is 30! Our back wall is 8'6" which is exactly standard and our playing wall is 16 feet – two feet higher than standard. I *do* hope it will be a success. It almost tempts me to go in for the game. I was at the Stores a few days ago (wish you had been with me!) and bought the rackets and balls – three rackets and half a dozen balls. I had no idea that the rackets were so heavy.

Mr Landon who has not been fit lately is coming down here for a couple of nights this afternoon and I expect that Hugh and Mollie Poynter will be down for the week-end – probably with Uncle Edward. *Voilà* all our news!

Did the Wawkphan powder do you any good? That's what Mother and I are dying to know. I have suddenly got the idea of another Stalky tale[1] which I hope will turn out a success. I can't tell you how rejoiced I feel to know that you got through your field-day with success. It feels funny, doesn't it to be with a beaten army? I've seen troops falling back once in my life and didn't like it.

With dearest love, and counting each day to the hols,

> Ever your lovingest,
> Pater.

[1] Perhaps the "lost" Stalky story rumoured to be at Haileybury College, where Cormell Price became a master in 1863.

> Bateman's,
> Burwash,
> Sussex.
> *July. 2. 1912.*

Dear old man –

Thanks for your long letter. Mother is awfully excited at the idea of your being beaten for the sinful offence of larking on a Sunday. Me, having been beaten much and often, I confess I am not unduly agitated. But it *does* seem to me fairly stupid that you aren't allowed to play tennis or something on a Sunday so that you can blow off steam naturally. I suppose by the time *your* son goes to school the schools will have a little more sense in these matters. It's *very* English. However, a rule's a rule and you were an ass to be caught. I will not rub it in. Glad to know that the motor barged into the Wykehamists [pupils of Winchester College] and not into your sacred behinds. The *Times*, where I saw the report, said it was gross carelessness.

Our news is entirely confined to engineering operations round the pond. Mother is having the time of her life with the 12″ eduction pipe which is being put in (or will be put in) by a man from Kendal to-day. I pity that chap. She is *also* having the edge of the pond bricked: *and* is going later to dig out the mud! Oh Allah!

Meantime your squash court is up – all four walls done. Three of 'em plastered and painted black: the floor levelled and concreted, and all that remains is to put down the bricks. E. went up there the other day with one of the new rackets and a ball and swiped about. E. is a great tennis player but does not savvy squash. She ducked and fled from the little hard red ball as it returned off the wall – rather as if she were shut up in a room with a buck-hornet. *I* think it's going to be a spiffing court. Likewise one can play fives in it.

We haven't even been out in the motor since last Thursday – all our work being in the garden. Did I tell you that Mother has now bought Keylands (under the Orchards) and has discovered that it is a superb spot for a house. She potters round there when she has nothing else to do and cackles over enlarging the little cottage.[1]

I feel it is about time the holidays began. Doubtless, Sir, you share my views. Do let us know how you have made up your mind about the camp. Surely if you can pull through a tough field-day like you did, you ought to be able to stick the training. You know, of course, that we hope to come over at the end of the week. I shan't keep this letter open for the "financial support" you hint at so strongly but Mother says she'll send you some f.s. this evening. Meantime I send you all our love.

> Ever
> Pater.

Bird is getting absolutely too cheeky to live and urgently needs being sat upon. Why should I be called "Doodles"?

[1] Renovated by the Kiplings for Percival Landon.

Bateman's,
Burwash,
Sussex.
July. 22. 1912.

Dear old man –

Splendid! (You will note by the way that the pot of jam was despatched at once!) 73 out of 80 looks like big cricket. And now Mummy
and I both hope, not to say pray, that you will keep your end up in the
exams. You see it's awfully important just at this year that you should
make a start forward. Otherwise you are in danger of being hung up
among the lumps and louts of the IVth form and of getting the reputation of being a fool. You are many things, but a fool you are *not*. So
dig out with a cool mind and a steady handwriting at the exams and
give us all cause to rejoice when the results come out. You will have
already got your train. You come to Tunbridge Wells, I believe, and
there the car will meet you. I wouldn't be surprised if there was someone
in the car.

We've just had a chap from the Dinka country (Southern Soudan)
staying with us. He has told me the most amazing tales I ever heard in
all my life about the elephant-poachers and about elephant hunting.
Dr Jameson is coming to lunch to-day, so I shall be fed up with Africa
at both ends.

But I am really thinking all the time about the exams and how you
will do in them.

Dearest love and best wishes from us all.

      Ever,
      Pater.

Bateman's,
Burwash,
Sussex.
Sunday [Sept. 22 1912] 6.30 p.m.

Dear old man –

The days since your lamented departure have been hectic – for
reasons which I shall now relate. For a long time past Mother has been
suffering from a trouble in her back which as you know made her walk
lame and gave her a great deal of pain. Sir John Bland-Sutton had a

131

look at it some time ago and said that there ought to be an operation. So, the day after we left you at Wellington, we went up to town and I had to take Mother to a Nursing Home at 16, Fitzroy Square so that she could rest for a night before she was operated on in the morning. The idea of the operation did not worry Mummy one-tenth so much as the idea of spending a night in this "home" where all the walls were painted with a hard pale green paint, so that microbes could be wiped off, and there were no pictures and the people who looked after her were uniformed nurses who alluded to her as "the patient". Imagine Mum's joy at being called a "patient". Well, I took her there at 5 p.m. on Friday afternoon and spent the night at Brown's. I don't think either of us had what you might call a good night and what Mummy must have felt all alone, Lord only knows. However, the worst night wears through and at nine o'clock Bland-Sutton performed the operation. It was, as doctors reckon these things, an extremely small operation and all the nurses, of course, looked down on Mummy with contempt for not having more of a trouble. Anyhow 'twas quite enough of an operation for Mums. I saw her at 10.30 when she was just coming out of the effects of the chloroform and ether. She was a bit tired but quite undefeated. Then I saw her again at 3 p.m., when she was, so to say, full of beans but rather stiff and uncomfy. Then I went down by the 4.50 (our 4.50!) and spent the night at Bateman's. Bird told me all about her dance at the Havilands which she had greatly enjoyed.

This morning at 10 a.m. up to town by car with Bird. We counted bikes and motors from Etchingham to Buckingham Palace Gate. Bird took motors: I took bikes and side-cars (push-bikes didn't count). Result:– 88 4-wheeled cars, 113 motor-bikes! Saw Mummy at 12.45: lunched with the Bland-Suttons: at 3 p.m. back to the Home, where Mummy horrid stiff but still undefeated sat *dressed*! to go home. So home we brought her in the car: reached here at 6.15 p.m.: undressed her and put her to bed in the big guest-room where she now lies *very* happy to be home again and going to stay in her little bed for the next two or three days till the wound heals up. I confess it's a great load off my mind. I'd have told you if it hadn't been just as you were going back to school. All's well that ends well. She bids me send you tons of love, and I am

     Ever your
     Daddo!

Bateman's
Burwash
Sussex
[Oct. 8 1912?]

HOW THE BALL LOOKS TO THE FULL BACK.

I see! Who was the chap who threw himself into the gulf? Quintius Custius? But I'm awfully pleased at the news. You know I always told you that you were more of a person than you think you are: and now that your first year is over you are beginning to find that out. You'll be rather somebody in the House henceforward. In my time the old maxim was "Collar *low*"! This was supposed to throw the other chap clear of you: but you are so light and active that you ought to be able to run rings round 'em. Does a full back have any chance of getting away with the ball or must he pass it the instant he gets it? I wish you'd send me details. I'm *immensely* interested. Now take my tip and eat enormously. You'll need a lot of grub this term.

Our weather has been something lovely – warm and sunny all day with bright sharp frost at night. Mother is improving. Yesterday she walked out in the garden and gave a lot of orders – sure sign of returning strength. I had a game of squash with Fipps [Elsie] yesterday. She beat 2 out of 3 games. Neither of us are what you might call star performers but Fipps has a better return than me. Gwynnie says he is coming down on Saturday for a squash game. Pity me! Gwynnie is as fat as an ox and can't run for nuts but he *can* play. I shall lather. Out shooting with the Colonel yesterday. He picked up a brace of pheasants on Rye Green. I nearly stepped on one old cock who got up almost between my feet. Wish you'd been with me. I didn't take your gun. Consequence was I put up two or three coveys of partridges.

Thanks for giving us the date of your exeat or what-ever you call it. So many of *our* arrangements depend on knowing what yours are. I go to Brighton to-morrow for a voluptuous day with the Dentist! Then up to town for the night where I meet Mummy who goes up for shopping. I'm glad (you don't know how glad I am!) that you are coming up in maths. I want to be hellish proud of you some day: to be able to swagger around and throw a chest (to your deep disgust) and to allude to you casually as "me son, don't you know".

I'm rather busy with work and odds and ends and our news is scanty. Jack was sick in my presence yesterday – over-fed little beast. It's all the maids' fault. They stuff him. Mother told you what an awfully sporting thing Moore did the other night taking Mr Dann to town at 2 a.m. He tells me he met nothing whatever between here and Lewisham (edge of London) when he met the Hastings motor mail having its morning coffee at a coffee stall. Doesn't that suggest desolation. You might write him a line saying what you thought of him. He nearly froze with the cold.

Dear love from us all.

> Ever your loving
> Daddo.

> Bateman's,
> Burwash,
> Sussex.
> *Oct. 16. 1912.*

Dear Sir,

The Kipling family were both pleased and surprised to receive your kind letter of the 16th as they were under the impression that you had either emigrated to S. Africa, or joined the Turkish Army. Mr R. Kipling suggested that you were at Broadmoor – for reasons of state. As it is only ten days since you have written, the wildest conjectures were naturally rife. (That's a specimen of dam bad journalese.)

We are still in England. Mother is much better after her operation though she is not quite her old self yet. Phipps has been having an irritated gum. (It makes her furious if you call it a toothache.) Her face swelled and she looked like a wet pillow.

All the family is much set up with your news. It's splendid but I *do* hope you've been vetted by your doctor. Remember it's dead easy to overstrain oneself in a long run. Mother of course is not pleased at the idea of the skin being taken off your chest by another chap's boots. It is, when you come to think of it, a somewhat rough and ready way of performing what a mustard-plaster would do cheaper – if not as quickly. The thing to remember is *not* to overdo but to slack in between when you can and to get all the sleep you possibly can. I suppose that now you are so well up in running you haven't got to hang about and wait for a bath. If you do the work for your House take care you get its privileges as regards baths etc. I expect by this time that you will have taken Oscar prisoner or *vice versa*. Give us full news of the bloody débâcle.

By the way, are you following the war in the Balkans? It will be, if the winter doesn't stop it, one of the most merciless wars that has ever been waged. The Turk is, to put it mildly, annoyed and intends to settle the question once and for all. Also there is a danger of Mohammedans throughout the world taking a hand.

Went out to-day for 2 hours in the woods with your 20 bore. Saw (and spared) four pheasants and a covey of partridges. Heavenly afternoon. Wished you were with me. To-morrow (if I live) I have to go and make a speech at Ashton-under-Lyne which is Sir M. Aitken's constituency. I've been sweating blood for days past trying to think what the deuce I am to say. Pity me!

We are busy in rebuilding the little cottage at Keylands as a week-end place for Mr Landon to rent. Also a new tenant has come to Dudwell, Dan having moved to a farm near Mayfield. The new man is a cowman employed by a big grazier called Hyland – a huge chap with chin whiskers and a tummy – who wants all the land I can rent him. He looks *and* talks like a man of substance who knows how land ought to be looked after. He wants it all for grazing cattle, and I think I shall let him have all the fields round the house.

Yes, we hope to be with you on the 26th. I believe we shall be at Chirkley for the 25th. I feel as if we were all bursting with news to tell each other when we meet. What about sausages at the Hotel if we have tea together? We have to go on to Basingstoke afterwards. I observe you say nowt about your work. Send us a line and let us know if your Dorothea [Ponton]'s tips have been of use to you.

Dearest love from us all.

Ever,
the Pater.

Bateman's,
Burwash,
Sussex.
Wednes. morn. [Nov. 6 1912]
(foggy)

Dear old man –

Your welcome letter – brief but to the point – came in last evening and I confess that I am rather pleased with your position in form – specially as regards mathematics which, I think, you owe to "Dorothy's" coaching in the hols. You might pull up a bit in Latin. I am more and more convinced that you are *much* cleverer than you make out to be. You have an ungodly gift of "jaw" and a faculty of putting arguments together which ought to be useful to you in after life. Only, another time you want anything, *don't* take it out of Mother. She was quite upset after your performances last Sat. I told her it was only your cheerful way of expressing yourself. I don't know whether you saw how near I came to laughing when you protested that it "was no pleasure to *me*, Sir, to have to say these things". Of course it was a great pleasure and you thoroughly enjoyed it – same as I used to do when I was a youngster and my people allowed me to jaw and ass about over *my* grievances. But, as I have said, next time you want to blow off steam – try it on *me* not Mother. I may not be so sympathetic but I shall be amused.

Glad your coat and waistcoat are a comfort to you. It can be no fun watching matches in this foul weather. Mother meant to go up to town to-day but I managed to stop her as it is a thick fog here and, most likely, will be black dark in town. What a giddy time we had with Oscar Hornung and at Virginia Water. I wonder the park keepers didn't hoof us out. It seemed to me that Charlie Law [Bonar Law's son] was much nicer than I had ever seen him before. He wasn't playing up to anything.

No news here except that we have let all our spare land (74 acres) to Hyland for grazing purposes at 34/- per acre which is a good rental all

136

things considered. Remember this if reductions are proposed later.

Did you ever imagine anything so dramatic as the smash up of the Turks – inside of 3 weeks! That's what comes of being unprepared. I don't know what is going to come next but I shall be surprised if the glutton Bulgar does not go straight into Constantinople and *hold a Christian service in the mosque of San Sofia there*. Then the fat will be in the fire with a vengeance! There is an awful account of the battle of Lulle Burgas in the *Daily Telegraph*, which I am enclosing in case you haven't read it. It gives a real notion of the lack of organization. Remember they were fighting within 40 miles of Constantinople and *yet* they hadn't provisions. Verily war is a queer thing.

Dearest love from us all. Bird goes up on Sat. to skate at Princes. She is in a blue funk about falling down – as she has a new pair of boots and, so far, can't get proper screws for her skates.

> Ever lovingly,
> Dad.

> Bateman's,
> Burwash,
> Sussex.
> *Nov. 16. 1912.*

Dear old man –

Well, I *must* say that, if you don't send news often, your news when it comes is quite exciting. As to the beating that doesn't matter. You probably took your chances of it when you went to Grubby's.[1] I am only *very glad* that you didn't show that it hurt. As to the Young Cup,[2] I want you to think over it well before you go in for it because you can't afford to lose it if you are going in for the event with the idea of beating Roberts. I mean you mustn't think you will win the event "sitting" as you say. You must go in and train and take particular care that you *do* win. Above all, you must *not* talk about what you are going to do, or why you are in for the Cup. You can easily see that if you get beaten for the cup it will be a double defeat. I have no objection to your going in for the Cup and have written to Pompey to that effect. But I want you to realize what a bad thing it is to keep chopping and changing your mind. You are getting too old for that.

Another result of your little experience ought to be to make you dig out and work like a devil to get up the school. You are fifteen and a quarter now and I want to see you in a position where it won't be possible for you to be beaten. I haven't the least doubt that you played for the wopping and if it spurs you up both to work and win the Young Cup it will be a good piece of work. Only whatever you do don't gas and jaw about the way in which you are going to win the Young Cup in order to get even with Roberts. That is vile bad form and hurts your own soul. I don't suppose for a minute that you have talked – if I know you you've kept your head shut – but there is always a temptation to do so. So remember.

I've written to Pompey explaining that I'd like you to go in for the Young Cup. *Don't* be confident: don't take chances: get to work and train soberly and whether you win or lose do it like a Sahib – *specially* if you win. God bless you, old man.

> With dearest love,
> Ever your
> Daddo.

P.S. We had one prefect at the Coll. who couldn't hit straight but the few that he got home on one's behind were beauties.

P.P.S. *Did* you read of the Tax Collector who got into the house of a Harrow school-master and went into the drawing-room and asked the man's wife if her husband had a shooting licence?

---

[1] Wellington College tuck (refreshment) shop.
[2] A running trophy for which the thirty members of Pearson's House at Wellington could compete.

> Bateman's,
> Burwash,
> Sussex.
> *Dec. 3. 1912.*

Dear old man –

Thanks for your good letter and for the news that you are 2nd in Maths. I *am* pleased. It would be a splendid thing if you alone of all us Kiplings became a mathematician! Elsie also is rather a whale at that game. She got 75% out of her last Algebra paper.

We are both of us pained and shocked and *horrified* at the price Hookham asks for a suit of clothes! Four guineas! It's too much but you must go ahead and get it and get it made quickly. *I* don't pay four guineas for my suits and my tailor lives in St James's Street. But see that that pirate Hookham makes it properly and *fits* you. I've just been having a regular siege with my tailor in town – five suits of sorts.

Incidentally I may mention that as your Christmas present is coming later in the year I couldn't think of anything to get you, so I got a whole lot of new gramophone records. Some of them are daisies! I duly note your choice of motor-bike – Douglas 2¾. I expect you'll change your mind once or twice before you settle definitely. I looked at all the reports of the bicycle show at Olympia for Douglases – but I couldn't see anything about 'em. Why was that? As to names, what about "Goblin"? The big kettle is "Green Goblin". By the way she is supposed to come back to-day from overhaul and the grey and silver "Spectre" goes back.

I distributed prizes yesterday at the Rifle Club. Hilder was very tight and *would* interrupt the proceedings. Wish you had been there.

If you want epitaphs I can put you on to a whole lot of 'em. The Prince of Wales' address I know. Here's one that is supposed to be true:–

> Here lie I and my three daughters
> Killed by drinking Cheltenham waters.
> If we'd ha' stuck to Epsom salts
> We shouldn't have laid in these 'ere vaults.

But in the old days people really used to put up the most amazing epitaphs.

All goes well here – Allah be praised – and we are counting days till you come back. The big trunk is being packed for Switzerland – which looks like business. I hope and pray you'll do well in the exams because I have a notion that you are going to shoot up all round in every direction. Life's a dam' interesting thing, my son, and I want you to have a good life. But you won't if you don't dig out. I've just met a youth who is a slacker. My gawd, such a slacker! He gave me cold shudders at the thought that you might grow into such another. Now I must get back to my work.

> Dear love from us all.
> Ever
> The Pater.

I've written this with the sun in my eyes. Hence the vileness of the fist.

Why did you chuck Humber? And what's the matter with Lea-Francis? Isn't that a motor bike firm?

Dear old man,

You know Elsie's silvery voice? The mail was a bit late at breakfast this morn as the old motor that brings it down from London had smashed up again. So Mother had left the table when your letter came in. I read it out slowly to fat Bird, laying proper stress on your success in Maths which she was pleased to hear. Then I read out the P.S. announcing that you had got the Young Cup. . . . I do *not* say that Fipps squealed like a stuck pig or even like a locomotive, but she let the house know the fact in one long clear high yell. She tore upstairs howling:— "Mother! Mother! He's got it", as if it was small-pox. A nice child that Fipps. I never saw her so pleased in my life. I sat at table and lit a cigarette and did a private gloat. Wait till *you* have a son of your own (God help the poor little kid!) and you'll know how *you* feel when your son does well. And *you've* done a double shot – maths and the Young Cup. I don't – between ourselves – much care if you aren't high in form subjects (one can always pull up on them any time) but I am *greatly* rejoiced about your going up in maths. You'll be rather a Duke next term because your Revered Masters will respect you for your maths and the Young Cup will. . . never mind. I'm not an unkind man at heart so I only say I'm sorry for Roberts. It was a well-calculated and nice little revenge. *Don't* rub it in.

So sorry you didn't enjoy your pleasant Joan of Arc evening.[1] She was a great lady but hardly the kind to interest a chap for an evening. And you didn't appreciate the company you were in! Shocking! Hope you'll like "Drake"[2] better. I'm looking forward to it no end. You know the programme. You come up, *summo engenio*,[3] by the first train (8.22 at Charing X) and get over to Brown's in time for a classic feed. I shall not be at the station because I'm dining at the House of Commons with Uncle Stan on Monday night. Then we perambulate about town, doing shopping and things. In the afternoon Mother and I may go to see General Baden-Powell. In the evening Drake – and then Bateman's next morn. Where there will be a lot of things to show you. We leave for Engelberg on Boxing Day – Dec. 26th and you may as well pray for snow, as I hear there isn't much at present.

I simply *can't* think of any presents for you this Xmas but if we go to

140

the Stores together I'll give you a look (that's generosity) at the motor-bike you're going to get in the Easters. I believe that Mother is getting you fine raiment and purple linen.

Dear old man, we're all very pleased and proud of you, and you'll get a high old welcome when we meet. It's only about 120 hours now. What *dam* folly to have a Cup run in the middle of the exams.

> Ever thine,
> Pater.

P.S. For goodness sake tell me what books you'd like for Xmas.

---

[1] On December 8 the Revd H. Bedford Pim had presented a lecture on Joan of Arc at Wellington.
[2] *Drake: A Pageant Play in Three Acts* by Louis Napoleon Parker was first performed at His Majesty's Theatre, London, in September 1912.
[3] With your great talent – but also a pun on "first train".

Next letter *care of Thomas Cook & Son, Cairo, Egypt.*

Hotel Regina,
Place Rivoli,
Paris.
Feb. 5. 1913. 1 p.m.
a beautifully fine day.

Dear old man –

We found your *very* wet and mournful letter waiting for us when we arrived at the Hotel Regina last night at 1. a.m. As usual the fool train we were in went wrong. Something attached to one of the carriages – the vestibule, I believe – broke or flapped or got loose. Anyhow we were hung up, eighteen miles outside Paris while the railway staff shouted and howled. What made it worse was that Mother was very far from well. I told you she had gone down with a touch of influenza at Engelberg. Well, the five days of continuous fog made it worse and she felt that if she didn't get out of the blind, narrow, dark valley, she would *never* get away. So we moved yesterday. We had a lovely day to go away on – *the first decent day since you left*! – but the journey across the lake and the slow crawl in the train was very trying to Mother. Elsie played up like a brick and we got her to Basle in an empty carriage: collared an empty compartment from Basle to Paris. (I dropped the tear of friendly remembrance at that little narrow buffet where one comes out of the *douane*. I felt that you had gone that way only a little while before me: but it looks nicer in the daytime.) Several people – French mostly – looked in on us but the sight of Mother and Elsie laid at full length on the seats in a disgusting state of déshabille, was too much for them and they fled and left us alone in our glory. Mother was pretty dead when we reached the Hotel but she is better today. Rummy thing – if our train hadn't been late (it was due at 11.35) we should have seen the last expiring minutes of the Cárnival in Paris. As it was, we found all the main streets literally *paved* with confetti. Our sober old motor bus was full of 'em. And this morning every crack in the pavements that a broom and water could not get at is red and blue and yellow and green with confetti. And that reminds me. What really broke Mother up was Monday night in Engelberg. She didn't get a wink of sleep all night. The whole village gave itself up madly to the business of revelling – and the latest revellers were going home in wavering but loud-voiced crowds at 8 a.m.!! You never heard such a row.

I am awfully sorry about your cold, old man. But you ain't the only one. Mother and Elsie and I have got 'em in various stages and we stink of eucalyptus and other devildoms. Miss Ponton was here when we came. As you know, Miss Howard's trouble with her car prevented her coming to Paris with Cecil. She doesn't expect to be in Paris till the 14th and so we had to send over for your "Dorothy" to look after Elsie till Miss Howard should come. Miss Ponton and Elsie go over to Madame Sabatiers this afternoon and settle down. At 8 a.m. to-morrow morning Mother and I go down to Marseilles leaving Paris at the ungodly hour of 9.15 a.m. We get to Marseilles at 10.35 p.m. – another long day for Mother – and on Friday at 10 a.m. we go to Port Said in the P & O *Persia*. How I wish that there were an epidemic at Coll. and that you were coming too. You may be sure that I will write you full and particular accounts of all that happens in the land of the Pharaohs!

Buck up! Easter is always a simply *bloody* term and you have our keenest sympathy in your wet and slush and general misery. All the same you seem like the chap in Horace who *"Vixi*[t] *semper puellis idoneus"*[1] [was] much in request among local society. But you didn't tell us who your three invites to tea were from. We are dying to know!

Your next letter must be care of *Thomas Cook & Son, Cairo. Please* let it be a full one. You don't know how one hungers for news of people one loves.

God bless you, old man. I hope that after six months of practically continuous rain we may get a decent February and March.

With dear love from us all,

Ever your loving,
Daddo.

---

[1] "Was always attractive to women", Kipling misquotes a line from Horace (*Odes*, Book III, no. 26), "*Vixi nuper puellis idoneus*" ("I was until recently attracted to women").

Hotel Regina,
Paris.
[Feb. 5 1913?] 8.45 p.m.

Very dear Daughter,

It seems about one year and a half since you went away – and that is why I sit down – I mean to say stand up at the mantelpiece to tell you how we love you. By this time I expect you will have met the other maidens and found them mildly interesting specimens of a breed of which you do not know much – the British Female Girl. In eight and forty hours you should be as thick as thieves together, and when the time comes for your return you'll grieve to be separated from them. Mother, who is going to bed, here interpolates that she has found a pair of nail scissors which you left behind but as she knows you have another pair and as these happen to be handy she intends to hang on to 'em. In other words, she says, she does not know how to get them to you.

I won't burden you with advice. I know you will be good: but what I want you to do is to be interested in your companions and your surroundings. Up to now you haven't had many companions, and you have regulated your surroundings to suit yourself. Now, my darling, you're in the world for a little bit on your own and (here's the whole secret of life) as you treat the world so will it treat you. Your esteemed parents do *not* treat you as you treat them but the world, which is chiefly busy with its own concerns, behaves otherwise. If you smile at the world, it grins. If you frown at it, it scowls. This is knowledge that you will learn before a week is out. I merely mention it that you may recognize it when it comes along. Selah!

Now I want you to write your little brother at Wellington a full true and particular account (much fuller than you'd write to *us*) of your feelings and experiences in your new life. *He*'ll understand because, you see, he goes out into the cold hard world three times a year – and also he remembers what his first day at school was like. Tell him fully and you'll find that he'll sympathize with you no end and that you'll have another bond of sympathy between you.

And I think that's all. We're going to bed (I hope you are there already!) Mother finds that the new feather in her new hat is insecurely placed and she is giving it a new "security". Gawd knows whether "security" means tin-tacks or resewing it but it makes her happy. Now she is in the scantiest of attire, lecturing away as she undresses. I will spare you a picture and I will subscribe myself

> Ever and ever
> Your most loving Pater.

I leave a space here in case Mum takes up this particularly vile pen. Do not mistake the following for poetry. R.K.

FORWARD TO JOHN   s.s. Persia.
      S.V.P.   *Feb. 10. 1913.* 10.30 a.m.
      Blue sky and sun – but *not* warm.

Dearest Family,

Here am I in the smoking-room of a P & O. You'd think it wasn't any way different from a Union Castle but, as Sunshine T. observed:– "There's no smell of paint – nor india-rubber". That was the first thing Sunshine noticed. Then she observed slowly:– "It smells quite different from other ships". That again is true. There is a queer faint mixture of curry, Lascars, and the East generally. It's precisely the same smell as I remember when I was a kid on the P & O. Nothing has changed on this venerable line. The saloon decorations are all pure pale whites: the smoking-room is a highly respectable arrangement in oak and pictures of mermaids: and the stewards are *very* quiet, highly respectable, soft-spoken gentlemen. Our cabin steward is called "Stevenson" but he might be Matcham. Our white-haired stewardess is called "Mrs Scott" – and she is like all the stewardesses one ever knew rolled into one. The Lascars – the native sailors in their blue clothes and red turbans – are the same (so it seems to me) as the ones I played with when I was five; and the big, fat-stomached *Serong* (Lascar petty officer) with his chain and boatswain's whistle might have been the very man who used to carry me about on deck.

You'd be amused over the ship. To begin with, she is a single-screw and she thumps along at about 13 miles an hour. The food is good – what there is of it – and it is served without any frills or flubdubs – dingy silver, table cloths not too clean, salad all dumped into a plate, glasses big and thick and like tooth-glasses. *But* the cabins are big and roomy. Everything in them is dingy and battered but clean. And the passengers themselves are a quiet crowd. No rowdy-dows on deck: no gambling in the smoking saloon: not even much laughing at dinner.

We left Marseilles with a strong sun, a blue sky and a calm sea. Even Elsie could not have found any excuse for being sick. But there was a lady travelling with a small, red-faced boy called Robert. She had hired a Scotch nurse (with false front teeth) to look after him. The nurse had never been to sea before. She understood, however, that people are always sick the first night out. So she solemnly turned in and was sick. She did it, I presume, from a sense of duty but *how* the deuce she could manage it, beats me. Then on Saturday the sea got calmer and calmer, till at last it oiled down and looked exactly like the Equator. But it wasn't warm. I never imagined that the terrible Gulf of Lyons could behave so prettily. And we went strolling through it – we haven't got the mails aboard, so it don't matter what we do – with this absurd old single screw going *wop-wop-wop* – sixty to the minute.

Last night about midnight we were roused by the old ship swinging and curtseying in a stately manner. Mummy, after much thought and some words, got up and shut the porthole. But we were on the leeside and nothing happened. Some people on the weather side, however, got the top of a wave or two through their porthole – and we saw their bedding to-day drying in the alley ways. A familiar sight!

There isn't a thing to tell you about. You never knew or saw or heard of so quiet a ship. A lot of us are getting off at Port Said for Cairo. We expect to get into Port Said about 2 p.m. to-morrow. If there are sixty of us they will telegraph for a special train to take us to Cairo. If there aren't sixty (and, between ourselves, I don't think there will be) we shall be left to knock our heels in Port Said till the regular train goes at 7 p.m. In that case we shall arrive at Cairo about midnight. But, as Mother says: "What *does* it matter? We have only our two selves to think about. No beastly little girl who has to be fed and put to bed. No outrageous boy who demands to be amused." Quite true: and in a way we feel free but (also between ourselves) we are lonesome – *very* lonesome. The first day we came aboard, as the luggage was being stowed in the hold, I saw – a pair of *skis* – SKIS!! going down. Now for what earthly purpose does a man transport skis – full size – black with white lines – to India for? It was a touching sight; and reminded me of ancient days.

Now as I write, I can feel the air getting a little warmer: and a big fat gull is sailing over the smoking-room sky-light. Mummy is somewhere in the music saloon doing her letters. She is *much* better I am glad to say. She has got rid of her cough and appears to be enjoying life. If only you two were along I couldn't wish for anything jollier. We are living in the hope of getting letters from you at Port Said. I think the time I miss you two most is when Stevenson enters with my tea and two bananas in the morning. Then I feel as if it were my duty to hunt for you and take you round the decks in bare feet.

I haven't found anybody interesting yet. There are not many young people and the small "Robert" (who calls himself "Wob") doesn't mind accepting a box of bricks (bought at the barber's) from me but he doesn't want me to help to play with 'em. I tried yesterday. "Wob" stood it as long as he could. Then he screwed up his face, and pointed towards the people walking up and down on the decks, and whispered:– "You – go – there!" So I went "there" and as I turned away "Wob" said "Good-bye" and went back happily to his bricks.

6 p.m. Smoking-room again. Nothing more to tell except that it has got cold and rainy again. This within a day's sail of Port Said. Sunshine, with a face like the butt-end of a pyramid, has packed most of our things ready for going ashore (it *is* settled that we can't have a special train) and Mummy has gone down for her bath. It remains only to subscribe myself,

> dear Sir and Madam,
> as ever
> Your lovingest
> Pater.

P.S. Forgot to tell you that there is a lady aboard with an eighteen-year-old daughter, going out to Egypt for the first time. *And* tho' the weather is as still as a mill-pond the 18-year-old persists in feeling sick. I told her that she ought to have a brother to rag her. She groaned and went downstairs. Perhaps she has brothers!

Hotel Semiramis,
Cairo.
Feb. 12th. [1913] 11–12.30 a.m.

Dearest Elsie and John,
  [Begun by Mrs Kipling and continued by RK]
  To the right there is a splendid bridge over the river, with one piece
of it moveable, thus:-

It swings round for an hour or so every morning to let the great
lateen-sailed barges through. This is the kind of animal they are - *very*
picturesque.

  Cairo itself is a cross between Rome and Florence with touches of
Cape Town thrown in. *But* it is cold - beastly cold and Mother and I are
surprised and annoyed. The train that met us at Port Said was, as
Sunshine T. remarked, exactly like a South African train - I looked for
the big coat of arms and the springbuck on the outside. The men (there
are no women in the street) are attired in long blue petticoats, thus:-

147

When they do anything that requires exertion – such as pushing baggage trucks – they hold one end of the petticoat between their teeth. This has the great advantage of reducing them to silence. The colours of their garments are mostly blue or black, with occasional white or orange. We have not seen more than half a dozen women in the streets and they are of course veiled.

The nice thing is to see the camel again – passing unconcernedly between motor cars and trams. Cairo bristles with motor cars and all the luxuries. Our hotel here is full of the latest appliances down to a glorious lift, worked by an Arab in gold-embroidered jacket. It stuck this morning, when I was in it and the Arab panicked.

The notice in the bedroom about bells says:—

> Once for the waiter.
> Twice for the chambermaid.
> Three times for the Arab!

This gives one a spacious feeling – as though, if one rang six times a Pyramid would enter. You never saw anything in the world so like their photographs as the Pyramids. We saw them this morning, across the Nile with the tawny grey desert behind 'em, and I only said:— "Huh! Of course. Those are the pyramids." Only when one looks at 'em for some time one realizes their enormous size. They dwarf the low hills behind 'em, and they change with the changing lights exactly like mountains.

If this were Cape Town, I should say that there was a south-easter blowing. I don't know what is the local name for the beastly thing but I am quite sure that they will try to explain it away. Lady Edward Cecil is staying here at the Semiramis. We haven't seen her yet. Enclosed you will find a nice little note from your Countess Isabelle. She sent it on straight to Cairo. You will be *delighted* to read the news she gives of the weather at Engelberg.

(The washing has just gone to the laundry. We expect to go up the river in the steamer to Assouan on Saturday morning but I don't *quite* know if the chambermaid – not the Arab – comprehends how important it is that we should have it back on Friday. More than ever I wish you were here to interpret for us. But this is a digression.)

Our window attracts us like the window on the Thames when we stayed with the Durnfords. There are always camels or dahabeeyahs [large sailing boats] or donkeys to look at. Our balcony looks slap on to the great brown silent Nile. Somewhere round the corner is a barrack of English troops (Sunshine discovered it first) and we can hear bugles and drums.

[no signature]

grounded but quite holthy
owner on stern surveying his troyes

Cook's steamer
Rameses III.
Monday morning 9.30 a.m.
[Feb. 24 1913]
running down the Nile.

Dear old man –

The only trouble in this letter is how and where to begin. We are in a Cook's river steamer – an elaborate house on a boat, as per picture postcard – leading a life like life on an ocean liner except that we tie up every night as we used to do on the Norfolk Broads.

We left Cairo by train at 8.30 a.m. last Friday morning. The train might have been going from Salt River to Johannesberg except that the dining-car (International Wagon Lits Co.) was pure white and the grub was a shade better than they give you on the Cape trains. The night before we left Cook's man came to us and said that our steamer "Rameses III" had stuck on a sandbank just off Assiut and that he didn't know when they could get her off. (Steamers are apt to stick on sandbanks when the Nile is low.) However, some way or another they got her off and when we reached Assiut (which is about 200 miles from Cairo by rail) we found her waiting for us – all clean and swept, with big carpets, and easy chairs and writing tables on the deck and the black stewards getting tea ready. Exactly like a house-boat.

We left Assiut in her about 4 p.m. and had to make a very awkward turn in order to get out into the river where a dredger was dredging mud. While engaged in this manoeuvre we hit the bank an awful wop – said bank being faced with stone. I heard a whack and a crack which were sufficiently familiar to me – reminded me of Boulogne in fact. Then we paddled out across the river which is about a mile wide and in less than ten minutes ran ourselves ashore on the edge of a sandbank just at sunset. It was necessary for us to do this because we had cracked one of our plates and we were making water. A naked diver went overboard to locate the leak and, I suppose, they must have puttied it up somehow for after two or three hours we got off the bank and began our journey up the Nile by moonlight. This isn't usually done but we had a good pilot, and the moon was strong enough to show us the outlines of the sand-banks and the sails of the native craft. Of course they carry no lights and take a hellish joy in tacking just under the nose of Cook's steamers. One has to slow up for 'em every few minutes just like sleepy carters on the road in a car.

Well, we carried on till 2.30 a.m. on Friday night, or rather Saturday morning. . . .

The landscape never changes – it runs for hundreds and hundreds of miles and it is always interesting. The Nile at present is low and one can't see over the dark earthen banks – exactly like the banks of the Dudwell when there has been a slip – but magnified ten thousand times. There is always a native village of square mud huts and big towers of mud for pigeon cots: there is always the solemn fringe of date-palms behind it: there is always the vivid blue-green of young wheat, or onions or the pale goldy-green of sugar cane and behind everything else, four or five miles away is the pale, pinkish grey of the utterly barren hills of the desert. One feels that one is sliding down a gutter less than ten miles wide. I had no notion Egypt was so long and so thin. It's an absolute length-without-breadth-country. *But* you never saw such cultivation.

They get three or *four* crops a year off this amazing Nile mud, which again is only the silt of the Dudwell: and, *on an average*, after all expenses have been paid, they make £7 (seven pound) profit per acre!!! At these rates our land at Burwash would fetch us in over £2000 a year. Of course all this cultivation is limited to where the water can be put on the land and where the Nile can deposit its honey-coloured mud. The traffic on the River is incessant. Boats loaded with chopped wheat straw for the beasts to eat when the country is flooded; pots for pigeon nests; pots for drinking water; lime, stone, sugar cane and all that sort of thing are always in sight. They navigate by the Grace of God but they don't seem to come to any harm. At least we have only seen one wreck of a dahabeeyah and that looked very ancient.

The rummy thing is the climate. It's – not to put too fine a point on it – rotten cold in the mornings and the evenings and to-day, within 2 or 3 degrees of the Tropic, it hasn't got warm yet at 11 a.m. I've been wearing my thick winter things till to-day and only wish I'd not taken 'em off. The sky isn't S. African blue but a sort of washed-out pale bluish grey. The river is a pale brown and the banks are dark brown and the natives are blue-black with a smile on 'em like a split water melon.

The night before we left Cairo we dined with Fitzgerald, Kitchener's Aide-de-Camp, the man who saved K's life on the last occasion when an Egyptian tried to assassinate him. Fitzgerald is a cheery bird – all medals and decorations and hard service with a cheery brown face. He is a Wellington boy of course – Hardinge dormitory – and knew all about Pompey. The man on my right was Captain Flower who runs the Zoo at Cairo and is *quite* one of the most interesting men I have ever met. He can tame anything that exists from panthers to snakes and knows more about the inner private life of snakes, bats, wolves and hyaenas than any man. He was a Wellington man of course (every one out here seems to be Wellington) and of course knew Pompey. Spoke of him with great affection. We are going to Cairo Zoo as soon as we get back and Flower says he'll turn out all the beasts for us to play with. Did I tell you that the Hippo's name is Kitty? And he has trained her to sit up and beg! *Quite* mad but as I have said one of *the* most interesting.

And last night, sitting on the deck after dinner, an old chap called Parley who used to be in the Navy and is now Secretary of the Royal Yacht Squadron told us a story which is worth preserving. We were talking about Marryatt's novels, which Parley knew by heart and someone said something about *Snarley Yow*. "Well", said Parley, "I'll tell you a tale (you needn't believe it but it's true) about another Snarleyow". And he began:– "When I was in the old *Blanche* (cruiser) on the Jamaica station, our Captain who was a bit of a brute, bought (or stole) or somehow procured at Havana an awful hound as bad-tempered as himself which he said was a Cuban blood-hound. He called the beast *Limon*; and Limon used to take a piece out of you whenever he got the chance. All the ship's crew and all the officers hated him and, after some weeks when we were lying in a harbour of one of the South American ports, a young officer of the name of Meredith saw the back fins of at least three sharks under the counter and promptly kicked Limon overboard, in the hope he'd be eaten. Devil a shark 'ud touch him. The Captain heard the splash, saw the splutter, ordered the life-boat away and Limon was rescued. Defeat No. 1 for the crew. A few weeks later, the Blanche being then at another South American Port, young Meredith went ashore with Limon under pretext of giving the brute exercise and tied him firmly to a tree with a rope. Came back and reported Limon as lost. Great hopes that the Blanche would have to sail without him. But half an hour before sailing Limon came flying aboard. He'd gnawed through the rope and escaped. A few weeks later, at some port in British Honduras where small-pox and yellow jack were raging, the Blanche sent a boat ashore with the mail. She wasn't going to let any of her men go ashore. Limon of course flung himself into the boat as soon as it was lowered, and being the Captain's dog no one interfered with him. The instant the boat touched the jetty Limon was off, up the street and fighting with strange dogs and out of sight. The midshipman in charge of the boat came back, apparently depressed but secretly elated, with news that Limon this time really *had* been disposed of. The Captain was pretty wrath but even *he* couldn't take a dog aboard out of an infected port. So the Blanche went away and continued her cruise from island to island and six or eight weeks later fetched up in the harbour at Barbadoes. I don't know how far that is from British Honduras – say 800 miles. Anyhow, the Royal Mail steamer came in as she was there and suddenly over its side leaped the undefeated Limon. He'd recognized his own ship and plunged at once to rejoin her. The crew received him with cheers; made him as big a pet as they'd made him a beast before; his nature was changed and chastened. He became the idol of the ship and after many years died and had a tombstone erected to him by his sorrowing owner. Do you know what he had done? No mail packet touches at British Honduras. The wise beast had stowed away in a tramp steamer to Colon on the Isthmus where the British Consul knew him and his owner and the Consul had shipped him on the R.M.S. packet to Barbadoes, to be sent on, as occasion served, to Jamaica which was the Blanche's dockyard. But Limon as soon as he saw the Blanche, made his own arrangements."

How is that for a tale? Doesn't it almost equal the original Snarleyow. Limon was always a devil – even when the Blanche's crew loved him. At least, he wouldn't bite them but he bit everything else that wasn't connected with his ship.

[no signature]

s.s. Prince Abbas.
Mar. 2. 1913.

Tied up at Assouan – a red hot early afternoon; waiting for the train that is to take us to our other steamer.

O Beloved Kids!

Your letters have come at last – John's of the 16th – your (Elsie's) diary, from the 12th to the 19th with John's letter enclosed: and we have just revelled in 'em. (By the way, all our passengers have also received their mail and are sitting round the deck devouring it with comments and outcries.)

Poor old John! Footer in half a foot of mud *and* measles and a partially insane form-master are a full portion for any unbaptized Heathen. No matter. If he lives he'll have his motor-bike in the Easters. He seems to be working well *which is a matter I shall not forget*. I was never so upset over anything as over poor Scott's death[1] – within sight almost of grub and warmth – and the letter that he left almost made me blub. What a good man he must have been – and how splendidly all his chaps backed him. Whence has come the new idea of going to the Varsity and why – oh why – Clare? Cambridge is sad enough but Clare – C-L-A-R-E – !!! Why Peg – unspeakable Peg himself! – came from Clare.[2] But no matter. Think it over and tell me in the hols what made you think of it. I am beginning to understand you (John!) a little. Every time you profess an earnest desire not to work and to confine yourself to ragging, I note that you always go up in form. But with 17 survivors out of 30, surely to goodness you can climb up like a rocket – even to Cambridge. Have you ever seen Cambridge? *I make no promise* but I think it would be good for you to look at Cambridge. Oxford, my son, you have seen.

As for Elsie, she lives in a whirl of delights – musées, lycées, boutiques and galleries – not forgetting to count her weekly wash. I can't tell you how pleased we both are (damn J's impudence for writing of me as his "Pa"!) that you are taking to your Paris and enjoying it so much. I expect that all the French in you is now coming to the top. Of course it was all right for you to go out with George Allen – he is a sober and improving young man – and it made us laugh to hear that his visit taught you how John felt when he is taken out on Saturdays. (I can see Johann gnashing his teeth afar off as he reads about what you do in Paris.) Equally of course it is all right for you to have elocution lessons. I expect when you return you will go round declaiming Racine and Molière to the listening natives of Burwash. Sorry about the mistake about Miss Howard – not that it made the least odds but I imagine it rather upset her. I hope the Ponton had a good time – and occasionally smiled. Glad you like the French girl.

'Wish – oh how I wish that you were both here for five minutes. Now I must go down to the cabin, and see that a horde of howling heathen (all labelled Cook's Nile Service, across their tummies) do not rush our baggage into the *Egypt* instead of the *Rameses*. Choko purred and grinned when I gave her your messages. She is a wondrous bird! Nothing moves her to any expression of feeling other than a faint rolling of the eyes and a smirk.

I will now conclude. Hoping this finds you well as it leaves us both at present and excuse spelling and a bad pen.

    I am
    Ever yours respectfully,
    "Pa".

(I'll give John a kicking for that last.)

[1] Captain Robert Falcon Scott, British naval officer and explorer, who died returning from his expedition to the South Pole.
[2] The "unspeakable Peg" who went to Clare College, Cambridge, remains a mystery.

154

Semiramis Hotel,
Cairo.
Mar. 11. 1913.

10.20 a.m. after having just read your diaries of 26th Feb.–Mar. 3.

Oh you Awful Kid! *Did* I send you to Paris for this round of delirious and unbroken delights? Did I save my hard-earned pennies that you may "froolic" in the Bois and with Betelheims and Laws, and at dinners and at theatres and among confetti? I'm afraid I did. But didn't I also tell you, darling, that you were going to have a ripping good time? Mummy and I rejoice, aloud and often and shamelessly, at the exceeding joyous procession of new experiences that are crowding in on our own beloved Djinn. True, the bottle, (with Ponton for a cork) is waiting but it will be a different bottle hereafter and a different Djinn – now that Allah has enlarged the skirts of your experience. And see also how your French – acquired with yells and protests long ago – has made this new life possible and rich for you as no other accomplishment could. Fancy having to study your Paris *now* with one eye on the grammar and the other on the accent! And Paris and France will be a permanent possession for you for all your days. You are entitled to them by birth you see, and I'm glad your blood realizes it.[1]

I can't pretend to answer your letter in detail. 'Tis a frivolous record – shockingly so. Let me sober you with the Stern Fact that we are leaving, Miss, on the *Cordillere* (Messageries Maritimes) from Alexandria on the 15th March, next Saturday, and should be at Marseilles on the 19th. Letters to be sent there care of *Thomas Cook & Son*. But we shan't come to you straight off. We hope to bring the car up to Paris with us when we have finished our tour with Landon and if you can manage to have some pleasant weather we want to take you and the girls for some excursions. But no more blizzards, please. Anyway we shall be on the same soil as you and within a few hours by rail which is a joyous thought! You wouldn't think it, but I too sometimes, want to see you – most dreffle! You see, I love you!

We didn't want you – we were glad you weren't there – and John too – and we kept on being glad you weren't there – when we stuck for 28 smitten hours on that dam sand-bank! The thermometer stood at 55° (this on the edge of the Tropics) but the wind it never stood still for one wicked minute. It blew like Hades and it cut like a knife and our miserable steamer swung round and round (but never got off the sand-bank) and other steamers (four others) came up and got stuck too and

a little express steamer who was taking cheap tourists on a cheap trip
had to stop and throw us a rope and help to haul us off bodily. *How* it
would have bored you and *how* it interested us – barring the cold. Then
the intelligent Thomas Cook whom we had told in a loud voice that we
were going to the Winter Palace Hotel (and it *is* a palace!) at Luxor
sent all our mail to the Luxor Hotel. That is why we didn't get any mail
at all from you till this morning. Damn Cooky!

While we were at Luxor we went out and spent a night with a Mr and
Mrs Winlock. He is a digger and digs for curiosities at a place called
Dehr-el-Bahri. The curiosities when found go to the Metropolitan
Museum at New York. There is a huge bungalow at Dehr-el-Bahri
(which is practically a huge cemetery of Egyptian tombs) where the
New York Museum people live. It is like living among gigantic
rubbish-heaps. Not a green thing grows there; not a drop of water falls
there. It is just one tumble of mounds of rubbish. Thus:–

The only view there is ends in one blazing amphitheatre of vertical cliffs – once white but now literally toasted by the sun to pale gold or rich red. *And* the heat! Everywhere tombs. Tombs reached by steps; tombs entered by descending stairways: tombs in one's backyard, under one's stables and in the natives' hut. All the great grey city of Thebes must have buried itself there in years gone by. The only people who didn't were the Kings. They had a terrible dry valley of stones to themselves behind the little hill in my sketch. I saw it – I'll tell you about it when we meet. At Dahr-el-Bahri the highest class were nobles. Mr Winlock showed us the tomb of a man who administered one of the royal farms. There were pictures – comic and serious – on the walls of the great gallery to his tomb (but the coffin of course had been taken away long ago) that showed exactly how he did it. The whole thing was like a picture of Egyptian life to-day – even down to the skin of water swinging in the shade of the trees and the tired man slipping away to have a drink. An Egyptian tomb is a set of rooms cut into the rock. This gentleman had a very pretty wife and their three daughters inherited their mother's looks. They were all drawn nearly half life-size. He used to go duck-hunting with one of his daughters and kill the ducks with boomerangs. But nothing is more useless than to try to describe things which the reader has not seen. So I suppress all account of how I went (Mummy was too tired) to the tombs of the Kings with Mr Winlock and was grilled alive in a huge rock-walled ravine of aching white and red rocks or how I came back by a short cut down the side of that almost vertical cliff I have drawn. It burned me a rich and lively chestnut colour. That was a day never to be forgotten.

[Letter finished by CK]

[1] The Balestiers were originally a Huguenot family.

Grand Hotèl d'Europe,
Avignon.
Mar. 21. 1913. 9 p.m.

Dearest child –

Your prompt letter in pencil, tho' you had to leave your food to write it, came in this morn, for which our best thanks. Now on receipt of this write to the *Hotel Boule d'Or, Bourges* where we expect to be on the 25th.

Yes. 'Tis true we have our car. It met us in Mr Landon's charge at

Marseilles but Mr L. was in charge of a heavy and severe and sodden cold which he was treating with ammoniated quinine by the gallon. He is at his worst to-day but vows he will be better to-morrow when we start for Albi, 180 miles across the lower slopes of the Cevennes. Je – your daddy – is in charge of the travelling arrangements. I hope they will turn out all right. To-day Mums and I drove to the Pont du Gard – our third visit. It was still as beautiful as ever. Our weather is grey, moist and warm with the spring racing across the hills in the most tender blues and greys.

We have quite given up trying to follow your amazing career! It seems a whirl of cubists and theatres and lectures. We love to hear about it all – give us the fullest news of Cyrano. I also love the play tho' 'tis ages since I read it. Apropos of plays, you may be interested (*this is strictly confidential*) to know that Vedrennes of the Vedrennes-Eadie Company, Royalty Theatre, is anxious to produce *our* play – the Pyecroft one.[1] At present we haven't quite decided the terms but if we agree 'twill be produced on the 22nd of next month as a curtain raiser. Shall you go? I shan't.

I have letters from John complaining that you haven't written to him. I think you are a *beast*. Write at once.

Dear love from us both. ('Wish you were here to help Mums to pack.)

> Ever affectuosisssimus,
> Daddy.

Write to Hotel Boule d'Or, Bourges. We can't yet tell when we get to Paris, but think it may be 28 – 29 – 30 – or 31.

---

[1] *The Harbour Watch*. In her memoir, Elsie says that she and her father wrote this one-act play together. Its production at the Royalty Theatre, she continues, was not a great success. Pyecroft is a character in a number of RK's later stories: a petty officer in the Navy, he is equivalent to – though less memorable than – Mulvaney in the soldier tales.

> Bateman's,
> Burwash,
> Sussex.
> *Monday*. [May 5 1913]

Dear Old Man –

Just a line to say I'm back at Bateman's after the Academy dinner – d----d dull: but I met Ward (Sir E. Ward, Under-Sec. for War) there and talked to him about your getting into the Army. He says he is going to write to the head of the Examining (physical) Board and suggests you might be examined privately just as a preliminary canter. This isn't a bad idea.

In the meantime I suggest that you wear your *pince-nez* as much as you can and try to get used to 'em. They give a man a different expression as compared to spectacles.

No news except it's beastly cold and I'm rather lonesome for lack of a Friend & Ally to play with. Remember to dig out this term and let me know what a "presentation" to Sandhurst means. Is it a sort of letter of recommendation from your Headmaster or what? You'll never get it if it is.

> Ever your own
> Pater.

> Bateman's,
> Burwash,
> Sussex.
> *Thursday. May 15. 1913.*

Dear old man –

I forgot to tell you in my last that I have applied to the War Office for a prelim. medical exam on you which, they tell me, will take place at Aldershot before a Medical Board. This means you'll be looked over by an Army doctor there. Word will be sent when that examination is to take place and I will come over in the car and take you to it. So be prepared at any time for the summons. I've written to Pearson about it and I expect you'll probably get off a lesson or two for the exam.

Meantime keep yourself as fit as possible and for goodness sake don't smash up all your available *pince-nez*: so that you can sport a pair before the Board.

> Ever lovingly,
> Pater.

> *May 16. 1913.*

Dear John,

There is to be a medical board to sit on you at Aldershot at 12.45 on Monday. I shall be at Coll. with the car at 12.30: and shall want you with your leave in order, *and dressed in your best kit* which you had better put on that morning when you get up, the minute you come out of school. I have asked Pompey to see that your leave is ready signed beforehand but I expect you to see that it is.

Then we'll rip over to Aldershot and see what the medical board says about things. It will be rather a rag.

> Ever
> the Pater.

> Bateman's,
> Burwash,
> Sussex.
> *June. 20. 1913.*

Dear old Man:

Your half-term report is just in with a letter from Pearson which troubles me. P. points out that you are now *one* term superannuable and in order to escape superannuation *next Easter* you must reach the *Upper Second* by Easter. He tells me that you will get into the Lower Second at the end of this term; then you will have to get into the Middle Second by the end of next term and then if you don't get the Upper Second at Easter you will be in a bad position. This is sufficiently serious. P. says that it is doubtful if you can get into the Upper Second by that date as so few boys leave at Easter; but the first 8 or 10 in the Middle Second can reckon on getting promoted. You *must* try for that, old man.

I will give you the reason. As soon as a chap is superannuable he lives on as it were by favour and has to keep very much up to the mark all round – in games as well as everything else. They naturally don't care to keep a boy who isn't doing the Coll. credit in one way or another. You haven't so far done much except in the running line, and I am afraid from P's asking me whether I am going to keep you on after next year, that you have been saying that you're going to leave anyhow when you're seventeen. This is a bad error because it gives them an excuse for chucking you before you chuck them. Also, I have an idea from your talks with me that you go about rather despising the Coll. That is another bad error. A man who has done a good deal can enjoy the luxury of despising his associates: but a man who hasn't must not try that game.

So I ask you now to take a big pull on yourself and work as hard as you know how, both in form and at whatever games you can make good at. Evidently they all expect a good deal from you. It's no good saying that nobody minds being superannuated. In most cases this is true but in your case, remember, everybody would know that *you* had been superannuated. I have done, as I think you will be the first to admit, everything that I can think of for your enjoyment and your comfort. Now it is up to you, dear old man, to show that you are worth taking trouble for. You simply *can't* afford to chuck the next term away. You *must* get as high a remove as you can. I don't suppose you can manage a double remove but I do hope and pray that your place at final exams will be thoroughly good. Your report generally is very decent but the fatal fact remains that you are behind the age-average of your form by about 9 months: and that has to be made good.

Also, I want to hear what you are doing in games. If you get the reputation of hanging around Grubby's and slacking you'll find that they'll be keener on superannuating you than if you even played up and pretended to play at something.

Think this letter over carefully, because this is a serious point in your career, and let me know how you feel about it. You're a young man now, not a boy and must act accordingly.

Ever your loving
Pater.

Bateman's,
Burwash,
Sussex:
July. 18. 1913.

Dear old man –

You must have been pretty tired out to have written that last letter of yours so I won't worry you about it: tho' it grieved Mother a good deal. This is just a line to beg you to take a pull on yourself for the last few days of the term which, as I know, when one is fed up, are the bad days for every man. The trouble is that your mind is a bit ahead of your body (I know the symptoms quite well myself and can feel for you). You will get your "responsibility" quite soon enough – as soon as you are willing to take it. We will talk about that in the hols. I was *very* pleased at what you did in the House-match and glad to know that Pompey appreciated it. As I always say, you could do anything you liked if you gave your mind to it, and top-score in a house-match is proof of it.

We've come down, as I think Mother told you, from seeing Aunt Trix at Scarboro. She is getting better but it is a slow job and we were rather tired when we came home to get your letter. Up to the present, we haven't got a new chauffeur. The R.R. needs a special type of man and he is *not* easy to get.

At last our dry weather has broken in floods of rain – not before it was needed for the brook has been nearly dried up. Did you know that Phipps of her own accord has taken to music again and sits strumming at the piano whenever she has a chance. She has a pretty little voice too – so you must look out.

I am looking forward *very* keenly to the hols when I think that a good talk between us two will clear up many of our present difficulties. At the same time I admit that, when excited, you have the rudiments of a very decent literary style.

Now I won't preach. I'll just sign myself,

Always lovingly,
Your Pater.

Bateman's,
Burwash,
Sussex.
July. 30. 1913.

Dear old man!

I am weeping salt tears at your luck. Pompey sends me a note to-day that you are "perfectly well" – I don't believe you had anything more than your usual glands – and I am counting the days till we can get you back. But there is no good in hiking you out of a warm bed into a motor for three hours without a minute's interval. So, as I said, I'll be round on Saturday as soon as may be. Oh Damn! Damn! Damn!

Did you catch the mouse or more mice than one? I very nearly sent the Ward a box of tin soldiers and a pea-shooter cannon but I reflected that it might lead to a sanguinary rag and riot. Do be careful, and tell the other chaps to be careful, about their behaviour (you know what I mean) during these few days. Pompey evidently don't think that sanatoria (when one is well) are good for the morals. I dam-well *know* they ain't. So I entreat and exhort and command you to hang on to yourselves.

We burst a tyre at Haywards Heath coming home – quite in the old Fleck style. It was a hot day and she went off with a bang like a seven-pounder – blew out the inner tube and spread it like a piece of tripe all over the wheel. All the same Fleck's driving is a wonder and a revelation. He *never* checks; he never hurries; he never skids on a curve and he *never* says a word to anyone on the road. Mother goes off this morn to Lowestoft to inspect the house there. I anticipate rather fun on the sea-shore. I can't go with Mummy because I am staying at home with Phipps, and we go to the flower-show at Laurelhurst this afternoon.

I've been through my books but I can't find anything decent to send. However I'll make another search to-day and see if I can send you off a packet of stuff. Tell Allen I'm afraid I haven't got a Wee Willie Winkie in the house.

Are you allowed to write me a letter. You might do me an adjective one. Write *exactly* what you feel, leaving out every adjective and when it's done get the boys to supply an adjective (respectable) apiece: not telling them the letter till all the adjectives are in place. The result is perfectly awful sometimes.

Meantime I have the honour to assure you and the rest of you lopsided lepers of my deepest and saddest commiseration. Here's to Sat. morning. Bless you and *keep straight*.

> Ever your loving
> Pater.

Bateman's,
Burwash,
Sussex.
Oct. 3. 1913.

Dear old man –

Not a line from you this week: so I take my pen in hand and hunt you up. Why have you not written?

Curse you,   why have you not written?
Confound you   ,,   ,,   ,,   ,,   ,,   ?
Damn you   ,,   ,,   ,,   ,,   ,,   ?

This seems an easy way of filling up a letter but for fear of shocking your infant mind and the morals of Wellington, I'll stop.

The Motor Lawn Mower machine is coming from Ransomes on

Monday with a demonstrator. I bet it will fizzle and stink just like the other but anyhow I'm going to get it and have these lawns of ours properly rolled for once. I've just been doing a new story about a dog[1] which is of so appalling a nature that Elsie runs out of the room whenever I attempt to read her extracts. She says it keeps her awake o'nights. It is a ripping good tale. The dog-hero squints! Also he is partly a devil dog. Thus do I improve the worldly tone and morale.

Landon came down to-day to Keylands (by the way the road up there is nearly finished) and this afternoon we went for a trip in the car into Romney Marsh – visiting Brooklands and New Romney, where we had an enormous tea. You know what a pig Phipps is about her grub. She managed to smarm her plate with an ungodly glue of shrimps and plum jam! It nearly made me sick. However it all went down inside her and none of it has come up yet. Yesterday Mother was out in the fields with me when she slipped slightly on an uneven place but in less than a minute was all right again. This was at 11 a.m. She walked about all day, went to Keylands and Dudwell, came home and at 6.50 p.m. took her usual bath. *Then* her foot began to hurt. At dinner she was in great pain: Phipps put Pond's Extract on it after dinner. It got worse and finally being unable to walk Mummy went upstairs and to bed *on her knees*!! Once in bed she literally wept with sheer pain. I was awfully scared, painted her with iodine on the ankle, and prepared to run her up to Bland-Sutton to-day. She woke in the morning cheerful and a little stiff but that was all. She said it hurt her a bit to-day but she walked over to Keylands quite as usual. It was a most mysterious seizure, and helped to turn me grey. That is the chief news of the week.

I wish I didn't miss you as much as I do, old man. You were a huge nuisance at times but I seem to have got fond of you in some incomprehensible way. I know you love the clergy[2] so you will be glad to know that His Grace the Archbishop of Canterbury is coming to Bateman's next week. *This is true!* I wish you were here to make him welcome.

This is just a scrawl of affection from

Your loving
Dad.

[1] "The Dog Hervey" in *A Diversity of Creatures*.
[2] At his own request, John was baptized into the Church of England, July 19 1914.

Bateman's,
Burwash,
Sussex.
Sep. 28. 1914

To the Hon.
Miss Lofter-Brassey,
Castle Driver,
Niblinks,
Nr. Bunker.
[to Elsie, staying in Scotland at Castle Menzies with Mrs Law]

But the idea of *you* as a hard-bitten golfer, oh my best beloved, fills me with amazement. I don't somehow seem to see you swinging your fat self round after the stroke – following through, keeping your eye on the ball and all the rest of it. But if it's going really to take hold of you it will be great fun. You'll have to join the Burwash golf-club and play with the Chamberlain. Words can't say how pleased I am that you are having a good time. Just like you. First:– "*Must* I go?" Next:– "I don't want to go. Tell me to come home as soon as possible." Then:– "Please may I stay longer?" Yah!

We too (or two) greatly wish we could come up but it's an overlong journey for a very short time and frankly I'm not up to it. You know I am not much given to lying abed (except o' mornings) but I was abed for four full days with a variorum mixture of neuralgia, toothache and temperature – at which I was in great indignation. Mummy was more different sorts of an angel to me than even *she* had ever been before – and you can guess how much *that* meant! Now I am dressed indeed but rocky, and Saturday came John in full canonicals by the 5.44. He *very* much becomes the uniform,[1] as you Scotch would say. It was a changed John in many respects but all delightful. A grave and serious John with an adorable smile and many stories of "his" men – notably Beggie his mad Irish servant whose idea of cleaning J.'s room is "to keep a broom about" – as an earnest, I suppose, of what he might do. The Irish Guards I gather are racially and incurably mad – which of course suits J. down to the ground. For goodness sake try to get some of his stories out of him – notably of drunken men trying to kiss sentries, while the sentries presented arms. He meant to write to you yesterday (he left at 6.30) but he didn't. I am immensely pleased with our boy. The old spirit of carping and criticism has changed into a sort of calm judicial attitude. Evidently he gets on well with his men – he talks to 'em when he can, which is one of the great secrets of command. He speaks well of the food at mess "almost as good as Brown's", says he; and I think he is growing. We had a perfectly lovely day together: broken by occasional grunts of "wish to the devil Phipps was here", which indeed we all did.

Tho' I am sorry for your disappointment Mummy and I both feel that he will appreciate you more when you meet. (Please forgive this abominable handwriting but the pen feels as strange to me as an oar, after all these days.) We talked and we talked, *and* we talked – this grown-up man of the world and I. Mother is trying to arrange a meeting between you and John at Brown's on Saturday but we mustn't be disappointed if it doesn't come off because he doesn't know five minutes beforehand what he can do or when he can be spared. When he came down to us on Saturday, for example, he had to change his train because, though he knew he was free, he had to go to the adjutant to report that he was leaving; and the adjutant was engaged with prisoners. The Irish Guards are rather given to prisoners – "not an ounce of vice in 'em even when they are drunk," says John, "but *quite* mad." He mimics their dialects perfectly.

And now I will stop. No one will be more pleased that you have had this lovely time than we shall be. But there is worrk, Madam – shirts and socks, Madam – to be under-taken. The fame of your socks has spread. Mummy's order for nine pairs (with shirts) has brought her a fresh order from the same troops – a modest man who says he is rather thin and five foot ten and 22 inches from elbow to wrist, or else it's shoulder. I enclose copy of his letter which Mother asks me to send you.

A whole heartful of love from us both and best remembrances and heartiest thanks for Mrs Law.

> Ever your own,
> Daddy.

[1] See illustration 11

> Bateman's,
> Burwash,
> Sussex.
> *Oct. 21. 1914.*

Dear old man –

Hard luck on you to be held up on your Warley-ward way but there's no accounting for the S.E. & C.R. [South Eastern and Chatham Railway] on *any* night of the week much less Sunday.

I enclose herewith cheque for the Singer. I suppose you bought through an agency and couldn't get any discount. I do hope she'll be a good and faithful handmaid unto you. Only, remember to look out for London lighting which gets progressively darker. *I* shouldn't risk her lovely form in traffic for some time. I'm awfully glad you like her and when next at Brentwood shall be charmed to be taken for a ride. I don't think, honestly, that there's a better car in the market. It's her amazing strength, speed and handiness that attracts me. What are you going to call her? Patti? It must be the name of some eminent Singer.

A note has just come in from Eric Gore-Browne telling us that his second inoculation, which he thought wouldn't hurt, laid him out on Sunday. So he couldn't come over. He expects to be at Crowboro' all winter, and wants us to come over when we can.

The 5th Sussex Battn has just been sent to the Tower. Ernest Marten is in it, very bucked up as he writes me that owing to the Battn's smartness it has been *brigaded with the Guards*! There's glory for you. If you go to the Tower you must let some of your glory shine on Ernest.

Yesterday Elsie went over to Hawkhurst to talk French to some of the Belgian wounded soldiers. She had a very gay time and enjoyed it much. I am going over to-day to take them some books in French.

No news of George Cecil. That is all our news so far. *Don't* I beg you burn the candle at both ends but get all the sleep you can as you never know when you will be wanted.

Dearest love from us all.

> Ever
> Dad.

> Bateman's,
> Burwash,
> Sussex.
> *22. Oct. 1914.*

Dear old man,

Yours with receipt for cheque came last night. All the family is most keenly delighted at the news of the car, the Sweet Singer in Warley as one might say. I knew they were as good as they make 'em. I betted myself that you would work in a Baby Claxton some way or other. Look out for your electric light installation! It's all beautiful till something goes wrong with the wires and then you have no alternative to fall back upon. Glad you ain't having a dicky. It isn't smart and tries the tail-end of the car too high.

Elsie swears that she is going to have first ride in the car when it comes down. Keep out of London traffic as much as you can of evenings (it's dee bad for new mudguards) and run about the county of Essex a bit. You ought to be able to stretch over half the county.

We expect to be up in town Friday morn. No news here except that Eaves is in bed with a chill and that the weather is beastly.

Much love from us all.

> Ever
> Dad.

P.S. Why not call her Car-uso (he's a great singer). So was David. So was Melba. You might christen her "Depèche Melba" which is a foul pun. Don't lend her to chaps who can't drive. Good luck and pleasant drives.

1915

There was, of course, no Switzerland trip for the Kiplings this winter; indeed, after the war, memories of John made any return to Engelberg impossible for the family. Rudyard spent much of his time promoting recruitment,[1] visiting wounded soldiers, and closely questioning officers billeted at Bateman's for his series of articles on "The New Army in Training". In February and March he was also writing "Sea Constables" and "Mary Postgate", two of the bitterest of his war stories.

At the same time, John continued his arduous training at Warley, though he had opportunities for occasional trips to Bateman's, or reunions with the family at Brown's Hotel in London, or visits to Bath, where Carrie had been ordered to go for her health. A taste for motor cars, music halls, and elaborate dinners marks the few of John's letters that have survived. Still, the young man's most often expressed ambition was the desire he appears to have shared with nearly all his fellow officers to see action in France as soon as possible.

Ironically, it was RK who reached wartime France first, invited there, as a famous journalist, to inspect French military preparations and to write about them for English readers. This he did in a set of articles published under the title "France at War". John soon followed his father, however, reaching the continent precisely on his eighteenth birthday. At times, the two could not have been separated by more than a few miles, but though their correspondence continued, now almost on a daily basis, they were never to see one another again. In early October the Kiplings received word from the War Office that John was missing in action. His body was not recovered.

[1] See illustration 10

Bateman's,
Burwash,
Sussex.
(*Sat.* [Feb. 27 1915] (a vile misty
wet morning) 8.30 a.m.)

Dear old man,

The billettees (I don't know how you spell it) have just gone to pick up their men in Burwash and to march back to Eastbourne *via* Dallington and Pevensey. I think they have had a good time of it. They turned up yesterday evening about 6.30 (having ordered dinner for that hour). They were preceded by a young transport officer (Preeston was his name) who rather reminded us of you. Also three or four soldier servants carried their kit to Bateman's - and you can imagine the joy of the maids.

There were six chaps altogether - a Captain Dryden with a North-country accent that you could cut with a brick; a Glasgow boy with a ditto Scotch accent; another Scotchman and the rest mixed and curious but all interesting - Dryden: Cooper: Brown: Goodman: Nicholson: Andrews was the full list. They had posted sentries and outposts over by Sutherland Harris's and had set the rest of their company to digging trenches near the golf course. Apparently the 10th Battn Loyal North Lancs love trench-digging.

We gave them a decent dinner - tomato soup: fish: mutton: mince pies and cheese straws and unlimited ginger beer and cigarettes. They, naturally, talked shop *all* the time. Three of 'em had been in the Public School battalions and had got their commissions from the ranks. They said it was a great pull in the New Armies, if a man had passed through this mill. They said that *the* weakness of the new armies was in the N.C.O.s and they told me awful yarns of Sergeants (aged 21) larking with the men. Of the men themselves they could not speak too highly. One of the officers was at Tidworth with the 6th L.N. Lancs - Henry Longbottom's battn before he joined the R.F.C. He said that that battn was a set of first class sweeps and rapparees [blackguards] but that they came to heel in a very short time. Four of the officers got out at ten to inspect trenches, outposts etc. They were hung with revolver, binoculars, water bottle and all whole mass of muckings.

The young transport officer and a senior sub. stayed behind and enjoyed 'emselves talking shop with me. Some of their tales would have made you faint. Here's a problem which you can submit to your mess.

A. in a Territorial Battalion is a private in billet. Owing to this fact letters for the privates can only be distributed on parade. A. on parade gets an official letter addressed to him as Lieutenant A., telling him he has been given a commission and must forthwith report himself to such and such a place. He tells his platoon commander of the contents and asks what he should do. B., the platoon commander, says to A.:- "Double out and tell the Captain." A. accordingly doubles out, salutes and acquaints C. the Captain with the contents of the W[ar] O[ffice] letter. C. says:- "Who gave you leave to leave the ranks? Get back and go on with the parade." A. returns rather sore. D., the Sergeant Major then comes up to B. the platoon commander, and asks him what the deuce he meant by giving a private leave to double out on parade and confer with the Company Captain. B. with great presence of mind retorts:- "It wasn't a private. It was a Looutenant"! At the end of the parade A. goes to C. and repeats to him the W.O. communication and asks leave to go to town and report himself to his new battalion. C. says:- "No. You finish your day's work here." A. then goes to the battn C.O. who gives him leave to go away at once which he does. But before he goes he has the pleasure of strutting up to C. (hands in pockets) as an *equal* and says to him:- "Look here. When I doubled out on parade this morning it was as a Lieutenant *not* a private". C. replies:- "Well if it was, you ought to have carried on till the end of the parade." *Query*. Who was right in this tangle. *If* A. was a Lieutenant from the moment he received the W.O. intimation, obviously he couldn't stay in the ranks to be ordered about by corporals and sergeants. Yet, on the other hand, my personal sympathies are entirely with C. the Captain and, had I been in his place, I should certainly have ordered the brand-new Lieutenant back to the ranks. Submit this to a senior and see what he says.

Well, at eleven, the 4 officers on duty returned. They were very pleased with the trenches etc. etc. We gave them drinks and sandwiches and they went to bed. One in the dimity room: two in the big guest room: two in the north room upstairs and one in the room that used to be my father's. They were as quiet as mice. We gave 'em breakfast at 7.45 and handed 'em their lunches to eat on the road and we parted with expressions of the highest esteem on both sides. It was a pretty wet day and I feel sorry for 'em. But there's no doubt that the new armies work like beavers and they *are* getting some sort of discipline. *You* seem to have come in for a lot of heavy work – digging trenches in snow storms is no catch. I wish you'd send us a line telling us when you are likely to be in town. It's more than a week since we met – or will be when this letter reaches you – and after the month at Brown's I feel that a week is a very long time.

Now I'll shut up and send this letter to the post.

> With all our best love,
> Ever affectionately,
> Your Father.

P.S. I've got my new fountain pen (a Waterman's) in perfect working order and don't intend to use any other till I've broken it.

R.K.

> Bateman's,
> Burwash,
> Sussex.
> *Thursday, Mar. 4. 1915.*
> (stinking wet and mild)

Dear old man,

Phipps and I had a look at the catalogues (A & N and Harrod's) last night to see what we could possibly find in the Games line which would be refined (but not too bally refined) and quiet and at the same time have *no* connection with War. There is a thing called Billiard Nicholas where you puff with a kind of nickel-plated enema at a ball. This seems rather promising. I couldn't see anything else that looked at all useful: but Phipps says that if we all actually go *to* Harrods and look for ourselves we are likely to rootle up something. Do you think a *small* billiard-table (like the one we have here at Bateman's) could be put into one corner of the ante-room? It's simply dam silly of them not to allow for any means of recreation.

And this reminds me of what I sat down to say. It may be that my mind is as mushy as my innards; owing to the fact that I partook of Epsom Salts last night – and a cheery night and a half I had afterwards. *But* as I lay awake wrestling with "conflicting reports from various channels" I reviewed the facts and surroundings of your present life – how damnably and unrelievedly dull the surroundings were and what a wet and grey and muddy and depressing existence it was in itself: and I felt exceedingly proud of the way you'd stuck it without yapping. So I made a resolve that I'd write and tell you so in the morning. Young as I was when I began, and hard as my work was in that climate, I did not have to *live* absolutely alone. As you know I lived in my Father's house. It was only when my people went to the Hills for the summer and the house was shut up, that I had to live for a few weeks at the Club. But *you* have had to face a certain discomfort (which is inevitable) *plus* a certain loneliness of the spirit which is awfully hard to bear; and a certain sense of isolation which, as I remember, almost frightens a young man. And you have stood it like a white man and a son to be proud of. I haven't said much about it, but I've noticed it, and I think I can feel pretty well what is passing in your mind. It is an experience that you have got to go through by yourself (all the love in the world can't take it off your shoulders) but it may be some help to know that another man has had to face something of the same sort (I mean loneliness *plus* news of a pal's death; *plus* dirt; *plus* a general feeling that the world is a wicked place which it isn't) and respects you for the way you are taking your dose.

But I babble! Put this down to the Epsom his Salt. Phipps has made a bloody graven image of your photo in her room. It's mounted in a gold frame. She has, *I* think, chosen the very worst of 'em all.

> Ever lovingly,
> Thy Parent.

Brown's Hotel
Tuesday. [March 16 1915] 8 p.m.

Dear F–

Just a line to say that I am off to Dublin to night to bring back a party of 34 recruits to Caterham.

You can faintly imagine what Dublin will be on St Patrick's day & the state of the recruits "falling in".

I have to march 'em right through the town.

So I will have my hands full till Thursday evening.

Well good bye old things; wish me luck.

Can the "front" present a worse prospect than this little "Dublin Stunt"?

"*Je pense que non*".

Love to Jerry.[1]

> Yours ever,
> John

[1] A current secretary at Bateman's. Not to be confused with Lt.-Col. "Jerry" Madden, mentioned later.

Shelbourne Hotel, Dublin
Wednesday, [March 17 1915], 2 p.m.

Dear F–

Here I am after a most bloody trip, stopping at what is called "the best hotel in Ireland"; it realy is jolly comfortable.

My party of men is being drawn from 4 cavalry barracks so I have spent a busy morning talking to strange adjutants, ordering meals at various stations & accomadation, etc. No troops can be shifted on St Patrick's day, so we are going by the 9 o'clock boat Thursday evening.

I am spending the night here in a most wonderful room, but without even a pyjama leg to bless myself with.

By gad Dublin is a frowsy hole, all slums and stinks but the faces are all the same, just like Warley.

There are wonderful carts, "outside cars". I nearly took a toss in one this morning.

I think I will go to a Music Hall to night. It ought to be good fun.

"The Lord's annointed" is at large again – the adjutant of the 12th Lancers – he is Kd, Frankie & the "grannies" all in one.

His orderly room was like a pig sty.

But He was adjutant of the 12th Lancers.

Have you heard of the 12th Lancers? I've never seen one of 'em before. I told him that if he didn't have his party ready by Thursday, I would let him bring them over himself. He

175

just gaped like the bloody old codfish he looked, all scent and cigar ash.

The cavalry are "some" freaks.

I hope his party won't take after him.

They aren't giving me a single N.C.O. but the W.O. knows best.

It will be good to see Caterham, though it is the most filthy hole.

> Yrs ever,
> John.

I have missed K's shamrock so my future spouse will have to go without the promised shruberry.

> Bateman's,
> Burwash,
> Sussex.
> *Mar. 18. 1915.*

Dear old man –

Your letter from the Shelbourne cancels our wire of to-day in which we said we intended to come up to-morrow on the chance of seeing you. By the time you have landed your rapparees at Caterham and reported yourself at Warley you will have had all the travelling you want for the day. So we will come up on Saturday, and stay the night at Brown's if that suits you. At any rate we will come up on Saturday to find out. The story of your Irish adventures will be worth hearing. Yes, Ireland is a rummy place and the Shelburne which plays at being an hotel is very like the country.

Elsie is better but I think that, as one can possibly pick up this fool disease a second time it is better for you *not* to come down to Bateman's this week-end. An ensign with chicken-pox is ridiculous.

We admire your trust in Allah in setting forth without "even a pajama leg to bless yourself with" as all the shops of Ireland are shut on St Patrick's Day.

The 12th Lancers rank themselves with but half a horse's length in front of the Lord God Almighty – as you have probably discovered. I suppose Cuthbert has found out that you are a person of cast-iron innards as far as the sea is concerned. So pray for a rough passage. As you haven't got a non-com (which I call trying a man rather high) it will be worth a Sergeant's guard to you.

With affection and pride and *intense* curiosity,

> Ever your
> Dad.

> Bateman's,
> Burwash,
> Sussex.
> *Tuesday Mar. 23. 1915.*

Dear old man,

Phipps got up yesterday and more or less dressed. She is almost "unspotted from the world" but there are one or two big ones left which have not yet disappeared. We told her all our adventures with you and she gave tongue like a beagle with sorrow and rage and envy and all those emotions.

Yesterday afternoon Mums and I went down to St Leonards to see old Mademoiselle [former French governess of John and Elsie] *and* Rider Haggard. Mademoiselle was in a convalescent home after a bad go of bronchitis. Among other things she has been acting as interpretress to the Belgian wounded in a hospital at Derby where *not one of the English doctors* understood one word of French! She told us with great pride that her name had been "mentioned in the papers". She was immensely interested in your career. "But *why*," said she, "is he in the Irish Guards?" I explained that our family blood was "prudently mixed" in view of all international contingencies and that there was some Irish in the strain. Then she couldn't understand why you were in the Army at all. "*If* there is no compulsion," she said, "why should John enter the Army?" "Precisely *because* there is no compulsion," says Mother and after a while Mademoiselle tumbled to that idea too. She sent her very best greetings but kept on murmuring from time to time "And *he* is in the Army".

Old Haggard was great fun. You would have exploded with joy to hear him. He too has been at St Leonards recovering from bronchitis and the effect of the disease apparently has been to make him say:– "What? Hey?" every five seconds and *much* louder than he ever did. Also his "vats" and "vens" and "ves" are more pronounced. He was in great form and I was sorry you weren't along to listen to his:– "Vat se

177

Devil – eh? What? Hey?" I love old Haggard. He hates St Leonards. Swears all the people are over 75 and diseased which, as far as I could judge from a fleeting glance, is quite true.

This is what I set out to say. We have got places for the Empire (Elsie Janis) on Saturday night. They are in the eighth row but the best we could get. We are coming up on Friday for Friday night and Saturday and we hope to go to Bath on Sunday night. So that's all right. Get it into your alleged mind.

Now I will walk up to the pillar box and post this. That *was* a day on Sunday.

> Ever your loving
> Dad.

> Bath Spa Hotel,
> Bath.
> *Mar. 30. 1915.* 6 p.m.
> (the sun shining hard)

Dear old man,

This is a rummy place – a sort of mixture of Madeira, the South of France, bits of Italy and Bournemouth all tumbled into a hollow between hills, and populated with invalids and soldiers. The town is full of soldiers. The 10th Devons have their headquarters in one of the most fashionable streets and what used to be elegant private houses now bristle with privates and great coats and rifles. They are going to have inter-Regimental sports in a few days. This explained the spectacle I saw this morning of six perspiring privates in obviously civilian knickers chasing round one of the squares hounded on by a long Corporal while the cooks of a battalion camped in one of the parks hung over the railings and criticized their action. I believe there is some artillery here too; though I haven't come across it yet.

Mother has started in on her treatment which means a hot bath one day and a hot bath and massage the next and a sort of dry massage every evening at 9 p.m. It is a devilish strenuous undertaking for so small a woman. Elsie and I went out this morning to the Pump Room where the hot waters of Bath are dispensed by two virgins at 2d a glass. It isn't an exciting spectacle except for the invalids. Some of 'em are fat – as fat as swine: others cough: others limp and the rest look like lepers. The hotel boasts one old gentleman who knits comforters for troops.

We overheard him say proudly:– "This is my third". I believe he finds it soothing for the nerves.

And talking of nerves, I owe you two bob – for I see in the papers that Wells was knocked out – a half-hook on the point. I don't know whether he has guts or not but surely this finishes him on the stage of pugilism. Did you see, by the way, that the much advertized Football battalion only roped in a few score men out of the 1800 pros. who play. *What* a stinking game is soccer.

We expect to have the car over by Friday morning, with the new man to drive; so if by any chance you can get to us for Saturday we might be able to go for a little run about the country. It's a pretty part of the world. You had better look up the A.B.C. and see how the trains go. There is one which gives you your lunch aboard – a most useful train and there is a splendid one (we took it) at 4.15 from Paddington which comes on without a stop, getting here at 6.6. There are also good trains in between – one at about 3 o'clock I believe but if you miss the lunch train you will find the 4.15 will give you tea. Uncle Stan always loved his food and he feeds his Great Western passengers well.[1] But you may be going to Bournemouth or somewhere.

We haven't met anyone we know yet but I expect that experience will not be long delayed. The Town Clerk is coming to call. God knows why. It makes me feel as though I were a deserter or a defaulting debtor. The grub here is good and the rooms are beautifully clean and comfy and as the hotel really *does* stand in its own grounds (see advts.) one feels decently secluded.

There's a prep-school at the back of us – up the hill-side, which moved us nearly to tears. Two kids began playing golf with cleeks. It ended in a hockey-match and a scuffle – precisely as it would have done with you and me not so long ago.

Best love from us all,

       Ever your
       Dad.

[1] Alfred Baldwin, Stanley's father and RK's uncle, had been Chairman of the Great Western Railway.

Dear old man,

A fine day after East wind and a little rain: with sunshine and clouds. We are off in a little while for a run to Bradford-on-Avon, nine miles away. Mother had rather a bad night with pain in her arm last night and is a bit tired out to-day. A bath and massage every twenty-four hours is a bit of a tax.

There was a dance – quite a big dance – last night. The company, as far as we could see it arriving by motors, was somewhat mixed, consisting of the usual mixture of privates, non-coms and officers. We took no part in the show. As Elsie said:– "I cannot gyrate with the Line!" They danced till pretty late and sat all about the hotel corridors. I found a couple camped outside our hall door and the whole place seemed to be full of 'em. In consequence, breakfast this morning was a rather disorderly and unconnected meal. Our small waiter looked very deboshed.

By the way I have at last found out something about your friend the Haberdasher who, needless to say, was got up to the limit of civilian splendour at last night's show. His name is Hurlbut or Hulbart – I couldn't catch which. His father who was a manufacturer (convenient term!) is dead and the old man who sits at the table with his Mother is his Uncle from Madras. Dr Milsom told me that the boy himself is "a very clever mechanic" – by which I suppose he mucks about with motor cars like most young men do. He was anxious to do something – drive cars at the front I believe but he is suffering from "bovine tuberculosis" and Dr Milsom has given him a certificate that he is on no account to go to the front. I think he is between 19 and 20, or perhaps a little older. Now "bovine tuberculosis" is the sort of tuberculosis you get from drinking the milk of a tuberculous or consumptive cow. It is not as fatal as genuine tubercle you will be glad to know but it causes enlargement of the glands and suppuration and, if not carefully looked after, may make the boy very ill. But there's no denying that "bovine tuberculosis" is a splendid name to have on a certificate of medical unfitness – a dam sight more convincing than mere "weakness of the glands". I expect his Mamma was at the back of that certificate.

I see by the papers which I hope are speaking the truth that your Band played with such success that 200(!!) genuine Irishmen presented themselves for enlistment at Dublin in one day – "several of them wearing the uniforms of the Irish National Volunteers". That strikes me as extremely comic but it looks as if the Band's Irish trip was going to pay.

What I really wrote this letter for was to condole with you over the Awful Result of the King's proclamation about Barley Water. I see that the Grenadiers are reported to be "considering" whether to drop all alcohol from their festive board. Of course the Irish, ably led by their Colonel-in-Chief *and* their Colonel must have sworn off liquor already and I hasten to send you my sincerest condolences. It will not affect tee-totallers like Jerry Madden and most of your fellow-officers, but to a hardened toper like you I fear the shock will be most severe. Remember that Delirium Tremens (which means seeing pink Irish shamrocks and green Irish pigs running round the latrines) always comes from breaking off drink suddenly. So you must try to diminish your drinks gradually. Knock off the eleven o'clock whisky and soda first: then the cocktail in place of afternoon tea: and later on the cocktail before breakfast. But do not, I beg you, do anything rash and if you begin to see blue or yellow parrots sitting in the fireplace and talking Erse, look hard to see if they cast a shadow. If they do, you are all right. If they don't – consult Jerry. But it's a great lark. Tell me as soon as you know what your mess is going to do.

Just as I had written this in came your note with cheque for £40 – for which many thanks. Not to be behindhand and to prevent your bank account from looking too lonely after the withdrawal I send you a cheque for £20 which I make no doubt can be used. I'm *awfully* sorry about your crawling "home" (fine word) at that ungodly hour. Didn't the silly trains connect?

Dearest love from us all and specially Mother. Just off in car.

> Ever
> Dad.

Bath Spa Hotel,
Bath.
Ap. 19. 1915.

Just in from town to find this for you – from the W.O. which I send at once.

I hope you got off the route march and on to the range. It was a good week-end and I'm very fond of you but I wish to God you wouldn't steal *all* the gloves I ever buy. The *second* after you left, the whole station filled up like a pantomime rally. I never saw such a sight. I wandered about there for nearly a quarter of an hour in the thick of this roaring, good-natured and slightly boshed crowd. I went home in a bus, next to a muzzy private who wanted to go to Waterloo Station. The conductor told him that the bus only went to Waterloo Bridge. He could cross that and get to the station on foot or take a bus across the bridge. Then the private said, confidentially:– "Look at me! I'm a stranger in the world. I've missed one train already. . . . *Look* at me. *Do* I look as if I could cross a bridge? I'm a *complete* stranger and I'm missin' *all* my trains. *I* shan't find Waterloo to-night. *Look* at me." The conductor looked, patted him affectionately on the shoulder and said:– "All right. I'll tell you when to get off." And when we reached Waterloo Bridge the private got off in one long lean limp wisp – like a Khaki towel – I wish I could give his general air of being *all* on a curve. I finished up my journey next to a servant girl, who had anointed her hair with essences and unguents – lemon verbena for choice. I nearly catted.

On the train down just now I picked up with a couple of Inns of Court training battn. Yeomanry officers just off to take their first independent or real regimental command at Chippenham in a Wilts Yeomanry Corps. My word, they *were* raw.

R.K.

Buck up and talk it over quietly with the Adjt.

Sunday
Warley Brks
Brentwood
30th May [19]*15*

Dear F-

There are great doings here as we are very short of officers – there are only about 10 – so it means three times as much work as before.

We had 18 casualties in one day out there, and 15 officers were sent out whilst I was sick – just my luck.

I have been warned to be ready to go out at 5 minutes notice, so it won't be so long now.

I have got the last of my kit together and am waiting. T.F.O. Hamsworth has been recalled and him, "Ringo" & myself will I suppose go out together, or I may take a draft out.

God knows where our officers are coming from.

To make up for last time, I went on the "Razlle-Dazlle" last night.

Diner at Princes, Alhambra & Empire next, then supper at the Savoy, then Murays & two other night-clubs of lesser repute.

I left Town in the Singer at 10 past 3 a.m. & got here at 7 minutes to 4 (43 mins); that is "going some".

I only met 2 taxies & a cart on the way down & being broad daylight I could move like hell.

This certainly is some war and the Germans seem to be getting into their stride, whilst our "ceaseless vigilers"[1] seem to be letting their ships sink all over the place.

Well it is only a matter of days now or a week and "I will be right there".

I will wire when I get my orders & will meet you in town if you come up on receipt of the telegram, "so stand by" as we say in the Brigade.

So long old things.

Dear love,
John

[1] Probably a wry reference to the journalistic cliché about men of the Royal Navy "keeping their ceaseless vigil". In his 1918 talk "The First Sailor", collected in *A Book of Words*, RK quotes a High Priest advising Nobby Clarke, "the first sailor", to "go and keep your ceaseless vigil in your lean grey hull and – and – I'll pray for you".

5th July 1915
"Somewhere in Brentwood"

Dear old F–

Just in from a 15 mile walk. Talk about heat. My hat!!

I commanded my company and walked ahead with Kerry. He told me definitely that I would be the first ensign to go out to France after the 17th of August,[1] and I would have been too young then if I hadn't had a years service in the Brigade.

So going in early was a damned good move after all.

It is nice to have a month clear notice, so I can get every little thing all ready.

I am going up to arrange about selling the car.

I am going to get the rest of my kit out of the money the Singer will fetch, & then turn the balance over to you.

So you ought to make.

Well I can tell you, though I ought'nt to realy, under the "Official Secrets Act," that the Allies great advance will begin after August the 17th.

I feel so bucked that the fatigue of the march does'nt trouble me a bit.

Love to Jerry.

So long old things,
Yrs John

PS

I will try to get down next week end to Bateman's.

1 John's eighteenth birthday.

Dear old man,

Just got your letter of yesterday. We had to be up in town on business for a few hours and we pitied you on the road for the heat was ghastly. How kind of Vesey *only* to take you out in his perambulator for 15 miles. "At him, Nipper!"

It is a comfort to get your notice in good time. Kerry, however, was wrong in one respect. It is not the mere fact of your having been in the Brigade for a year that has made you what you are. It is because you deliberately went into it for a purpose and gave yourself up to the job of becoming a good officer. (I have heard indirectly from another source that you are considered to be "damned smart".) Lots of men, as we know, go into the Brigade for a year and haven't made anything but a bloody show of themselves. *You* went in and you stuck it out without a whimper through that foul winter, and you shouldered any responsibility that was going and you laid yourself out to know and understand both your men and your profession. We are both more proud of you than words can say. It's a record that can't be beaten.

Now as to arrangements. Don't bother to sell the Singer. Turn her in to the makers and tell 'em to repair her. I'll allow you £100 for her as she stands (you told me she was worth about that much). If you want the £100 I'll pay it into your account. If you don't, I'll let it stand over and put it aside towards a new car when you come back. Of course I'll pay for having the Singer repaired.

We shall be up in town on Thursday before lunch and shall go down in the evening: so if you can come up for lunch or tea or dinner so much the better. I do hope you'll be able to pull off Bateman's this week-end. There are reliable rumours of strawberries. And now, old thing, keep fit, so that you may go out with a full banking account of sleep and strength to your credit. I hope you've got the rifle with you and that you're fully supplied with a first-class compass.

Dear love and great pride from us all, my veteran.

Ever,
Dad.

Warley Brks
Brentwood
16th July 1915.

Dear old things

Isn't it awful about poor old Oscar?[1] There is another of the "old Brigade" gone.

Many thanks for the laces, etc.

I am going up to town this evening to be fitted for the 'specs' at C & P & get one or two little things

Warley is more sanguinary than ever – a living Hell on Earth –

I can't get off on Saturday as I have a thick week end. Worst luck.

but tell Tibalds I will see him Sunday week (the 25th) "so help me god".

Dear love

	John. 2nd Lt.
In case	Irish Guards
you have	Brigade of Guards
forgotten	2nd (res) Battln
my position	Warley Barracks
	Brentwood. Essex O.H.M.S.

---

[1] Oscar Hornung, recently killed in France.

2nd Batt Irish Guards
Warley Brks
Brentwood
Tuesday, 20th July

Dear Old Things,

You may have seen, in yesterday's paper, that his "Majesty the King has been graciously pleased to sanction the formation of a new battallion of foot guards – the 2nd Battallion Irish Guards."

That's us – a regular battalion – what ho!!

Vesey told me this morning that I was to get 16 trained signallers ready to go out with us in 10 days.

As it takes a year to make a trained signaller, it is a rather

16th July, 1915.
Warley Brks
Brentwood

Dear old things

Ri'nt it awful about poor old.

Oscar? There is another of the "old

Brigade" gone.

Many thanks for the laces etc.

I am going up to town this evening

to be fitted for the 'specs' at C.A P

& get one or two little things

Warley is more sanguinary than.

ever. — a living Hell on earth —

A LETTER BY JOHN KIPLING COMMENTING
ON THE DEATH OF HIS FRIEND OSCAR HORNUNG.

caval order. But I am allowed "carte blanche" about taking any man I like, so I have got hold of 5 old 1st Batt Signallers and a sergeant who got a DCM for good signalling in September.

I beat up the proffesion sheets of all the men here, and got hold of 4 G.P.O. [Post Office] men who are splendid at the "Buzzer" (the only thing used out there) and a corporal who can mend anything that has electricity in it. Also I have got the champion middle weight boxer of the Army who is a damned fine signaller but an awful swank; and two pretty good fellows who have been at it six months.

So there are 13 for a start.

"Jerry"[1] came back last night as he is going to command us, which is pretty awful. He is in great fettle. Shook me hard by the hand & said pleased to "see you looking so fit my boy" – which being translated is – "I'm glad to see you looking so fit for a good term's work my boy."

One of our officers, a captain, on patrol the other night at the Brick stacks killed a German officer & took his map. On it was printed the "Hymn of Hate"[2] as they print "Bartholomew sheet 34".

I have got practically everything ready now.

So long old things. Love to Jerry

> Love from,
> John.

PS

Will wire about Sunday. Please continue with shirts as I showed.

> JK

[1] Lt.-Col. G.H.C. Madden.
[2] A German propaganda song whose theme, "One foe and one alone – England", was meant to alienate the British from their allies.

Bateman's,
Burwash,
Sussex.
July. 21. 1915. 8.25, p.m.

Dear old man,

Just got your letter announcing your present lack of Reserve (that's a dam' fine joke if you only had the mind to see it). We are *highly* delighted with the news. Question now is, when and where and how do you get your Colours? I don't see how the Battn. can go away without, at least, having them presented.

We gather from your silence on the matter that, after all K.[1] did *not* come to inspect you on Monday. If not, why not? Your promptitude and resource in the matter of signallers is very striking. I can't see, myself, what is the use of anything but a "buzzer" at the front.

Now about the Dentist. Norris who lives quite close to Brighton will come *specially* into Brighton to attend to you next *Sunday* if we can only give him warning. He thinks it is very important that you should be overhauled as to your teeth. It doesn't seem unreasonable that, under these circs., you should ask for dentist leave – specially if you can get the job done on Sunday. There aren't many dentists who would do that for anyone. But we will wait your wire on the subject.

Mother sends word she has got you a perfect duck of a little electric lamp and the shirts are progressing. That I think is all for the moment.

> Dearest love, O Veteran,
> Daddo.

[1] Field-Marshal Earl Kitchener who succeeded Field-Marshal Earl Roberts as Colonel-in-Chief of the Irish Guards.

The Bath Club,
34, Dover Street, W.
Thursday 4 p.m.
[July 29, August 5, or August 12
1915]

Dear Old F–

This is a very thick week. We did 19 miles on Monday. The heat was awful & the men fainted like flies. We started at 7.30 a.m. I wasn't back till 4.20 p.m. as I had to bring in all the men who fell out for the last 3 miles.

There were about 60 of them. I got hold of all the water I could find & washed their faces & gave 'em a drink. Some revived enough to be able to walk back but a few were too bad to be moved.

A great number had cramps in the belly & I had to rub them hard whilst someone sat on their legs, they writhed like shot rabbits; it was hell.

I commandered every sort of vehicle from wheelbarrows to 30–40 Peugots and got 'em back somehow.

There was no room in the carts for rifles etc. so I came back with a rifle and two men's packs. My God I was done. I have been attending a memorial service at St Paul's this morning & to night at 9 p.m. we start on a night march of 20 miles. We ought to be in about 6 tomorrow morning.

      So long, John

PS

I can't put off paying my E F & subscription any longer as I have been elected. So will you be a sport and pay £42-0-0 into my account?

                Southampton
                Monday [Aug. 16 1915]. 11 a.m.

Dear old Things,

Just arrived here after a putrid trip.

We left Brentwood at 7 a.m.

The men are behaving splendidly and the weather is top hole; we are the first train & are now waiting for the two others to come in we cross at about 6 this evening & ought with luck to to be over there at about 3 a.m. Tuesday. I believe we are spending a night at Havre & then going straight up to St Omer.[1]

Please send first parcel of goods off now. 2nd Btln 1 Ggds Div. B.E.F. [British Expeditionary Forces]

Please excuse pencil & dirt.

      Dear love, Yrs ever
      John

---

[1] British mobilization centre and headquarters in France.

Although away from Bateman's this is a fine birthday.

Dear old Things,
You will notice by the above that we have arrived in France.
We had a good crossing, getting over in 7 hours.
I, worst luck, was chosen for Picquet Officer and had to pass
the night visiting all parts of the ship posting & visiting
sentries for submarines and on the lifeboats.
We got over at about 1 a.m. this morning & I had still to keep
prowling round the ship till 4.30 when we had breakfast.
We got off the boat at 6.
We were escorted by a destroyer all night about ¼ of a mile
on our left flank.
We are now under canvas for the night and are moving right
up tomorrow morning – a 30 hour train journey.
Have you heard anything about the Singer yet? do write &
say. This is the most lovely day you ever saw, hot & balmy.
As I have had only 4 hours sleep this last 48 hours I am going
to turn in.
  Writing again shortly,

    Yrs ever
    John

Please send   1 pair roomy carpet slippers
        2 towels seize of face towel but rough
        2 pairs civilian black socks
        1 pair brigade braces
This is the life

        Verdun.
        Aug. 17. [1915] 9 a.m.

Dear old man,
  A line of welcome and blessing if you are in France as I suppose you
are by now. If you have been one of the disembarkation officers you
won't feel like blessing.

I've had rather a good time. Been to several nice places including a bombarded town; had a squint at the Crown Prince's Army in the Argonne; seen Rheims (they weren't bombarding it for the moment) and have greatly admired French artillery. The men I saw in the trenches were mostly Saxons and didn't want trouble even when the French stirred 'em up.

Now I'm in this queer place - all searchlights at night. I'm off this morning to see *your* Colonel [Kitchener] review an Army. Odd isn't it? But it's true. The review is some distance from here but we travel *en automobile* (20-30 Renault Limousine for me and Landon - 60 Merks for the baggage) and we go about 40 the hour steady.

I'm having a splendid time and hope to return to Paris about the end of this week. If you can send me a line to the Hotel Brighton, 218 Rue Rivoli, I'd be very grateful.

Dear love.

Ever your
Daddo.

I'm *awfully* glad your inspection was such a success. I wonder what K. will think of the lot he reviews to-day.

Wednesday *18th* [Aug. 1915]

8 p.m.

Dear old Things,
I am writing this in a train proceeding to the firing line at 15 m.p.h. (its top speed). Well –
We left camp at 12 this morning.
At 7 a.m. there was a parade for the whole battalion, presenting arms & skip driling.
We marched down to the station, 4 miles of downhill pavé, the hotest weather I have ever known & as I was carrying a very full kit I sweated some.
It took 3 hours to entrain.
Their methods here of transport are very sketchy –
They put the whole battalion – 73 horses 50 carts, 1100 men – in one train! With one engine to pull the lot (it is breathing very hard at the moment).

There are [140] men to each cattle truck. The French cattle truck is a bit smaller than the British ones, the poor men are packed like [flies]. The ones that can't stand are sitting on the footboards. We have 3, IInd class compartments for 26 officers so you can imagine what it is like.

But it is grand fun we sit here with naked feet out of the window singing & smoking.

At each stop (which is about every 15 mins) the men get out and step dance on the rails or platforms to the sound of melodians. The French can't make it out a bit; they think us mad. It is a funny sight looking down the train when going at our "top speed", the men sitting on the footboards smoking; right down the whole length 50 trucks (15 for the horses) and the melodians going.

On the platform from which we left there was a small coffee stall run by 3 English ladies – they were splendid.

Without any fuss they filled all the men's mess tins with tea or coffee, gave them great slabs of bread & butter.

I take my "[ ] latest" off to those women; they were wonderful (& quite pretty.)

We have just had dinner: Bread, sardines, jam Whisky & water, A-1!!

We are due at our destination at 11 a.m. tomorrow; till then we Black Hole of Calcut.

Its a funny feeling going & getting hot water off the engine for washing.

Am sending enclosed cutting about dad, I follow his movements in the paper.

Will you send me an *Orilux* service lamp for officers?

It is a leather covered lamp for the Sam browne.

It comes from Stewarts Strand.

Please send me one with a refill.

So long old things.

Will write again when engine stops for good.

It will be damned hard to read this if possible.

Yours
John

Somewhere in France
Friday 20th August [1915]

Dear F-

Here we are billeted in a splendid little village nestling among the downs about 20 miles from the firing line. It is an awfully nice place – a typical French village about the size of Burwash Wield.

I have the great luck of being billeted with the Mayor, who is also the school master, in his house. I am awfully comfortable, having a feather bed with sheets & a sitting room for 3 of us, the whole place being absolutely spotlessly clean. The old Mayor is a topping old fellow who can't speak a word of English, but the kindest chap you ever met & awfully funny. He possesses a very pretty daughter – Marcelle – who is awfully nice and we get on very well.

The old lady too is A-1 & they will do anything for one.

The only disadvantage is, that there is very little food & what there is very 2nd rate. All the other Regiments have gutted the place, & one can't get a cigarette for love or money. Our food in the Mess is mostly bully beef & jam.

I can't of course tell you where this place is, but it is quite near the place I told you I thought we would go.

The country is looking awfully nice, with all the [crops to] get in yet.

We haven't had any letters yet since we left, but are hoping that they will arrive tomorrow evening.

Motor bike despatch riders abound here, tearing along at fearsome speeds, and big lorries going "all out".

How goes old Vincent?

The French here are the dirtiest I ever saw, their ideas of hotels are simply unspeakable!!

The men talking French are screamingly funny, but they manage to get on very well with the French girls.

As we have to censer all the letters at our platoon we get some very funny things; also some rather pathetic ones.

The men are sticking it wonderfully considering they haven't had a square meal since they left England.

The idea is I believe that we stay here about a fortnight before we go up to the trenches but one can never tell from one moment to the next what is going to happen to one next.

Please send me

> a pair of my ordinary pyjamas
> that *stiff* hair brush of Dad's.

Grayson has discovered a French girl who rather resembles [Gaby] in appearance and very much so in morals so he is quite happy.

You might send me out one of those letter block letters & envelopes all in one,

Please remember me to Jerry

> Much love to yourself
> John

Please send me my stocking putties, which were with the lot I sent back I think if they are'nt there please get some & send 'em on.

> so long
> JK

NB
They trust the officers not to give away the names of places & regiments without opening our letters, and we have to frank them on the envelope see outside.

> JK

> Hotel Brighton,
> 218, Rue de Rivoli,
> Paris.
> *Tuesday, Aug. 22. 1915.* 9.30 p.m.

> No. 316. Just opposite your old
> suite No. 301 with the bath that
> you had when last here.

Dear old man,

Got in here from Troyes and found a batch of Mother's letters with copies of your two letters from S'hampton and Havre. What one hell of a time you must have had hunting pickets round the deck. Were they sea sick? I pitched two or three letters straight to the Guards Camp Le Havre: and I hope to God you got 'em. One described *your* Birthday review – Kitchener and the IV French Army corps which was a splendid sight: and the other my little tour among the trenches in Alsace.

I hope you'll never get nearer to the Boche than I did. The quaintest thing was to watch the N.C.O. gesticulating to his Colonel and me to keep quiet – and to hear a hopefully expectant machine gun putting in five or six shots on the chance and then, as it were, stopping to listen. I don't mind trenches half as much as going in a motor along ten or twelve miles of road which the Boches may or may not shell – said road casually protected at the worst corners with thin hurdles of dried pine trees. Also I hate to be in a town with stone pavements when same is being bombarded. It's a grand life though and does not give you a dull minute. I found boric acid in my socks a great comfort. I walked 2 hours in the dam trenches.

I saw Hermie's father at the Ritz just before I left for my tour. I shall try to see Hermie at Boulogne on my way back. I have to go out and see Joffre to-morrow. He wants to see me! Hide your diminished head! No. I did *not* wear my Khaki uniform *at all*. I had an idea I would be photographed too much (and I was) for anything except civil costume. So I wore my blue clothes and slouch hat.[1] You will probably see ferocious pictures of me. I also saw a batch of 50 Boche prisoners – awful beggars to look at and I saw a captured machine gun. The new idea is to put as much strength as you can in your blockhouses, where the pompoms and machine guns are, and to hold the trenches as light as possible.

Don't forget the beauty of rabbit netting overhead against hand grenades. Even tennis netting is better than nothing.

Well, good-bye, my own dear son. I wish you were here for one good dinner and a jaw. I'm going to Bateman's for a day or two, but I don't think it will be long before I'm over in the English lines. This is a life that grows on one. Good luck.

Daddo.

Forgive this bloody pen; but you know French ideas.

[1] See illustration 9.

France
Sunday August 22nd 1915

Dear old things–

I have just received that splendid parcel of supplies etc this morning for which I can't thank you enough. You simply can't realize how topping it is to get parcels & letters from home; we wait for the post from one day to another. The cigarettes, tobacco, chocolate, clean shirts socks etc were *most* acceptable. You sent me enough kit to carry on with for a long time. It was all very well packed. In fact it was about the only couple of parcels that hadn't been burst in coming out.

Our post system will settle down soon I hope as it has been very uncertain lately.

Today is Sunday & it is a very sad sight to see all the girls & women dressed in black going pour *"la messe"*.

The crops here I should think were a record & they are being cut & brought in by old women & girls entirely.

An old lady thinks nothing of cutting a 2 acre field of wheat with a sickle.

They all work like horses as they have to get the crops in somehow.

One old soul told me that this was the best year for crops since 1906.

It is hard to realize the war is going on so near; if it wasn't for the occasional booming of the guns it would be like England. I have to sit on my first Court Martial tomorrow as I am the only Ensign or Subaltern with a year's service. It takes place 20 miles away in some town where a regiment of guards that has no bearskin plume are stationed. I don't know how I am going to get there; it will most likely be on the back of some old A.S.C. lorry.

I have'nt heard from Dad yet; I suppose it is pretty hard to get a letter between the two lines.

Can you tell me where Landon is? I could get him to take
back a far more interesting letter than any of these.
Well so long old things.

> Love to Jerry,
> Yours ever
> John

Thank you *ever so much* again for the parcel & letters

JK

Please put B.E.F. in full when addressing letters, etc.

JK.

> Hotel Brighton
> 218, Rue de Rivoli,
> Paris.
> *Monday Aug 23. 1915.*
> 9 p.m. (and a d----d hot night).

Dear old man –

I am hanging on in Paris waiting for Joffre to send for me. G.H.Q.
(French) aren't more than an hour (by car) from here but as one can't
telephone and must not telegraph it's a shade difficult to establish
connection with the Staff there. And my orders were that I was to get
into touch. Staffs are alike all over the world.

There are *awfully* few British officers in Paris nowadays. Mr Landon
and I dined at the *Café de Paris* (which is supposed to be the smart
place) and only saw four. One was young Rodman, (Isn't he in the
Brigade?) and his mother. One of the others was a fat and fleshy general.

I am up to my eyes in all sorts of letters and other muckings but I
hope to clear out the day after to-morrow. Then, after a bit, I can make
a shot at coming out to the English lines. I have conceived rather a high
opinion of the French infantry and if our trenches are better than theirs,
we deserve gold medals. Of course, in hilly country it is easy to drain
'em. Their latrines (which I took care to see) are first-class. Any god's
quantity chloride of lime and *no* flies. They bury their dead a little bit
outside the rear trenches if they can and plant oats over 'em. Their one
inch "revolver-cannons" (pom-poms) are beautifully placed and their

trench mortars only weigh 120 pounds. At least that's what they told me. They throw a huge "torpedo" with tin fins to steady its flight. They all agreed that the Boche is not happy with the bayonet *but* (I got this from at least three generals at different times) they all agree the Boche is a *very* keen observer and imitator. If you change your plan of attack or defence, they think over it for a day or two in silence and then produce *their* counter-measures. *When they are quiet they are thinking*. They *hate* blockhouses because they use blockhouses themselves. They don't object to trenches much, *unless* they are bombed, which means their aim is to establish moral ascendancy in bombing by virtue of a lot of bombs. They are improving in their aviation – more planes and better trained fliers but the quality of their rank and file is falling off. The French interpreters who deal with the prisoners tell me the proper thing is to ask the private *first* for information; then the non-com and last the officer. Collate all three answers and trust the private before the officer. They *are* hard up in their homes for food however much the German papers may deny it. You have only to examine prisoners' letters for this. *Always* collar their correspondence.

Forgive me yarning like this but you may find a bit of it useful. Anyway let your C.O. or O.C. or anyone you think fit hear what I have written.

Need I tell you, my dear old man, how I love you, or how proud I am of you.

     Daddo.

Don't forget about overhead rabbit netting, and a man with a whistle to signal descent of first *minen werfer* [mortar].

> Hotel Brighton,
> 218, Rue de Rivoli,
> Paris.
> *Tuesday. Aug. 24. 1915.* 9.40 a.m.

Dear old man,

This morning's post brought in copy of your letter (Jerry typed it I expect) describing your train journey to the music of melodeons. Don't fuss about the French thinking you are mad. They are used to it by now and their own troops on the move (what bloody ink!) make a regular bean-feast of it. But "skip-drill" in this weather is simple rot. I've had to wash in water out of an engine in South Africa. There is a tap just close to the cylinder which supplies it but if you use it too freely the driver begins to grouse.

It's curious to think of you following my movements about France. I am held up in Paris because Joffre wants to see me and I expect orders to come out to his headquarters. There is no way for a "civvy" (beg pardon "damned civilian") getting to his headquarters without all sorts of permits etc. etc. – so here I am in the little old Brighton trying to catch up with my account of my journey.

I think even you would have had your bellyful of motoring if you had been with me. We wound up by a little run of 400 kils. from Alsace to Troyes – *never* less than 50 kils. per hour and generally 70. Our spare car the Mercedes was driven by a Devil from Connecticut U.S.A. He was a Frenchman who had been road-racing there and running a stud of six cars. I never saw driving to touch his driving. When our fat limousine stuck on the hill-side we got into his Terror and – by God we skidded within half inches of precipices but he whirled us up the hillside and was rather disappointed that he wasn't allowed to bring the car on up to the very crest, where the Boches could have had a mile of fair running shots at her.

Well, this is just the usual line of the day to my boy. If J[offre] sees me to-day I get away to-morrow for Bateman's. Now I have to go to the British Consulate and the Prefecture of Police with my passport in order to get permission to leave France. I tell you, they look after the stray civilian pretty close here. It's necessary: for Paris is still fairly thick with spies.

Did I tell you how a soldier at Troyes (he knew all about "me works") came up to me, and when I told him my name, uttered a long and friendly "Ah-haa. God-dam"? It was the first time I'd ever heard the oath as a sort of *entente cordiale* greeting: and it fairly winded me for a second. Aren't the women good to our people everywhere. I've met hospitals all over the face of the country run by the English.

I'm *awfully* wondering where you are likely to be sent. If it is anywhere outside our present front – in the direction of the Argonne or that way, west of Soissons (which may be possible) I think you'll find it useful to chip in with my name occasionally among the French. This isn't swank but they all seemed to know me.

Dear love. I'm going out in a French taxi. They are burning petrol mixed with pee. At least that's how it smells.

Daddo.

Hotel Brighton,
218 Rue de Rivoli,
Paris.
Wed. Aug. 25. [1915] 9.20 a.m.

Dear old man –

After keeping me hung up here for two days I find that Joffre can't see me. He's busy somewhere else. D––––d impertinence, isn't it? But he sent a message to "excuse himself". Can you see K[itchener] doing that?

Well, yesterday I worked like the deuce, and in the evening, having a desire to keep away from interviewers, editors, etc. L[andon] and I went to the Palais Royal Music Hall. It's close to that theatre where we saw *Le Monde où l'on s'ennuie*. I would have given a heap if you'd been there. 'Twasn't anything in point of scenery or chorus (12 people fill the stage) but there was an English subaltern in khaki who did the English accent. He wore a sporting Khaki jacket; light *fawn coloured gaiters, with leather buttons* and heavy *motoring* gauntlets! He placed his hands on his hips and struck attitudes while the audience howled applause. His English ran mostly to "Arl raight". Well, even K 6 would have slain him with a shovel. *Then* (and I thought how you'd have liked it) an English naval Sub-Lootenant came in and sang "Mary of Tipperary" with an indelicate female in a short green skirt and green holland drawers fastened with red tape bows. She represented the Irish! You've no notion how

flamingly indecent red and green drawers can be. The navy Lootenant's uniform was correct in every detail. That rather shocked me but as you don't care for the "ceaseless vigillers" you'd have liked it. The khaki gent in the motor gloves was however the great draw. He never left the stage. When he wasn't chanting about being an interpreter he took a chair at the back and received applause. The girls were awful bitches – all except one who was enough of a bitch to be interesting. There was a full house and about a dozen British officers (*all* senior) who seemed to be having a good time. We couldn't stick more than half the performance and walked home through the quiet sticky night to our hotel.

I leave to-morrow by the 10.5 train and should be in Folkestone at 6 p.m. where I hope the car will meet me. By the way, the concièrge here met Eaves(!) the other day in uniform. Eaves was on his way to the front *via* Paris. If you ever get over to Paris you'd better come here. They'll give you your old suite (301) with bath at ridiculous cheap rates and I fancy you'll find 'em a sort of French Brown's.

Now I'll get back to my work. "Me 'eart" as they say on the music hall stage is ever thine and I am consequently

    More than ever
    Your Dad.

                        Hotel Brighton,
                        218, Rue de Rivoli,
                        Paris.
                        Aug. 25. 1915. 7.30 p.m.

Dear old man –

As I leave to-morrow at a perfectly ungodly hour in order that there may be time at the railway station to examine the passports, I write my little daily letter to you now. I hope to be in Folkestone by 6 o'clock to-morrow evening but this is a deceitful world and there have been several delays in the Channel boats. I expect the submarines are on the rampage again. Yesterday's train went off crowded to the lee-scuppers (if that is the right word) on account of no boat going the day before.

I have been working all day at my accounts of my travels and saying pretty things about the French Army. I really think they are excellent and I expect as time goes on, you will be of that opinion too. Really, there isn't much difference between the way in which the officers of the English and French armies look at things. I was talking the other night "Somewhere in France" with a delightful old General. We were some miles from a town and the German and French searchlights were playing all around us. I asked him if he knew who was his opposite number on the Hun side. "Quite well," he said. "I've known him for months".

(He told me his name.) "He's an old man and I think he has gout. Every now and again I keep him awake all night with my big guns. He *always* loses his temper. He gets excited and begins to fire away all round the landscape. I should say he cost Germany a lot in ammunition". Now isn't that very much as an English officer would talk.

11 p.m. Just back from an idiotic cinema theatre at the Ambassadeurs. There were lots of faked pictures of the war and the only funny turn was about a kid who was spanked for throwing stones into a river where a man was fishing. So he went back to his father's caravan (he was a gipsy), got a crocodile's skin and fastened it over his dog. This was the result. Well, as you can imagine the sight of a sky-blue crocodile

on four legs running at him like Hell rather upset the fisherman and then the dog-crocodile got loose all over the country and the usual upsets and panics followed.

Thursday morn 9 a.m. Just off for Boulogne and have just received copy of your letter of 20th describing your billet with the Mayor and the maid Marcelle and the immoral luck of Grayson and the local Gaby. I'm sorry about the food but Bateman's will do its best to supplement. You *ought* to get a whole lot of letters from me when they arrive as I've written you regularly. Now for the Gare du Nord and a hell of a crush at the station.

> Ever,
> Dad.

> France
> *Aug 26th 1915*

Dear F

Just received Mum's letter of the 23rd.

We have a rotten system of post delivery out here. The parcels are only delivered every 4 days.

Please don't send any more underclothes, collars, shirts &

handkerchiefs, as I have ample now & too many will get lost. But chocolate is most acceptable as the food here – what there is – is *rotten*.

Many thanks for the Sunday Express, Pictorial & Sketch.

The heat here is tremendous & the flies the limit.

A very funny thing happened the other day.

In the billets where my platoon sleep there is a great big sow which wanders around the yard. The men sleep in a corn shed just next to the stye.

The old sow is always ravenously hungry & I suddenly heard a tremendous row & shouting & out of the yard gate onto the main road rushed the sow with a man's emergency ration bag in its mouth.

The bag was full of biscuit & bully beef.

After her rushed all the billet with clubbed rifles, sticks, stones, etc.

But the sow ran much faster than they did & they chased it for about 150 yds till it was turned back by some men coming down the road.

She never let go of the ration bag but rushed back.

Again the chase went on till just by the gate of the yard the old girl slipped.

The men at once pounced on her, the sergeant hitting her a great swipe in the belly with the butt of his rifle.

But she didn't drop the bag till she had everyone hitting & kicking her.

The owner came out & was very fed up but she was smoothed down & the old sow lay down on a dung heap quite exhausted.

I don't think I have ever laughed so much in my life.

I wonder the sow didn't die with the bangs she got.

I went into a big Town quite near here yesterday on a motor lorry to see the sights & get supplies, thousands & thousands of pillar boxes in [] or on foot or riding all doing nothing, & came back in the evening in a racing car.

I wish those pyjamas & civilian thin socks would come out, but all the post is hung up at present.

Will you send me 2 pairs of those thick Khaki socks I had at Warley?

> Love to all,
> John

Am sending Insurance paper filled in

> JK

> *Aug. 26.* [1915] 10.20 a.m.
> In the train on the way to Boul-
> ogne.

I shall post this in Boulogne which, when you come to think of it, can't be more than 20 miles from you. I wish I could have a look at you with Marcelle. By the way the best dictionary for French is a dictionary in skirts. (While I am trying to write a damned Yankee in the same compartment is holding forth on the sinking of the Lusitania in a voice that would drill holes through steel plate. It is so awful that Landon and I have had to get out and are now sitting in the restaurant car. It seems that the Yank was aboard her when she was struck. I am almost inclined to sympathize with the German point of view.)

About half this train seems full of Yankees who have been getting contracts for arms etc. In the Hotel Brighton I met a round hairy pinkish Canadian who told me he was the son-in-law of "Mr Ellis of Burwash". It takes a fair amount to surprise me nowadays but I own I was a little bit astonished. He had come over, he said, to sell arms to the French and was disgustingly prosperous.

It's a very hot day in the train. I hope you and Marcelle are having a cooler time. Talking of Grayson, did I tell you that one of the private soldiers (the Colonel's orderly) who took me round the trenches at Hartmanweilers Kop might have been Grayson's twin brother. In civil life he told me he was a lawyer. He had exactly Grayson's slow way of trickling out his sentences and rolling his eyes. I expected him to talk English every minute.

2.50 p.m. Three English officers got in at Amiens since which we have had a lovely time. The Yankees were crushed and silent. They are on leave (8 days) and I am trying to smuggle 'em over with me instead of their waiting for the 10 p.m. boat.

Dear love.
Your Dad.

Bateman's,
Burwash,
Sussex.
Aug. 28. 1915. 8.20 p.m.

Dear old man –

Your letter of the 26th with the joyous tale of the Emergency Ration sow just came in this evening: and Mums and I howled over it. But for a pig to rob the Irish is rather like "seething a kid in its mother's milk" isn't it? Where, if anywhere, are some or all of the letters that I've been writing you for the last ten days. French postal arrangements are specially putrid but some of 'em ought to have turned up by now.

Uncle Stan turned up last night. He sent a wire but we were out. So he had to walk most of the way from the station. I gather from what he said that Ollie is about fed up with Eton and refuses to stay on. At any rate Stan talks about getting him a tutor for the next six months, with an eye to coaching Ollie for the Diplomatic. This, I think, will be "all my eye" for Stan added that as soon as he was old enough Ollie wants to go into the Guards – Grenadier for choice as Stan knows a lot of old Grenadiers. Well, everyone to his taste. I expect that Ollie may have written to you about it. Oh! And he also told us that he was dining with Kerry t'other day (some weeks ago). He and Kerry got into the House of Commons together. Kerry said to him:– "I've just discovered that I've a nephew of yours in my regiment – young Kipling. He's a very good boy and he's done very good work. All his work is good and thorough. I shall let him go out when he is eighteen because he's had a year's training and he knows his work." So even the v.p.g. has an eye in his head.

To-day has been filthy hot and I've been digging out over my letters about France – observations on their Army. I repeat, for about the 5th time, that they employ rabbit wire over-head in their trenches to guard off bombs. The little pitched roof is supposed to make the bomb roll off before or behind the trench. Now I'll stop till to-morrow morning.

observations on their Army.
repeat. for about the 5th time. that
they employ rabbit wire over head in
their trenches to guard off bombs
thus:-

or in section thus

the little pitched roof is
supposed to make the bomb roll
off before or behind the trench.
Now I'll stop till tomorrow
morning.

Sunday 4.30 p.m. It's been raining
hard, all the day and that's all over
it. Hope you're dry. The Colonel has just
written with best greetings to you.
so if you can something of your work (it won't
do to tone) Do you carry on with your signallers
or do you continue with your gym work? How
is Gibson. Our greetings to him.
That's all. A heart full of love.
Dad.

♣ BURWASH
🚂 ETCHINGHAM

BATEMAN'S
BURWASH
·SUSSEX·

Aug. 28. 1915
8. 20. p.m.

Dear old man —
Your letter of the
26th with the joyous tale of
the Emergency Ration Sow just
come in this evening: and
Mums and I howled over it.
But for a pig to rob the Irish
is rather like "Seething a Kid
in its mothers milk", isn't it?
Where, if anywhere, are some
or all of the letters that I've
been writing you for the last
ten days. French postal arrangements
are officially perfect but some
of 'em ought to have turned up
by now.

ONE OF A NUMBER OF LETTERS BY RK RECOMMENDING
THE USE OF RABBIT WIRE IN THE TRENCHES.

or in section the

Sunday 4.30 p.m. It's been raining hard, all the day and that's all *our* news. Hope you're dry. The Colonel has just left with best greetings to you. Tell us if you can something of your work. (It won't assist the foe.) Do you carry on with your signallers or do you continue with your gym work? How is Grayson? Our greetings to him.

That's all. A heart full of love.
Dad.

> 2nd Guards Brigade
> France
> *Aug 29th 1915*

Dear F –

Not having a letter for four days I get nine all in one post yesterday. Many thanks for them.

The heat here is incredible, far hotter than the Cape, & by God the flies!!

There isn't one of us who hasn't been tickled up by a wasp. This seems to be their "happy hunting ground".

We look like a Colonial regiment, we are so sun burnt, & my visage is the colour of a well smoked briar pipe.

In fact we are quickly assuming that "lean & bronzed" appearance so inseparable from the heroes in the *Daily Mirror* serials.

I don't think I have ever felt so fit before.

We work like blazes & have 8 hours sleep a night (lights out at 9 p.m.).

Many thanks for Dad's letters.

His "tips for the trenches" are rather quaint. Surely you know it is a standing order never to have any thing over the top of a trench, even rabbit wires. If the Bosch comes, he has you like rabbits underneath it.

Remember our C.O. was 7 months on a "Brigade" staff & what he doesn't know about the game isn't worth knowing. Of course you were only allowed to see specimen trenches, not those which a French battalion had made in one night, the great test of Trench digging.

Good old Max Aitkin has gone & given a commission to the wrong Rgm in spite of the fact that we gave him initials, etc. Some Colonel!

Many thanks for parcel No 5.

I have not as yet received Nos III & IV but they are doubtless hung up somewhere.

There is ceaseless drill here all day & route marching; the dust is simply unspeakable.

You never saw anything as smart as the men are now, & by Gad the discipline!

The Brigade bands (that play at Guard mountings) are taking it in turns to come out & play at the base to the troops there & at rest Camps.

We are forming our own "drums" here as all the Battalions in the "Brigade" have got them. We have a lot of drummers & fife players in the ranks so it won't take long. When the "Colonel in Chief" comes out we are going to have the massed drums of the Division that will be a grand sight.

By the way, I am running rather short of note paper & envelopes. Will you send me a writing block in a canvas cover, you know the thing. "The Linesman's friend" I think they call it or "Active Service letter pad", some thing like that.

Please don't send any more underclothes, shirts, collars, but thick socks as per agreement.

About refills, Please send a refill for the "Orilux" once a fortnight; for the Holzabel about every 10 days.

Please send a bottle of Colgates tooth powder, also a tin of Colgates shaving powder.

About food –

The only food I want sent out is plenty of chocolate as the

rest we get (like sardines) from the mess. Also things like chocolate biscuits, not Digestive.

The chocolate biscuits were A-1.

When you send out the ¼ lb Tobacco would you mind sending it in 2 2oz tins as it is more handy.

I am really rolling in shirts & good things here but any little Knick Knack is most acceptable.

Would you send me a portable glass in a strong case for travelling, about the size of this sheet of note paper.

Bad luck about [?]

But I am going right there the next time I am in England.

Funny old Phipps being way up in Scotland!

Do please send me some literature: Nashs (Sept.), Royal, Strand, Pearsons etc.

There is simply nothing to read here.

Many thanks for the Tatler, Punch & Sketch.

Well having spun my wants to the tune of three pages I will now close.

> Dear love to you all,
> John

France
Aug 30 1915

Dear F –

I got the parcels (III & IV) this morning; also three letters from Dad for which *many many thanks*. It is awfully good of you to send me all these things.

Dad's rather "fruity" letter of Wed 25th arrived with a big notice over the flap "Opened by Base Censer".

Some damned interfering Linesman who enclosed a printed slip.

Damned cheek!

I wish I had seen the music hall, especially the Sabaltern.

Well about our doings.

That Court Martial.

There were no lorries so I got a horse, a streamline one with "bulbous stern & disc wheels"; also raked steering, really quite a fast animal.

It skidded a bit to start with but I let the clutch in gently & soon had it under control.

It didn't take long to get there (it was about 9 miles off). In fact, in one place I'm sure I touched 25 m.p.h.

It was a "Field General Court Martial" which holds the power of "life or death" (rather impressive don't you think it sounds?)

As the junior member has to propose the "finding of the court" first, I had to keep my wits about me.

The President was a Major in the Grenadiers & the 2 members a Captain in the "Kiddies" & myself.

One man came very near the extreme penalty & I didn't like it at all.

All offences on Active Service are regarded twice as seriously as in England & quite right.

There were 4 cases & it lasted 6 hours.

Having acquitted myself "Comme Monsieur Edoward Carson",[1] I again climbed into my bucket seat & letting in 2nd gear I wasn't long in getting back.

Rather a long day: an 18 mile ride & a 6 hour Court Martial. By gad I was stiff the next day!

Yesterday we had a grand time.

Our first Battalion is in billets about 15 miles away.

Jerry is now a Lt. Colonel commanding the 1st Batt I.G.

We both marched out to meet each other halfway & had a great picnic.

Sgt O'Leary was there looking very smart. He has got the clearest eye you ever saw, really quite good looking. It was awfully nice seeing all the officers. Old Jerry rushed up to me & shook hands effusively.

The men looked very strained & [pulled] & it was hard to recognize the ensigns. Some realy looked like animated corpses. They say they never get a moment's rest & they looked it. By Jove their arm drill was a treat.

They have a very funny trick; they have removed their felt coverings from their water bottles & as it is dark blue japaned tin underneath it looks damned smart against Khaki.

About one man in 4 wears a ring of aluminium made out of bits of German shell casing.

We both cheered each other lustily & Jerry let out some

frightful bellows, to intimidate the young officers, no doubt.
7.30 a.m.

Aug 31st [1915]

2 Companies (ours & another) are off in an hour in motor buses to help dig the 1st line trenches for the defence of the seaports.

We are due back at 8 this evening.

Tomorrow their is a "Divisional Field Day" which means Frightfulness.

We parade at 4.30 a.m. & march off at 5 a.m. as we have 12 miles to go before we get to the place where the Field Day is held.

We walk back 12 miles when operations are finished, which will be in the evening.

Rather a strenuous day. 24 mile march & a day's moenuvres. This sort of thing brings the war right to your front door and drops it there with a bump.

Lady B[land] S[utton] sent me a topping big sponge cake and I have just written to thank her.

Our Brigadier is Ponsonby, a Coldstreamer, one of the best out here. 2nd Guards Brigade.

Well old things I must be getting on my goggles & motor gloves for my trip "en Bus-Auto".

> So long.
> Dear love,
> John

[1] Lord Edward Henry Carson (1854–1936), at this period Attorney-General, had been a neighbour of Kipling's at Rottingdean and was admired by R K for his stand against Irish Home Rule.

France
Sept [2 or 3] *1915*

2nd Guards Brigade
Guards Division
B.E.F.

Dear F –

It keeps on raining here like old Hades.

Will you send me an oilskin coat just the same as those sailor chaps use in the North Sea, etc. Big black things that don't stick. Not a civilian one you get in a shop which is only good for a week, but the standard Naval article. You could perhaps get it at Portsmouth. You could try it on on Dad. It must be good & roomy & reach just below his "fatted calves". No "Burbury" or Mac will stand up to these soaking rains. You must have an oilskin & a good one too.

Will you try & get one for me as a real Waterproof is $\frac{1}{2}$ the fight. I know it is asking rather a lot of you to go hunting for a Naval Officer's oilskin & it is a great "comedown" for me to utilize the kit of the Senior Service.

I am sending you a "fiver" which I enclose in this letter to cover any little bills that roll to Bateman's for me.

Will you also pay a little bill I have at Dunhills, Duke Street, out of it.

We are going to be out all tomorrow night.

The trenches ought to be rather a rest.

We go up to them some time next week.

Well, so long old thing. Love to Jerry.

Sorry to trouble you about a "slicker".

> Yours ever,
> John

Will you also pay enclosed bill to Slazengers.

> J.K.

(The cheque is quite valid in indelible pencil)

> Bateman's,
> Burwash,
> Sussex.
> *Sunday. 5th Sept.* [1915] 8 p.m.

> Bateman's drawing-room, with a
> small brisk fire.

Dear old Warrior:

Your orders *re* oilskins (Seadog and Ceaseless Vigiller pattern) received and Jerry at once laughed. It will be long before she forgets that: but naturally she knows all about oil-skins.

This afternoon at 5 p.m. Lady Aitken turned up with her brother Chipman now a captain on the divisional staff and another officer and his wife. Lady A. looked awfully pretty and well. She says that Sir Max has a house and a staff of his own at St Omer. She came in an *eight-cylinder* Cadillac. I've never seen one before. The cylinders are set V shape four on each side. It's a wonderful smooth goer and develops any power you like – between 60 and 90 I believe. *She* drives it. She'd drive anything. I studied the self-starter for the first time. Alan Aitken, whom you met at Cherkley at Christmas, is coming back from the Dardanelles. They all asked after you and your true friend Gladys [Mrs Max Aitken], to whom I gave your address, says she is going to send you chocolates. I much admire your taste in admiring her. She's living at Folkestone for the time being.

I shouted with joy over your tale of the court-martial horse. You used to have a very good seat and hands in your early youth. Did it come back to you at all, *en route*?

(Mums and the Bird are fighting over another one of your d----d socks – the toe or the heel or something. Bird has gone to Mum's room to get it – *and has left the door open as usual.* That girl wants talking to.)

I have nearly done my last letter about the French Army[1] and expect to be a human being again to-morrow. Bird says I'm a mushroom at present! You will I'm sure be glad to know that Wiggy whom we allowed to come into Bateman's for lunch yesterday *only* peed twice in the hall in half an hour! A well-brought up little animal!

I've been about with your gun and have valiantly missed my usual amount of partridges. Jenner who is bandmaster of the Burwash band, has had a full-dress performance in the village (we heard 'em from afar) last night. They collect money to get tobacco for the "Burwash lads at the front". *They don't give any to the Home defencers* which shows that J's heart is in the right place.

I hope you've got your 2B packet. I have picked up several unwritable pink stories for your private ear. But I will now conclude.

> With a whole heartful of love,
> Dad.

P.S. If the Censor opened my "fruity" letter, it probably cheered him up.

[1] Collected as *France at War* (1915).

France
Saturday 10th Sept 1915
7.30 p.m.

2nd Batt Irish guards

Dear F –   ,

Many thanks for those parcels you sent me. I now lack nothing but a pair of sock suspenders.

Realy I am rooling in good things.

The oil skin is A-1.

I have *ample* socks now so please don't send out anymore till I write for them.

You might send an Orilux battery.

I want no Holzapel Batteries any more as the lamp was no good.

The Orilux is the finest lamp you can possibly have.

Everyone uses them out here.

Lady Aitken sent me a topping box of chocolates & Lady B-S sent me a huge cake. Really it was awful nice of them.

I am writing on the letter block that arrived the other day.

No more *shirts collars* or *underclothes* till I write.

Well, about our doings.

We were out till 12 last night digging trenches.

We have been at it all morning & are going out all night (till 5 a.m. Sunday).

Dad most likely knows what is going to happen out here in ten days. That is what the Guards Division have been formed for. Sounds mysterious but I can't say what it is if you don't know.

So we are moving up shortly.

The heat still continues & it is very very hot.

Many thanks for the mags. They are always most acceptable.

Yours ever,
John

France
Sunday Sept 19th 1915

Dear F –

Got your letters (Dad's & Elsie's) of the 16th for which many thanks.

The post was delayed owing to submarines playing around in the Channel.

I am awfully pleased to hear about Phipp's Singer – they *are* rather nice little things – if I live to get back again I'm going to get myself the smartest 2 seater Hispano-Suiza that can be got & get a bit of enjoyment out of life with it.

By Gad to think of it makes me grip my pencil like a steering wheel, which accounts for the writing.

We work like fiends; if we get two hours for meals & stand easyies in a day we think ourselves damned lucky.

Usually getting up at 4 a.m. & going to bed at half past nine in the evening.

We move off again I believe on Tuesday.

I've done enough marching the last month to sicken me of it for life; it is simply indescribable! – these long blazing strips of dusty roads where you can see about five Kilometres ahead of you, & staff cars & lorries covering you with dust.

Many is the time I've thought of a hot bath! evening clothes! dinner at the Ritz! going to the Alhambra afterwards!!

You people at home don't realize how spoilt you are. You don't realize what excessive luxury surrounds you.

Think of a hot water tap alone.

I find that I didn't bring out any studs with me. Would you please send me out 3 front studs & 3 back studs; also another pair of pyjamas exactly similar to the last you sent me.

By the way, the next time you are in town would you get me an Identification Disc as I have gone and lost mine. I think you could get one at the Stores.

Just an aluminium Disc with a string through it like this

about this size

It is quite impossible to get one out here or I wouldn't trouble you about it.

It is a Routine order that we have to have them.

Well so long old things, good luck to the Singer. I hope PHS learns to manage it expertly soon.

> Yours ever,
> John Kipling

France
Thursday Sept 23rd 1915

Dear old F –

Just a hurried line to let you know what we are doing. We have begun what I said we were going to do; have been marching for the last two days. It is awfully hot, but we do most of our marching by night so it is a bit cooler.

The dust is realy appaling.

There isn't much food or sleep flying around as we keep at it pretty hard.

I slept last night on the floor of a farm parlour. The bricks were a bit hard but I slept like a log for four hours. We are off in an hour so I must be getting on.

We have had to chuck a good half of our Kits away as the waggons are very heavily loaded.

I will write and tell you what to send later on.

It made my heart bleed to leave a lot of my splendid Kit by the roadside.

Please send me a really good pair of bedroom slippers (fluffy & warm with strong soles) (*not* carpet) also a good strong tooth brush.

> So long old dears,
> Yrs John

Saturday Sept 25th [1915]
5.30 p.m.

Dear F –

Just a hurried line as we start off tonight. The front line trenches are nine miles off from here so it wont be a very long march.

This is THE great effort to break through & end the war.

The guns have been going deafeningly all day, without a single stop.

We have to push through at all costs so we won't have much time in the trenches, which is great luck.

Funny to think one will be in the thick of it tomorrow.

One's first experience of shell fire not in the trenches but in the open.

This is one of the advantages of a Flying Division; you have to keep moving.

We marched 18 miles last night in the pouring wet.

It came down in sheets steadily.

They are staking a tremendous lot on this great advancing movement as if it succeeds the war won't go on for long.

You have no idea what enormous issues depend on the next few days.

This will be my last letter most likely for some time as we won't get any time for writing this next week, but I will try & send Field post cards.

> Well so long old dears.
> Dear love
> John.

Love to Jerry.

> J K

G v R I

HE whom this scroll commemorates was numbered among those who, at the call of King and Country, left all that was dear to them, endured hardness, faced danger, and finally passed out of the sight of men by the path of duty and self-sacrifice, giving up their own lives that others might live in freedom. Let those who come after see to it that his name be not forgotten.

Lieut. John Kipling
Irish Guards

ACKNOWLEDGEMENTS

It is a pleasure for me to be able to acknowledge here the help I have received with this collection from many quarters. My thanks first to Robin Wright, Managing Editor of the National Trust, for his early and continuing support of the project, and to Elizabeth Burke, whose enthusiasm and imagination in the production of the book have been contagious. Then, to the staff of the Documents and Manuscripts Section of the University of Sussex Library, especially John Burt and Elizabeth Inglis and their colleagues David Kennelly and Sheila Schaffer, my gratitude for unfailingly patient and cheerful assistance. Also helpful at Sussex were Diana McLaren, who collated the holograph letters with the typed transcripts, and Keith Wilson of the Media Service Unit, who photographed the drawings.

My particular thanks to Charles Carrington for sharing his notes and other records with me, and to John Shearman, Secretary of the Kipling Society, for reviewing my work and making invaluable suggestions. I am indebted, too, to George Webb, Editor of the *Kipling Journal*, Mark Baker, former Wellington College archivist, Roger Lancelyn Green, whose *Kipling and the Children* was a constant guide, Susan Gubar and Thomas Pinney. From the start, my work has been supported by a series of travel grants from the University of California at Davis, and for these I am grateful; my gratitude as well to the Berg Collection of the New York Public Library for permission to quote from their Kipling letters. Most of all, I wish to thank my wife, Sandra M. Gilbert, for generously taking time away from her own many literary projects to help me complete this one.

E.L.G.